UNTIED

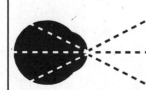

This Large Print Book carries the
Seal of Approval of N.A.V.H.

UNTIED

A MEMOIR OF FAMILY, FAME, AND FLOUNDERING

MEREDITH BAXTER

THORNDIKE PRESS

A part of Gale, Cengage Learning

GALE
CENGAGE Learning™

Detroit • New York • San Francisco • New Haven, Conn • Waterville, Maine • London

GALE
CENGAGE Learning™

LIBRARY OF CONGRESS CATALOGING-IN-PUBLICATION DATA

Baxter, Meredith, 1947–
    Untied : a memoir of family, fame, and floundering / by
Meredith Baxter.
        p. cm. — (Thorndike Press large print biography)
    ISBN-13: 978-1-4104-3865-2 (hardcover)
    ISBN-10: 1-4104-3865-1 (hardcover)
    1. Baxter, Meredith, 1947– 2. Television actors and
actresses—United States—Biography. 3. Lesbian
actresses—United States—Biography. 4. Large type books. I.
Title.
PN2287.B3915A3 2011b
791.45'028'092—dc22
[B]   2011011220

Published in 2011 by arrangement with Crown Publishing, a division of
Random House, Inc.

To Allan Manings

AUTHOR'S NOTE

I have told the truth about my story as best I can recall and up to a point. There are a few names I have changed to ensure privacy. There are some incidents that have been truncated or eliminated because full disclosure is often tedious, dreary, and redundant.

A few of my children posited their opinion that for me to write about my life automatically meant I was writing about theirs, which I think they experienced as a form of trespass. So, although our lives are inextricably linked, I tried to limit telling my children's stories because, after all, those stories are not mine to tell. In truth, I felt awkward even writing about their feelings or perceptions, believing it was not my right to represent them with any particular slant. Consequently in this book, for the most part, I've avoided talking much about them at all, which belies that they were and are the center of my life; they have taught me

7

great love, patience, and compassion, which have shaped me in the richest ways.

PROLOGUE

On the night of November 29, 2009, I was sitting in the bathtub at the Four Seasons Hotel in midtown Manhattan, having a meltdown. The following morning I was supposed to go on the *Today Show* so I could come out on national television. Even my partner of four years, Nancy Locke, was concerned for me. Would it look like a pathetic career move? Would it look like a desperate bid for attention? Were there factions in my family that didn't yet know? How would people in the industry look at me now? Would I look foolish? Would my waning career be perceived as going up in a small ignoble puff of smoke? I was fraught with uncertainty.

It was the offer of two free tickets to the Caribbean a few weeks earlier on the inaugural voyage of Sweet, a lesbian cruise line, which had culminated in my sitting in this now lukewarm tub in New York City. The web series I was appearing in, *We Have to Stop Now,* would be filming more episodes on the cruise; would I like to join them and film some added scenes? I was a little wary of being so exposed on a lesbian cruise, but it took very little discussion for Nancy and me to decide we really wanted to go. So I called the show's producers, took a deep breath, and said, "We're in!"

We departed out of New Orleans and headed to Mexico, sailing right into Hurricane Ida. Our huge ocean liner was tossed around like a Coke can and Nancy and I just held on to each other for dear life but we made it through to Belize City, then to Honduras, then back to Cozumel. We had so much fun. Nancy and I kept it low key, reading, sitting in the sun, enjoying the day trips, meeting new people. I knew that there was press on board as well as a lot of cameras, but except for the few scenes I had to do, we steered clear of them. On the last night of the seven-day cruise, we saw our amazingly funny friend, comic Suzanne Westenhoefer, perform. At the end of her act, she looked out into the crowd and, echoing the words of gay rights activist Harvey Milk, said, "Come out. If you're not out, come out."

Okay . . . that got me. I had been struggling with the idea for some time. I was on a lesbian cruise, but who was I really out to? I had been letting my friends and family know since 2003. But I wasn't out to the world; I always told myself I had too much at stake. At that moment, I looked at Nancy, my darling Nancy, who had been out for thirty years, and I just knew it was time.

That night, back in our cabin, I started flailing around for a plan. I'd put an ad in the newspaper! I was thinking it should be modest, sort of like a birth announcement, and it could say something like, "Hey . . . Just thought I'd let you know I'm gay, (signed) Meredith Baxter."

We returned home to Los Angeles on Sunday, November 15. On Monday morning, I put a call into the office of my manager, Alan Iezman, to broach the idea of the coming-out process and what that might look like. Well, Alan had wanted to talk to *me* because he'd already gotten some calls from *National Enquirer, Star,* and the celebrity gossip website *PerezHilton.* They all knew that I was on the cruise, and they had photographs of me and Nancy. No! This was my worst nightmare!

My manager suggested I talk to Howard Bragman, a well-known Hollywood publicist who specialized in guiding celebrities through the coming-out process. Howard's first words were, "Well, aren't you full of surprises?" Then he said, "We have to take control of the story or you will have no say in it at all." He said, "We'll get you into *People* magazine and then we'll go to New York and you'll do the *Today Show.*" No! This was horrible! This was even worse than the *Enquirer!*

What? No ad? A major *network?* A major *publication?* No, no, no. *This isn't warranted!* This was way over the top. But Howard was already moving. "First I have to see if the *Today Show* wants you." Fifteen minutes later, he called me back and said, "The *Today Show* wants you and they want you *next week,* so we have to get *People* magazine over to your house within the next few days." I didn't have time to react. This was appalling but — I just went on stunned autopilot. "Okay. Okay."

Cut back to me crying and now shivering in the Four Seasons bathtub. *Why* am I doing this? Why should anybody have to do this? I just wailed. I was going to make a most personal announcement on national television and people were going to say, "Her? *Family Ties* has been off the air for twenty years. Who cares?"

Then Nancy came in and talked to me as

I wept. Nancy talked about the shame she felt when she first came out, how she hid being gay from those around her because she was scared how they would react. She told me how comforting it would have been to her back then to see someone like me, a known actress, someone people seemed to like, coming forward and being open about who they were.

Ah. This could be helpful? This was *being of service?* As long as I kept a tight focus on the bigger picture, it made what was about to happen much more meaningful and relevant, almost spiritual. Research has shown that when people have a friend or someone in their family who is gay, they seem more open to gay issues. All right, I haven't been in the limelight for a while, but people do still seem to respond to me. So maybe people will think, "Oh, Meredith. I like her! She's nonthreatening! She's friendly! She talks to you! So, she's gay! She was the same as she was before we knew; nothing has changed."

And perhaps, the next time those people will go to vote, they'll think about me and other gay people they know, and perhaps they won't so quickly vote away gay marriage rights; maybe they'll vote with real equality in mind.

And perhaps, for someone who's been fearful of coming out, this will give him or her courage to take the next step. Okay. I can do this.

I'd met *Today Show* host Matt Lauer back in 2008 when he interviewed Gary David Goldberg, the creator of *Family Ties,* me, and the rest of the *Family Ties* cast for our 20 Years Later reunion. So, before the interview began, I asked for a few minutes with Matt. He couldn't have been lovelier to me. He said, "Boy, I didn't see this coming. I'm here with you, Meredith. This is fine. It's all going to be great."

When we were seated on the set, I looked out the window behind Matt where New Yorkers congregate outside the studio, waiting to watch the show, and they were all excitedly waving and yelling, "Hi!" NBC was pretaping my segment and, since this episode wasn't going to air for a couple of days, our conversation wasn't piped outside, but I couldn't help imagining a live TV scenario: the crowd would be watching and waving, trying to get my attention, and then I'd blurt out, "I'm a lesbian!" The smiles would collapse and the waving hands would quickly be stuffed back into pockets and *whoosh,* the crowd would disperse. That's what was going through my mind as the cameras started rolling.

Matt Lauer gave me a nice intro, something like, "She's one of the most beloved TV moms of all time" and "This morning she's going to disclose something." He looked at me expectantly and I was horrified. I might have said, "Don't you *know?* Do I have to *say it??*" After a bit of stammering I just spoke from my heart. I announced that I was a lesbian, that it had been a later-in-life discovery. I said I hadn't fought the discovery but embraced it, that it had clarified some aspects of my relationships with men. I told of my wonderful relationship with Nancy and the unqualified love and support I'd found in my family and friends. I said I felt that coming out like that, on the *Today Show,* was a political act and that perhaps knowing I was a lesbian might free people to be more generous and understanding of the rights of others in the gay, lesbian, and transgender community. I hadn't memorized anything, but I think I said everything I wanted to say. Then it was over and I wondered, "Did I just set myself on fire on national television?"

Nancy and I walked out of NBC into a gentle, calming winter drizzle, leaving all the hoopla behind us. We were high and shaky on the adrenaline of the morning.

Strolling the city streets, huddled together under a large umbrella as taxis swooshed by, was the perfect antidote. We watched people ice-skate; we window-shopped; we lunched in a bistro; I bought some great cheap boots and then we wandered into Tiffany's on Fifth Avenue. It was packed with shoppers on each floor. Like everyone else, we tried on jewelry. I really liked a squarish silver ring with some letters stamped on it. It read T & Co. I didn't have my reading glasses with me — it looked like TACO, which I thought was a pretty whimsical touch for such a highfalutin outfit. Nancy found a similar ring, with the same letters, but round and convex; we bought each other rings to commemorate the day and wandered back out into the rain.

Over the next few weeks, I started to give some thought to writing about this experience. About two years earlier, the subject of my writing a book had been broached by someone I work with. So I toyed with doing something slim showing my paintings and drawings, and perhaps throw in some fab recipes and a few words of pithy, learned wisdom appropriate to each. I had even made a few selections from my artwork but never really moved beyond that because the project felt just a little lifeless and nonspe-

16

cific. What would be different now? I didn't want to just write about the coming-out experience. I hoped I had more to offer than that. (Although, if you googled me, you'd think that announcing I was a lesbian was just about the only thing I'd ever done.) What have I learned in my sixty-three years? I'll tell you the truth, everything I know I learned in a 12-step program or therapy. So I decided I could talk about my life and how I changed my thinking.

As a child I was held captive by feelings of fear, shame, anger, loneliness, and a profound sense of being unloved. I developed a belief system about myself based on these feelings that shaped and directed the trajectory of my entire life. I was defined by that thinking and undone by it. Every decision and relationship was governed by it. I decided I wanted to write about where the belief system sprang from, the choices I made because of it, and how, slowly over time, it is metamorphosing. For years, I saw myself as a victim; I wanted *you* to see me as a victim too, because if I were a victim, then I wasn't responsible, was I? Learning to accept responsibility for myself and my choices has been a rough and often reluctant path to trudge but the rewards have been copious and surprising. Becoming healthier and more mature, I attract like people. I'm no longer looking for someone or something outside myself to make me okay; I'm discovering I'm just fine as I am.

It is a lifelong process, thank goodness, because I'd hate to think I had to be done anytime soon; I still have work to do. And it is a spiritual experience. I believe that when something as deeply ingrained as my belief system changes, it has to come from a power greater than me. Which, really, shouldn't have been hard to find.

CHAPTER 1

To know me, you must first know my mother, Nancy Ann Whitney. More than anything else, my mother wanted to be an actress — a *famous* actress — which in the 1950s was all about being young, sexy, and available. She was all that, and more. She had big blue eyes, alabaster skin, a heart-shaped face, a beautiful figure. She was just a knockout.

But my mother seemed to feel there was an obstacle to her making it in show business in Hollywood. Children. And she had three of them by the time she was twenty-three — my two older brothers, Dick and Brian, and me. The fact that we existed made her seem older than she was. Her solution was to have us call her by her new stage name, Whitney Blake. We were not to call her "Mommy" anymore. We were to call her Whitney. I think she was hoping if we called her that, people might assume she was our aunt or maybe an older sister.

I can remember coming home from first grade, walking through the front door of our little white Craftsman-style house on Indiana Avenue in South Pasadena, and calling out, "Mommy, I'm home!"

No answer. I was confused; her car was out front. I stood very still.

"Mommy, I'm home!"

Still nothing. Then I remembered.

"Whitney?"

"Yes, dear?" her musical voice rang out from the middle bedroom, where she kept a vanity table at which she'd do her makeup.

Although I believe she had no idea about the psychological impact this might have on her children, now that I'm older I realize that Whitney was probably just giving us what she got. Whitney's mother was born Martha Mae Wilkerson — my brothers and I called her Memaw. She was a scrappy, tough, smart, and wily survivor. She wasn't the soft, fuzzy type; she didn't coddle Whitney and she didn't coddle me. Whenever I would complain about my clothes, as girls do, Memaw would tell me in her dry, crackly voice, "When I was little I had a red dress and a blue dress. When I was wearin' the red dress, I washed and ironed the blue dress. When I was wearin' the blue dress, I washed and ironed the red one. I didn't have choices."

Memaw was from Arkansas and married five times over the course of her life. She kept burying husbands (and sometimes I think there should be some exhumations to find out why). Whitney was only six when her real dad, Harry C. Whitney, a Secret Service man who guarded President Woodrow Wilson, died from alcoholism. Memaw's replacement husbands came at such a clip that Whitney never formed much of an attachment to any of them.

One of her stepfathers, Al, patented a fitting for oil rigs — his last name was Wells, ironically. He and Memaw would drift from oil field to oil field around the country. Sometimes they'd drag Whitney and her younger brother, Buddy, along. Just as often, Memaw would leave her kids behind, once with a couple of former missionaries and another time with her elementary school teacher.

It wasn't until the fifth grade that Whitney discovered drama class, when the boy who was supposed to play Oberon in Shakespeare's *A Midsummer Night's Dream* came down with a case of stage fright and she took over the role. From that day forward, Whitney realized that no matter what school she was in, the drama department would become home until Memaw announced it was time to pull up stakes and move again. Whitney said that the nearest thing she had to a real family when she was growing up were the casts of the plays that she appeared in.

Whitney was instead devoted to her brothers and sisters of the theater. One story she delighted in telling was about the time she was appearing in a Pasadena City College production that had a furniture dilemma: one scene needed a table, chairs, and a couch for the set, and none could be located. On opening night, Memaw shows up to watch her daughter perform, and when the curtain rises, she sees her entire living room set onstage. How Whitney managed to get the furniture out of her mother's house without anyone noticing is one thing. To reveal it in such a fashion required real chutzpah, which Whitney had in spades.

So in a way, Whitney's maternal model was someone who put her ambition ahead of her maternal responsibilities, and that's how she was with us. Dick, Brian, and I didn't talk about it much; we just lived it. It's what *was*. My brother Dick, the eldest, is very philosophical about her. He says, "Well, she did the best she could." But I think Brian and I took her actions more personally. They really shaped me; I had a strong sense of having been abandoned by her, that she didn't want me, that she didn't want to be my mother.

My mother was so intent on becoming an actress that eventually even Memaw got on board and told her that after she graduated from high school, she'd support her financially for one year. After that she would be on her own. Whitney attended the lower division of Pasadena City College, a sort of accelerated high school program for students interested in the performing arts, and she helped out at the college radio station, which was where she met my father, Tom Baxter. Just after Whitney turned eighteen, she got her high school diploma, she and Tom got married, and Whitney was finally able to move away from her mother. My father supported his rapidly growing family as an engineer with the Southern Pacific Railroad and later as a sound engineer specializing in live radio and television.

A couple of times, when I was very young, I visited my dad's studio at the ABC Radio Center on Vine Street in Hollywood. He would sit in his booth with a bank of electronic equipment in front of him, monitoring whatever show was on the air. He sat in front of a large window, through which he could watch the actors read from their scripts in the sound booth. He loved to tell about the pranks he pulled that invariably involved compromising the actors while they were recording. This was my favorite story: Because the rustle of papers is to be avoided in radio, anyone reading from a script typically holds the script pages in the left hand, separates the page to be read with the right, and holds that page next to the microphone, speaking directly into the mike. When that page is finished, it is allowed to waft silently to the floor and the reader continues with the next page. So, midrecording, my father would quietly enter the actor's sound booth and set fire to the top of the single page being read, which would initiate a kind of race for the actor to calmly read his lines before the paper burned up the text, while not betraying any tension to the listening audience.

My father said that he quit the business in the fifties when radio and television went to tape because it ceased to be fun. I think there was nothing for him to set fire to.

By 1953, after about ten years, my parent's marriage was on its last legs and Whitney filed for divorce. I was only five. The last day my father lived with us, my mother was away from the house, and he was in a state of turmoil and despair, just pacing, pacing, pacing. He sat my brothers and me down in the living room and said very seriously, "When I leave, you're never going to see me again." We all started crying like crazy.

My father was hurt, his life had fallen apart. I think his drama-filled master plan must have been to have Whitney return home to find her husband gone and her children sobbing inconsolably because she'd driven him away.

Before my father made his grand exit, without telling us he called my mother to tell her to come home, that we kids were alone. So when he drove away, we were scared and Dick called the only number we knew, which was our grandmother's, our father's mother. My grandparents arrived at the house followed closely by Whitney and Art, a guy she was having an affair with. Bedlam ensued with lots of yelling, accusations, and hysteria, and that was the end of my nuclear family.

Being single with three kids didn't mean that Whitney gave up on her hopes of becoming a star. She was dedicated and a hard worker. She worked as a bookkeeper and stenographer at the Lockheed Aircraft plant during the day, but at night she'd take acting classes and appear in plays at small local theaters like the Pasadena Playhouse, leaving us in the care of a string of housekeepers and friends. When she couldn't find anyone to watch us, she'd take us kids with her and we'd entertain ourselves in the dusty prop room, wardrobe room, and the cavernous wings and bowels of the theater until she was ready to go home. I remember those times fondly because not only were all of us siblings playing together but I also knew exactly where my mother was.

Although she herself was independent, Memaw's biggest message to Whitney when she was growing up had been: You need to find a man to take care of you. With my father out of the house, Whitney decided that my eldest brother, Dick, had the right chromosomal makeup — forget that he was about eight at the time — to fit the bill. She told him, "You are now the man of the family." But she kept looking for grown-up men as well; there were always plenty of them around our house, guys she'd met at class or in Playhouse productions. I remember two in particular: Ray, whom I liked because he fixed our sagging garage door, and redhaired Art, whom I didn't like. He mocked my fear of the rats that sometimes crawled out of our attic and ran across our backyard.

After the divorce, my father, Tom, remained part of our lives, but a small part. We'd see him every other weekend, and on the occasional Wednesday he'd pick us up after school and take us to his mother's house in Pasadena.

That grandmother's name was Jean Lawson Baxter and there was nothing soft about her, either. (What is it with my grandmothers?) She always spoke regretfully of being called Grandmother, instead of Memaw, the moniker she was hoping for. Unaccountably we called her husband Pepaw, but it was my maternal grandmother who was dubbed Memaw. Consequently, I always felt a silent competition between these strong women, whose paths rarely, if ever, crossed. Grandmother was tall, stout, formidable, very old, and had white hair that she wore circled and pinned. She didn't try to hide the fact that she had never been Whitney's biggest fan. One of my clearest memories is of her standing in the middle of our little house on Indiana Avenue, running her fingers over the mantel, saying negative things to Whitney and making it clear that she didn't think much of her housekeeping skills. She wasn't above interrogating me, either. She would sit me down on her porch swing and ask questions about Whitney — "Was she home at night?" "Were we left alone?" — making me feel very defensive. I didn't always understand her questions, but the tone was unmistakable. To my grandmother, as pious and self-righteous as she was, Whitney must have seemed irresponsible, flighty, and downright non-Christian.

Grandmother was too stern, imperious even, to bring much real coziness into our lives when we were little, but she did try. Once as a gift she gave me a pair of large, beautiful, fairly fragile, hand-painted boudoir dolls, more appropriate for window dressing than play. They were blond and brunette, stood about two feet high, and were dressed in gorgeous long satin and lace dresses. Though they were quite valuable in their day, I played with them until their gowns hung in tatters and their wigs were askew. At a certain point I decided that the dolls needed friends, so she made me two male dolls, sort of in the style of Raggedy Andy, with suits, ties, and shirts. But their faces were flat, and when I asked her to give them features, she obliged by figuring out how to gather the material together and make a seam that gave them little noses.

In my grandparents' long, deep yard was a huge two-story garage. On the second floor of it, my father had built and painted a complex miniature electric model railroad setup, complete with papier-mâché rocks and mountains, plastic forests and houses, railway stations, streams, small towns, and small townsfolk. It was magical. On rare occasions, he'd delight us by taking us up there, where, in the attic's hot motionless air, he'd let us stand on stools with our heads poking up between the mountains and watch as he made the trains traverse the rails around some snowcapped peaks down into a sagebrushy desert to the depot. There a train would take on water or perhaps let go a few cattle cars, then proceed out through a valley with livestock and a few ranches. We weren't allowed to touch, but I drank it in whenever he'd allow.

Grandmother and Pepaw, who was barely a presence, had a little one-room playhouse built for us. This small gesture, this act of making something just for my brothers and me, loomed so large in my tiny psyche that years later, when I was filming *Family,* and realized that we were shooting less than two miles away, I had to scratch that nostalgic itch and go visit.

My grandmother's house was at 95 Columbia Street in Pasadena. For some reason I have in my memory that they'd bought the house in 1900 for $800, a tidy sum in those days. It was a beautiful old Victorian house, white clapboard with beveled glass fans over windows and doors. I'd remembered it as huge and imposing: steep steps up to the grand pillared porch and a very heavy, important oak door. What I found on the day I visited was a less imposing house with the beautiful beveled windows and a cement porch with three steps leading up to it, flanked by two modest round white supports and a heavy, important oak door.

On which I knocked. An older woman came to the door and when I explained who I was and that I'd largely grown up in her house, she was most gracious and invited me to come in, look around. What luck! On the left of the entry were the drawing rooms, divided by high pocket doors, which still slid silently closed as smoothly as if made yesterday. To the right, another set of stairs I'd remembered as steep and threatening seemed so tame. Upstairs I was aghast to see that the heavy porcelain claw-foot bathtub had been replaced with a shower and countertop of turquoise Formica. Another room had a wall covered with a woven fabric, peeling just a bit, and a zebra print rug on the floor. Okay, enough of the house. I had to see the playhouse.

Unbelievably, it was still standing. The owner couldn't find the key, but the windows were open, and when I stuck my head in it was like Marcel Proust's famous bite of the "petites madeleines." The musty smell instantly took me back in time and there I was with my brother Brian, reading stacks and stacks of Big Little Books or playing school with my grandmother's companion, Kate Frazier.

Back in Springfield, Missouri, where my grandmother was from, she and Kate ran a boardinghouse together. When my grandparents moved out to California in 1900 with baby Tom and his elder sister, Jinny, Kate came with them to help look after little Tom. In fact, when Dick, Brian, and I would spend the night, I would sleep in Kate's room, which faced the street and had a big cut-glass fan window. This was wonderful to me because Kate was probably the first person I ever felt bonded to. In the constellation of an elusive mother, unsmiling grandmothers, and faceless housekeepers, Kate was the only grown-up who seemed to want to be with me. I remember her sweet patient old face and small, wrinkly, blue-veined hands. I'd trace the veins, pushing gently on them, marveling at how soft, pliant, and collapsible they were. And she'd let me. Unlike Grandmother, who usually seemed to have high expectations of us little ones, that we should live up to some kind of standard, Kate was just loving.

When pretend class would be in session out in the back playhouse, I would be the seven-year-old know-it-all teacher and Kate would dutifully make mistake after mistake, which I'd correct with exasperation and rolling eyes. When Kate would bake pies in the big kitchen in the main house, she would collect all the leftover bits of dough and make crisp piecrust cookies for us that she'd sprinkle with powdered sugar and cinnamon. I make them too, to this day, every time I bake a pie.

Many years ago, Whitney told me that once divorced from my father, she'd wanted to relocate from Pasadena to Hollywood to fully pursue her career but was afraid to move there as a single woman. She said it wouldn't be smart and she felt vulnerable, that it might not "look right" for a pretty young thing to come to town unprotected. And that was why she latched onto Jack.

My mother met Jack X (the lack of a period was what he called his signature)

Fields, a theatrical agent, when he came to see her in her first professional part: a production of *The Women* at the Hollywood Playhouse on Las Palmas. Jack must have seen promise in Whitney's performance because afterward he sent word backstage that he'd like to represent her. Jack was not an attractive man, but he was six feet tall, distinguished-looking, graceful, and solidly built like the boxer he'd once been. Most important, he believed in Whitney enough to orchestrate for her a Hollywood-style makeover.

He came up with the stage name of Whitney Blake. He had her lighten her dark hair blond and — as I saw one day in the second grade when she came to pick me up — get a nose job. It's a vivid memory: her hair was curled, she was wearing high heels and a tight gray pencil skirt, and there was a big bandage over the center of her face.

With that, the transformation from regular pretty girl to dazzling ingenue was complete. In fact, she'd often be mistaken for Kim Novak or Carroll Baker.

A year after they met, Whitney and Jack were married, and we moved from our small South Pasadena bungalow on Indiana Avenue to a ritzy (for us) split-level hillside house at 6722 Whitley Terrace in the Hollywood Hills. It was unbelievable: We walked into the upstairs! In our new house, the master bedroom, kitchen, and dining room were on the top floor and the kids' bedrooms and an elegant all-white living room and bar were downstairs. There was a big, sloped terraced yard and a view of the Hollywood Bowl parking lot. I remember my brothers and I went crazy when we first moved in . . . running up and down the yard steps . . . hiding in bushes . . . racing through the house . . . and getting lost. It was so much grander than the modest house we'd come from.

After our move, Whitney's television career started to take off. We had a series of housekeepers but she basically abdicated child-rearing responsibilities to Jack. She was busy guest-starring on popular TV dramas like *Whirlybirds* and *Circus Boy.* In "The Case of the Restless Redhead," she played a café waitress named Evelyn Bagby, who is wrongly accused of murder and seeks the help of Perry Mason in the hard-boiled legal drama's premiere episode of that series. I don't remember seeing her much in those days, just a few images of her in curlers rushing off to work early.

When I was much younger, I'd get in front of my class at school to tell the kids my mother was going to be on television. I think I was hoping this would earn me some friends or admiration; my subtext was always: Do you like me now? When I was older, in junior high, though, I switched to telling kids my mother was Anne Baxter. No one recognized the name Whitney Blake. Anne Baxter sounded like she actually *could* be my mother. And *she'd* won an Academy Award.

Jack had been an air force colonel during World War II and the Korean War, so, in lieu of any previous experience in bringing up youngsters, he practiced a bullying, military-influenced style of parenting that involved endless lists and schedules. What time we had to get up. What time to brush our teeth. What time to make breakfast. Who was to make breakfast. What time we were supposed to leave for school. What time we were to be home. The chores we had to complete. Whose turn it was to feed our three pet dachshunds, Faust, Tina, and Oedipus.

When I neglected to clean my room properly, I lost it; I forfeited any right to enter it for a period of days or weeks. On those nights Jack had me sleep in the "den," which was really part of the basement, a damp unfinished room built into the side of the hill; there were exposed overhead pipes and a dirt wall. I'd make a bed as close as possible to the door, bring in a lamp and a radio, and pray for daylight.

This, however, was preferable to what happened when my brothers forgot to put out the trash on collection day, which on rare occasions they would. Jack's way of making sure they'd never forget again was to take the garbage cans out of the garage, lug them through the kitchen, then down the stairs and up the hall, and deposit them in my brothers' bedroom. And there, not two feet from where my brothers slept — and these were the days before in-sink disposals and plastic trash bags — the cans of rotting, week-old garbage sat, the sound of writhing larvae and maggots growing louder and the stench worsening. It was Jack's plan to leave the garbage cans there until collection day the following week, but nature intervened. When fastidious Jack saw that maggots were wriggling out of the can and onto the carpet, he had them move the cans out into the hallway. Eventually he gave up and ordered my brothers to return the bins back to the garage where they belonged.

Jack controlled most elements of our lives. We weren't allowed to argue. We weren't allowed to be angry. We learned the hard way about why we should be wary of him while his back was turned. Over the years, one of my brothers or I would make the mistake of trying to get his attention by approaching and tapping him from behind. He would spin around and punch us in the stomach with a closed fist and then apologize. "Oh, sorry," he'd say. "It's my boxer instincts. Don't do that."

There were also infractions that Jack considered so egregious they could be remedied only by sending the transgressor out to the backyard to collect a thin branch from a big carob tree and bring it inside to him. Then he'd administer an old-school whipping on the backs of our legs. I understood the concept of "If kids do something wrong, they should be disciplined." But with Jack, the punishment rarely fit the crime. One trip I took out to the carob tree occurred after Jack found out that I bought candy after promising him that I wouldn't. I paid the price by being switched and arriving at school the next day with ugly red welts on my calves.

When Brian was about ten, I can remember Jack taking him into the downstairs den and switching him until his pained cries could be heard all over the house. I thought someone had to save him, so I ran up the stairs until I could see the door to Whitney and Jack's room. It was closed. I knew she was in there. The policy was that if the door were open, you could knock on it and see if anyone answered. But if the door were closed, that meant Don't Even Knock. We did not ever, under any circumstances, walk in. So many times, I remember standing on the stairs, just watching that door, willing it to open; willing her to notice what was going on in our house.

If there ever was a pure Hollywood agent, it was Jack. On one hand he was a master manipulator, the kind of guy who liked pulling strings, making things happen quietly behind the scenes. He'd build his credit by exacting favors when needed. Because I found him so harsh, I was surprised to discover that he actually had another dimension. In the late '40s and early '50s, when blacklisting was at the height of its power, he lent a hand to many folks who'd found themselves on the wrong side of the House Un-American Activities Committee, who were blacklisted for supposedly being Communists or Communist sympathizers and unable to find work in Hollywood. Jack helped actors like Zero Mostel, Jack Gilford, Woody Strode, Marsha Hunt, and Strother Martin get back on their feet by finding them gigs on commercials and other work situations.

And there was Jack's Home for Wayward Actors, a little guest room off our backyard where Jack would install clients who were between jobs. I'm not sure how the wonderful character actor Frank Silvera ended up there, but he was one of our more permanent residents. He stayed with us for about two years so we teasingly called him The Man Who Came to Dinner. He appeared in everything from Elia Kazan's *Viva Zapata!* to the action-adventure classic *Mutiny on the Bounty,* and the hilarious part was that in every movie Frank was cast as a different ethnicity. Black and born in Kingston, Jamaica, he managed to sidestep being racially pigeonholed because he was so light-skinned. In one film he'd play a Mexican heavy and in the next he'd show up as a Native American.

Memaw, who grew up in Arkansas and was not known for her racial tolerance, didn't know what to make of Frank. On his first Thanksgiving with us, we were all seated around the table and Frank was sitting next to Memaw. We noticed she'd been watching him attentively out of the corner of her eye. She leaned in very close to him and said hopefully, "Maybe you're . . . *Polynesian?*" And Frank, possibly the sweetest man in the world, put her at ease with, "Why yes, maybe I am."

When I was in the seventh grade, Jack asked me if I'd like to audition for a television series. I was beside myself with excitement over the idea; it sounded like so much fun! NBC was doing a half-hour black-and-white television remake of the 1944 family classic movie *National Velvet,* which had made a huge star out of Elizabeth Taylor, and I was going to audition for the lead part of Velvet. Jack prevailed on Frank, our handy in-house actor, to help prepare me for my scene.

When it came to acting coaches, I couldn't have found one more gentle, encouraging, and patient than Frank. I owe him a debt of gratitude for a good part of what followed. For several days, Frank and I sat in the dining room, rehearsing the long monologue I was going to give. It was a very emotional speech and I'd had no acting experience, but I threw myself into this task with total abandon. More than nine hundred child actors tried out and I was one of four who made it to the screen test. Three other young girls and I were sent to the hair and makeup department, where they tinted our hair so we'd look just like Velvet did in the movie. The jet-black rinse was so cheap that it turned my hair brush gray and left a sooty shadow on my pillow. But I thought I looked sultry; I thought that with my blue eyes and newly darkened hair I looked terribly glamorous.

On the day we all showed up for our screen tests, I guess I did my scene as required but what I remember most was the great fun the four of us girls had as we ran around the NBC studio lot. We were a quartet of nearly identical black-haired girls hyped up on adrenaline and postaudition exhilaration, racing around the cavernous soundstages and shrieking in unison. It was such a thrill to be running around with other kids, being part of a happy girl pack instead of the quiet loner at Le Conte Junior High School.

After several days of anguished waiting, Jack called me into the living room and told me that I didn't get the part. Apparently, they didn't want me to star in their series because I didn't know how to comport myself. I'd played around the studio lot too much. I was unprofessional.

"Oh, all right," I said to Jack as coolly as I possibly could.

Then I went downstairs to my room and collapsed. I sobbed for hours. I was blind-sided. It never occurred to me that I wouldn't get it. I'd blown it horribly. Jack said I was "irresponsible" and "unprofessional." I was wracked with humiliation. Rejected at twelve.

Only recently did I find out what might have *really* happened. The girl who landed the part was named Lori Martin and had been acting professionally since she was six. (Which was six more years of acting experience than I had.) I also read that after dying Lori's hair she was the mirror image of an adolescent Liz Taylor. In other words, the producers didn't necessarily reject me because I'd misbehaved. They probably went with the most seasoned young actress who also happened to be a ringer for a popular movie star.

How like Jack to leave me with the imprint of a self-inflicted loss. I might have fared better if I were a Communist.

CHAPTER 2

So my big break didn't happen. It was back to the seventh grade for me.

Meanwhile, Whitney's star continued to rise. For a while, it seemed like you couldn't turn on the TV without seeing her on popular shows like *The Millionaire* and *77 Sunset Strip*. An entire Whitney montage could have been assembled of her waltzing around in period costumes on every high-rated western series — *Rawhide, Cheyenne, Bronco, Maverick, Pony Express.*

The show she really loved doing was *M Squad,* a moody, black-and-white cop show starring Lee Marvin, on which she guest-starred at least once a season. Marvin played Lt. Frank Ballinger, a scowling plain-clothes tough guy from Chicago who wore a bent felt fedora. Whitney would play characters like a coldly glamorous girlfriend of a murdered mob lawyer, requiring her to be flirtatious, conniving, sneaky, vulnerable, and frightened and maybe even die, sadly, at the end. Those roles had real dramatic arcs; they involved real acting and they thrilled her.

The exciting guest spots ended, though, in 1961 when Jack got Whitney cast as a regular on *Hazel,* a new CBS sitcom starring Oscar-winner Shirley Booth as Hazel Burke, a problem-solving maid who runs roughshod over her employers. When *Hazel* debuted that September, it was an instant ratings winner. The only problem was that no one seemed interested in fleshing out a part for my mother. The energy of every episode came from Shirley Booth butting heads with her boss, corporate attorney George Baxter, played by Don DeFore. Meanwhile, Whitney's role — George's amiable wife, Dorothy Baxter, an interior designer whom Hazel called Missy B — stood on the fringes of every scene, relegated to silently smiling and nodding at Hazel and Mr. B's banter.

Whitney took her acting seriously enough that she never stopped trying to breathe some life into Dorothy, but from that first year, she hated everything about the series. She complained volubly and frequently that she hated being third banana on that show, hated the lack of variety, always arriving at the same set at the old Columbia/Gower Studios in Hollywood. She missed the excitement of appearing on different shows with new casts and going toe to toe with strong leading men like Clint Eastwood and Efrem Zimbalist Jr. She felt that Shirley Booth was always protecting her own territory, always making sure that my mother couldn't steal any of the spotlight. One perk for Whitney, though, was that initially her character was always fashionably dressed, wearing sexy, form-fitting suits.

During season two, Whitney began to feel as if even Missy B's chic wardrobe was being taken away from her. For the first year, the half-hour show was filmed in black and white, but when it returned the following September as a color program, Dorothy's costume color palette had a new range, from drab gray to mousy beige. My mother told me she believed that Shirley had issued a mandate that she never wanted her to wear anything pretty or that might be construed as flattering. I can remember Whitney sitting at the makeup table in her room, putting on false eyelashes and cursing the lighting man, who she thought was in cahoots with the star. Whitney was sure that Shirley was telling him how to light her so she looked jowly and unattractive.

Since Jack was her agent, Whitney blamed him for talking her into doing the series. She felt that he'd sold her out, that he'd imprisoned her in a multiyear contract with Screen Gems so that he could then use her regular stream of paychecks to buy into the Sid Gold–Jack Fields Agency, his boutique talent agency on Sunset Boulevard in Hollywood. Even after it went off the air after a five-year run, she always referred to *Hazel* as "the graveyard" of her career. The only upside that *Hazel* had to offer was that with its high ratings and Shirley Booth's two consecutive Emmys, it brought industry cachet and regular money. In the span of a few years, mealtime for our little family had gone from modest macaroni and cheese dinners in South Pasadena to more elaborate white-tablecloth and candle-lit affairs in our Hollywood Hills dining room. Whitney even had a large ceramic bell that she'd ring — this still makes me wince to think about it — to summon our dear Guatemalan housekeeper, Anna.

Whitney and Jack really loved to entertain at home for their friends in the business. Ed Asner was a regular, as well as the casting director Lynn Stalmaster and his wife, Lee, and film director Arthur Hiller and his wife, Gwen. Marlon Brando came once; he and

46

my old *National Velvet* acting coach Frank Silvera became friends while making *Mutiny on the Bounty.*

Jack and Whitney seemed to prefer inviting people over when my brothers and I were out of the house, especially as the years passed and we got older. Having three teenagers contradicted the young, glamorous TV star image Whitney was still putting out there. In fact, there are no home photos of my brothers and me from this time. There were never *any* family photos taken at the Whitley Terrace house. There are no photos of us with our mother until we were adults. It was a preventive measure: Not having snapshots of us around meant that there was nothing for a reporter to dig up about Whitney Blake and print in a magazine.

I can count on one hand the times my brothers and I were present at their parties. I have a faint memory of being about ten years old and being instructed how to offer cocktails on a tray to Martin Landau and Barbara Bain. I helpfully made sure I addressed Whitney by name in front of guests once in a while just to keep the "niece" possibility in the air. I never had to be reminded.

47

■ ■ ■ ■

While filming *Hazel,* the only time my mother was around was on the weekends. Monday through Friday she'd leave for work at 5 a.m., before I woke up. She'd return home at night looking exhausted, retire to her bedroom, and I'd rarely see her. I was essentially being raised by housekeepers, trying to catch a glimpse of Whitney on the fly. Because I saw her so rarely, I didn't want to aggravate her by seeming to need her. Once, I really wanted her to sign a permission slip so I could see a movie they were showing to the girls in our grammar school class called *The Story of Menstruation.* I wasn't sure what it was about but since it was "for girls only," I didn't want Jack to sign the slip. I didn't know anything about "the mysteries of womanhood" at the time, so I probably thought the movie was about a girl named Menstruation. I was inordinately excited to see it.

I think Whitney knew how clueless I was and her goal must have been to prepare me. So she came into my bedroom that night, sat down at the end of my bed, and gave me a short speech about cows and little calves, then said good night and went upstairs. I guess I understood it was somehow about our changing bodies but was not much more enlightened than before we spoke. I did get a profound sense of Whitney's discomfort around the subject. I am grateful to the Los Angeles Unified School District for making that film available or I'd have been left totally confused about how I was to relate to the bovine population.

When I eventually got my first period, I was thirteen. I was with Whitney, Jack, and my brothers in Palm Springs for a few days, staying at a small rental house with a pool. I had just come in from swimming and saw the blood in my wet bathing suit. I had to go to Whitney with the news but I remember feeling shy; it was so personal a thing to tell her. I was not quite sure what I expected to happen but I begged her urgently to not tell Jack. Whitney said something about my needing pads and a belt and sent me off to get dressed. I went, asking again that she please not tell Jack.

"Oh, of course not," she said.

An hour later, I saw Jack driving away.

"Where's he going?" I asked.

"To get your Kotex."

What? Did she not care? Didn't it matter that I didn't want Jack to know? I just walked around and around in panicked circles, choking on feeling so betrayed.

Meanwhile, even before I hit puberty, I started getting very different signals from Jack. My stepfather was very appreciative of young, attractive women and would always comment on their appearance. From the time I was twelve, we'd play this game where I'd stand on the stair above him and I'd say, "Kiss me like the movie stars kiss," and we'd mash our tightly pursed mouths together and go "Mmmmmm . . ." While it had been appealing to me when I was younger because it won me some attention, it was starting to get creepy as I got older. It wasn't until the time I could feel his tongue pushing forward against the inside of his lips that I didn't play the game anymore.

Then there was how I looked. I had these breasts. I went from almost flat-chested at thirteen to huge at fourteen. I felt it was because of them that I got so much undesired attention from men when I walked to junior high: whistles, guys yelling at me, some jacking off out their car window at me; I felt like a moving target and was always on the alert for *who's going after me today.* No wonder I have always leaned toward clothes that minimized my bust.

I had blossomed so unexpectedly that I

didn't have a bra and wasn't sure how to go about getting one. Then I thought of the Lerner Shop on Hollywood Boulevard. I walked past it on my way to Le Conte. I stopped in one day after school and prowled around. God knows I wasn't going to ask for help. That would probably involve showing some saleswoman my breasts and, well, asking for help. I didn't want to do either, so I decided to figure it out myself. I grabbed a tape measure and leapt into a changing room, where I measured myself, over my clothes. Going around my back and across the fullest part of my breast, I measured 40 inches. So that's a size 40, I figured, amazed that anyone would consider using a salesperson when this was as obvious as pie. I snagged a very white, starched, torpedo-shaped size 40 from the rack and tried it on. It was pretty scratchy and a bit big so I hiked the straps up really high to get it to fit me tightly, which put the back way up high across my shoulders. I wasn't clear just what was accomplished but I thought it was fabulous! I took it off, plunked down my bucks at the register, and sauntered out of the store. A bra owner.

When I got home, I was surprised to see my mother standing in the kitchen as I zipped past and headed straight downstairs to my room. She must have seen my parcel because she called out, "What did you buy?" I just yelled back, "A scarf."

I frankly can't recall where my clothes would come from. I only remember one shopping trip with my mother, which ended in disaster, probably typical of many mother-daughter shopping trips. She wanted me to wear something I didn't like and I ended up in tears. The dress came home with us anyway and I never wore it. Typical.

When I was about fifteen, I couldn't find swimwear that fit me properly, basically because my breasts were so full, and it was Jack who offered a solution. He could have a bathing suit custom-made for me. I could pick any fabric I wanted. He needed me to give him one of my bras for the tailor to copy. Giving my bra to my stepfather felt desperately creepy; everything in me recoiled. But I was a self-centered teenager and I wanted a nice swimsuit.

He brought it home a few weeks later when they had guests over to swim.

"Try it on," he said. "Let's see how it fits."

Well, he did get me this suit as a favor, I thought. I guess he can ask to see it on. I reluctantly went into my room, changed, and returned to show him. Jack had a way

52

of looking at me that made me look away. I guess Jack liked how the bathing suit fit. His friends Lynn Stalmaster and Arthur Hiller were out by the pool.

"Go show them," he told me. "I'm sure they'd love to see it on you."

"Jack!" I protested.

"Go on, go on, go on," he insisted.

So I did as Jack asked. I walked slowly around the pool in my new custom bathing suit while his friends checked me out. They made complimentary noises. I hated doing this. I died a thousand deaths before going back into the house. But I was getting the message that my looks, my breasts had some power; that no matter how much shame I felt, how self-conscious or insecure I might feel, how much I knew that the attention my breasts brought had nothing to do with *me,* they were my currency. That maybe they were all I had to have. And deep in my heart I craved the attention, no matter what.

Harvey was a client of Jack's, another houseguest who came to stay and lived with us for almost two years. In the late sixties, he'd make it big with his own TV series. But back then he was happy when Jack got him bit parts on shows. He had a beat-up James Dean quality and soulful, hooded eyes. He moved in when I was fourteen and he was an artistic, wonderfully funny and moody twenty-one-year-old. How could I not fall in love with him?

I flirted with Harvey. I tried to get his attention by wearing a pair of cutoff jeans and an oversize button-up shirt knotted high so my bare midriff was exposed. I had pictures of my mother in a publicity photo dressed similarly and it seemed to work for her. I felt more silly than sexy, but I kept trying.

I felt he had to know that I coveted the nights he'd sit with my brothers and me and play bluesy records in front of the fireplace. Harvey would tell stories and we'd play memory games. He must have had no other place to go; why else would he spend evenings with a bunch of teenagers? But then he gave me his sweater. To keep! A gray pullover with patched elbows. I loved it; it smelled of him and I wore it everywhere. Then he started dating this very delicate young woman. They'd frequently have dinner at our house with Whitney and Jack and I'd be *so* jealous. One night, I was going out and stopped in the dining room to say good-bye. As I walked out, I heard Harvey's date say, "Isn't she wearing the sweater I gave you?" I'd no idea it had been a gift from her. I was so confused. She gave him the sweater but he gave it to me, so he must care about me, but he was spending lots of time with her. And then, they were married at our house about a year later. I was crushed.

It was probably around this time I started putting more energy into getting boys' attention. I was desperate for attention but my shyness retarded the process. When I was in ninth grade, I had started attending youth group activities at a local Presbyterian church, where I'm sure I met some girls, but they were really only vehicles to the boys. There were about twenty of us in the youth group and we would have dances and serve dinners to the elderly members at Wednesday-night church gatherings, then we'd pair up and go make out down in the church basement. I was out on a date one night with a guy from the group named John and we wound up necking heavily in his car behind a drive-in. If I recall, small articles of clothes had been removed when suddenly flashlights were blinding us through the windshield and we were ordered out of the car by Los Angeles's finest. They talked to us separately, I think to ascertain that I was there willingly, because John was older and although I was fourteen, I looked younger. They threatened to call my parents but didn't, thank God; we were let go and I went home pretty rattled and embarrassed.

Shortly after that, someone must have read my diary — I'm not sure if it was Whitney or my father — and thought that I devoted too many pages to the opposite sex, so, much to my dismay, it was decided that I would go live with my father about fifteen miles away in the San Fernando Valley. Right around this period my brother Brian fell in love with the theater department at Hollywood High and began sneaking out in the early evening to go down the hill to school to rehearse. I don't know what Jack's aversion was to this activity but somehow he found out and grounded Brian. So Brian ran away from home and never returned. At seventeen, he preferred to sleep wherever he could — with a schoolmate's family, in a friend's garage apartment — than live with the über-controlling Jack. Brian was my emotional anchor at the Whitley Terrace house. Once he wasn't living there it was easier for me to leave.

The move turned out to be fun for me in many unexpected ways. I'd thought I'd start tenth grade at Hollywood High, as had my brothers; instead I found myself at James Monroe High School in Sepulveda, two blocks from my dad's house. I seized the opportunity to reinvent myself. I changed my name to Mardi, thinking somehow that would free me to be a more interesting person.

And I actually was popular at school for the only time in my life. I went out on a couple of dates. I made a good friend named Judy, who lived just around the corner, and we would spend many afternoons at her house, singing and playing the piano together. Living in my father's simple tract house in the flats was so different from living in the isolated Hollywood Hills, far from school with no friends nearby. I really felt, Wow, I'm a different person!

I'd never really spent any serious stretch of time around my father. People found him very charming and energetic with a nice sense of humor and a penchant for bad puns. ("How's the flying business, Tom?" "Oh, up in the air." He had been a pilot and worked with charter aircraft at Van Nuys Airport.) He *was* very charming and amusing but not very interested in me, it seemed. I'd come in the house, whether from school or back from a week away, and he'd be sitting in his chair next to the floor lamp, buried in and obscured by the newspaper. "Hi darling," he'd say energetically but without lowering the paper. "You look great!" So, yes, that was amusing but not inviting, not bonding.

The only physical interaction I ever recall having with him was when my brothers and I were three, four, and five, and we started playing a game we called 1–2-3-GO! My father would lie on the floor while we stood, eagerly poised in various corners, while he counted, 1–2-3, and on GO! we'd all race to see who could sit on his stomach first. His job, of course, was to keep that from happening. I loved the physicality of it; we'd shriek when we made it to his stomach and shriek to play it again and again. We milked that game for what it was worth for *years* until my father opted out because he thought he was going to get hurt. I also remember that he had taken us to Yosemite for a few days after his divorce from my mother. And while I was living with him he gave me a driving lesson in a parking lot across from his house. That was pretty much it.

I was very fond of my stepmother. If there was going to be any substantive mother figure in my life, it was Ginger. She and my father had two of their own children by the time I came to live with them (and two more shortly after I left), and although she worked part-time as a Tupperware dealer, too, she always made time for me. Ginger was the youngest of three sisters and came from a very protected Baptist family. Occasionally, my brothers and I would get to be part of holiday celebrations with Ginger's family out in Alhambra in the early years of their marriage. There'd be the usual spread of food and chatter, but what I loved most was when all of the women in her family would go into the kitchen after dinner to wash and dry the dishes, and they'd be singing and laughing. There was a real sense of warmth and family. I can remember Memaw, my aunt, and Whitney being in the kitchen together, but there was never a feeling that they were enjoying one another's company. Because of Ginger's family, though, washing dishes and singing and chatter in the kitchen is something that I've tried to re-create with my children. When my daughters come home and we're cooking together, we're always singing and laughing, baking and throwing flour at one another.

I was doing okay at Monroe High School and had an unparalleled social life: I had a few people I went to football games with. I tried out for the B Team cheerleading squad, which I didn't make. I think I was a respected part of the drama class. But I got homesick. I don't understand why. But halfway through the semester, I told my father, "I miss Whitney." Which is funny, right? What did I miss, her absence? I think it hurt my feelings that she was just continuing her life without me. So I moved back to Whitley Terrace and finished tenth grade at Hollywood High.

It was right around this time that two new preoccupations came into my life: the high school drama department and LSD. It was 1962, just when the acid craze began to take hold in this country, and my brothers jumped right on the psychedelics bandwagon. Dick was the first to offer me a tab of acid. I remember him standing there with two little white pills in his hand, one for me and one for him. At the time he was eighteen and way cool and usually paid little attention to me. If those tiny squares were worthy of an interaction, that was good enough for me. I don't even think I asked what it was.

It was Brian, not Dick, though, who became my LSD partner. He was living with friends but still going to Hollywood High when I moved back home, and we'd meet up and take it together on weekends. At this point he had full-on hippie hair: beard, mustache, and a long, red ponytail. Brian, his friends, and I would drop some acid, go out to Santa Monica, and walk around the beach at night, holding candles, just laughing and laughing and laughing at everything, interspersed with the occasional shriek of "Wow!" Then we'd go to the International House of Pancakes. We'd watch way too many plates arrive at our table and eat six bites before something about the color of the ketchup distracted us. Or the pat of yellow butter melting. Or the golden maple syrup oozing slowly from the dispenser. Or our waving hands leaving afterimage trails in the air. Once some guy walked into the IHOP dressed as a clown with a bulbous red nose and big floppy shoes and we thought we'd lose our minds! "Wow, man! *Wow! Far out!*" Afterward, we'd head up to Mulholland Drive, and, as we came down from the high, have long, convoluted discussions about what we'd seen, experienced, and hallucinated.

Taking LSD made me feel connected to the others; I loved that we were sharing insights, beauty, and laughter together, even though it was totally forgotten the next day. I started taking play production classes at school in search of the same connections. There wasn't really any other place for me. I was one of the last to get picked at team sports because I was not very agile. While

Hollywood High had a Greek system in place, none of the sororities wanted me, even though Dick leaned on an old girlfriend who was a Delta and got her to pull some strings. The Deltas passed anyway. Then I tried to get into the Lambdas. No deal. I wasn't unfriendly, but I had no people skills; I didn't bring much to the table. I was just looking for a place to *be*.

The theater gang was a different story. We were all on the outside of the Hollywood High social whirl. I was never assigned the important parts. A typical role for me would be playing Hera, the goddess of marriage, in *The Tempest*. But at least I felt I belonged. One day in drama class an eleventh-grade girl, Tory Thompson, casually mentioned to me that she and two of her friends were going to a football game that night. Tory was very tall and slender and I thought she was just beautiful. I must have mentioned that the game sounded like fun because she then asked if I wanted to come along.

"Really?" I asked. "Of course!"

I didn't have permission to leave the house that night. But I figured that since Jack and Whitney were going to be out, they'd never know. That evening after the football game, Tory's friend offered to give me a ride home. So Tory and I climbed into the bed of her friend's pickup truck facing backward. We turned off of Sunset Boulevard and, while heading toward Whitley Terrace, we stopped at a red light. A pale blue Cadillac pulled up behind us and I froze. In it sat Jack and Whitney. The flat, deadly look in Jack's eyes was terrifying. I don't think I even looked at Whitney . . . it was Jack I feared. I think I stopped breathing. He smiled faintly, nodding slowly. I was in such big trouble that I've totally erased from my memory what happened when I got home.

For Tory and me, this turned out to be a bonding experience. Tory, whose father was a raging alcoholic, knew what it was like to live with an unpredictable parent. I'd managed to make a friend who actually preferred the strained, pretentious atmosphere of Whitely Terrace to the wine-fueled turbulence she might find at home.

Tory and I spent a lot of time together and at some point she met my brother Brian, and they began dating. Around the same time a sweet, unassuming senior I knew from play production class named John Herzog asked me out. John was a very good actor and had most of the choice leading roles in our high school productions. We dated for about a year and I still have the photo from when he took me to his senior prom. He's handsome in a pale tuxedo jacket and black slacks; I'm in a spaghetti-strap gown that barely supports my DD-size breasts (I remember losing many cookie and cheese crumbs down my ample cleavage that night) and my hair is up in a circle of heavy braids with tiny white roses stuck in it. It was like I had a big flowered Danish on my head. I looked pretty goofy but I remember having a good time. There was normalcy and routine, both in school and in friendship, that felt stable.

I liked being with John. He was a good, gentle guy, and one year after the prom, I will lose my virginity to him. I won't be in love; I won't be eager to *do it;* I will sadly feel a little dead with no connection to him or the event. That pretty much is the end of us.

In the summer of '63, my mother was starring in a summer stock production of a romantic comedy called *Janus* at the Cherry County Playhouse in Traverse City, Michigan; Jack, Dick, and I came, too. For a sixteen-year-old who hadn't been much of anywhere, that part of the country was breathtaking. Traverse City sits right at the tip of a bay that feeds into Lake Michigan; it was a small town with a river running right alongside the historic downtown area.

Even better, Whitney was happy. In northern Michigan, my mother's role on *Hazel* made her a huge celebrity, and after another ego-bruising season as Missy B, she just drank in the attention. We stayed in a tiny white house out on the peninsula that my mother rented from a woman named Mrs. Wysong. She was warm and friendly — sort of like a white-haired, bespectacled Mrs. Santa Claus with a Michigan accent.

All of these images were part of the attraction the following summer, when I returned to Traverse City to be an apprentice in the same summer stock company. It was Jack's idea to pull some strings with the Cherry County Playhouse and get me an apprenticeship. Jack said I could bring a friend, so Tory came along. Jack paid any expenses that Tory's parents couldn't afford. I found Jack's occasional bursts of generosity confusing but welcome. At the time, my older brother Dick was working as an editor and features writer at the *Los Angeles Herald-Examiner,* and although he still lived at home, he wasn't there very often. Looking back, I can see that for all intents and purposes Jack and Whitney would have the house to themselves for two months, and I imagine they relished that.

For the first time in our lives, Tory and I

were free to do whatever we wanted. We shared a rented room in the house of a local doctor and put in long hours at the theater, but no one monitored our comings and goings. Apprentices showed up at the playhouse very early in the morning to help out with whatever needed to be done — cutting gels for the lights, printing out playbills, getting wardrobe ready. We stayed late into the night, taking tickets, delivering wardrobe to dressing rooms, running and then taking inventory of the concession stands, and waiting until the play was finished so that we could strike the set. I loved it.

The Cherry County Playhouse was a theater in the round held in a huge red- and white-striped circus tent. On hot nights or afternoons, the intense heat collected under the high peaks of the tent and the apprentices had to ventilate it by rolling up the side flaps. When the weather turned blustery or it rained, strong winds would blow in through the entrance flaps and literally lift the tent up. When this happened, it was up to the apprentices to hold the tent down. I remember times when Tory and I, working with the others, tied the flaps closed and climbed up the sides of the tent, mooring ourselves between staves during the performances, our full weight stabilizing its vibrating panels. The part that always made us laugh was when a powerful blast of wind would catapult us into the air, loose ropes whipping like lariats. It was wild. The work we did was varied and demanding but always exciting.

During that summer of '64, I worked with the comedy legend Joe E. Brown, who starred in our production of *Harvey* and who was best known as the millionaire Osgood Fielding III, who falls for Jack Lemmon in drag in Billy Wilder's *Some Like It Hot.* My part was to stand in the wings and belt out a song intentionally off-key, but I still considered it a feather in my cap that we shared — *kind of* — the same stage.

This summer was also the first time I really tried my hand at alcohol. I'd not paid much attention to it before, being put off by the noxious taste. Here, everyone drank a lot: cast, crew, and apprentices. I had a crush on the stage manager, Barry. He drank Cutty Sark and water. That became my drink of choice. It was *disgusting.* I can remember one strike night there was a cast and crew party in the tent for the closing of a show, and I began counting out loud how many drinks I'd downed. I think I hoped I was impressing Barry. "I've had eight!" was the last thing I recall shouting. The next thing I knew, it was morning and I came to — where I'd passed out — smack in the middle of the stage floor. I probably wasn't the first apprentice to spend the night there.

Barry and I got involved. It didn't seem to take me much time, maybe because I was no longer a virgin, and in retrospect, my decision seems capricious and cavalier. And it was tricky because he was thirty-five, married, and had two small daughters. Just like my internship, Barry's stage manager stint was only for the summer. His family stayed back in whatever city they lived in, while he had a tiny rental in the town.

I don't remember how the affair evolved; I can summon up a vision of myself kind of standing around, being available, wondering if I caught his eye. (Do you see me? If you see me, I am worthy.) Barry was short with dark eyes and a narrow face and resembled a skinny, not-as-handsome Al Pacino. What drew me to him was how nice he was to me. He gave me books: the collected short stories of Charles Lamb, some Shakespeare, a few John Steinbeck novels. I felt like he really understood me, that he grasped that I was the kind of girl who was interested in these sorts of things.

To be honest, the fact he was married

hadn't made much of an impact on me until the day of the crew picnic, toward the end of the season. I was so stupid I went even though I knew Barry's wife and two little daughters would be there. But why did I go stand near his picnic table while his wife was unloading their food?

"Who's that, Mommy?" said one of his little girls.

"Oh, darling, that's your father's girl-friend," she sighed. She seemed to have a world-weariness and acceptance that far surpassed anything I understood. How she knew or why I went over to the table is beyond me. Seeing her reaction made me realize that Barry had a life and responsibilities that had nothing to do with me. And I felt terribly foolish and small.

My internship was over at the end of the summer stock season. I was sad to see my independence come to an end. Tory and I had had great fun, although my being with Barry had cut into our together time. Now she was going home by bus and Whitney and Jack, who had been in Chicago, drove up to get me. They surprised me by announcing that there was a famous performing arts high school called Interlochen Center for the Arts about nineteen miles from Traverse City and that before we headed home we were going to check it out as a place for me to enroll the following semester. This was the first I'd heard that I wouldn't be going back to Hollywood High. I was very unsure about the whole idea. Six weeks away for summer stock had initially seemed daunting; being so far away from home for a whole school year was paralyzing.

Interlochen Center for the Arts sits on 1,200 woodsy acres of land with two lakes and an outdoor amphitheater. There was a year-round academy and a summer camp. Kids come from all over the world to study writing, dance, theater, and art. But the central focus was music. Years later, in fact, my daughter Kate would go there for three summers in a row to study piano. By the end of her first summer she knew how to take apart and reassemble a harpsichord.

There were few basketball games or mixers at Interlochen. Students were too busy putting together brass quintets or composing six-part cantatas. Walking through the shady pine forests where the practice cabins were located, from one you'd hear a flute student teasing out a Poulenc sonata, from another the soaring sounds of a voice major practicing an aria; farther on a wind ensemble would be working out their different parts. It was thrilling, transporting, and electric with artistic invention. If only it had been contagious.

It's not easy to get into Interlochen. Everyone who went there was put through a rigorous audition process. I enrolled as a voice major. Now, while I had a nice singing voice for a seventeen-year-old, "nice" was about the extent of it. Before I arrived in September to begin my senior year, I had sent an audition tape of me singing show tunes, which is what I'd usually focused on at home. That tape just couldn't have had any bearing on my acceptance to the school.

Standing in the soprano section of my first session with the choir — I can remember so clearly to this day — copies of the Vivaldi *Gloria* are passed around, and the darling, round choirmaster, Mr. Jewel, takes his place in front of the choir, raises his hands, and . . . obviously expects us to start singing something we've never even seen before! Except, I realize, everyone *does* start singing . . . except me. They are sight-reading the Vivaldi *Gloria* in Latin! I could belt out "I Cain't Say No," but I cain't sing in *Latin.*

I felt ashamed, disheartened, and out of my league. I was thousands of miles from home at a place I never asked to come to, where I was so ill equipped. Why would they send me away to a place I wasn't qualified for? How could they not have known?

The campus itself was exhilarating. I knew this school was a gift and was rich with opportunity for me to grow and become a stronger, more varied singer. I really wanted to love being there, but I just couldn't. Perhaps at another time in my life — but not then.

I was so lonely. I made three friends — my roommate and the two girls who lived in the room next door and we did have fun together. We got drunk on alcohol smuggled into the dorm in poorly rinsed shampoo containers; I threw up Coke and liquid Prell into my wastebasket. I often tried to call home. I rarely found anyone; there was so little contact; I felt so abandoned. I'd take long showers with the lights off, lying on the floor of the shower for an hour, the hot water pounding down on me, my suitemates pounding on the doors. I learned to sight-read the music a little and I loved the singing and think I improved some; I went to concerts; I added my voice to the others in the woods' rehearsal cabins. In the winter, I went on long, long walks by myself, loving the silence of the snow. I attended my classes. I went through the motions but didn't overapply myself.

In April, I went home for the two-week spring break. Whitney and Jack were very interested in Interlochen's academic program: Jack was particularly impressed when I told him we were comparing More's *Utopia* to Plato's *Republic* . . . a fact I might have made up. No one wanted to know how I was adjusting to living away from home. Inside, I was screaming to tell them, but I was afraid of sounding needy and incapable. I wanted them to ask me, "Who are your friends?" "What pieces are you singing?" — it would have made a difference.

When I returned to school, everyone seemed so excited to see one another, giddy to resume life in this creative Eden. But I felt like I was greeted by thudding silence. I just didn't feel like anyone here, or at home, for that matter, cared. Everything was tempered by the colossal weight of loneliness I carried.

One night when I was attending one of the mandatory concerts, I had a panic attack and started hyperventilating. My heart was pounding like crazy and I was desperate not to cry. I didn't know what was happening to me. I asked to go back to my room. Despite the rules — students weren't allowed to be in the dorm unsupervised for some reason — they granted me permission. When I got there, I was frantic and sobbing. I don't know why but I started trying the doors of other rooms, went into any of them that weren't locked, and began to gather pills. I took Midol, aspirin, sleeping pills, asthma medication, cold tablets. Anything. I didn't care what I took. I wasn't thinking. I didn't have a plan. I just took everything I could find. Then I went back to my room and wrote a farewell note: *"I leave my clothes to Tory . . . Brian, you can have my records . . ."* I swallowed all of the pills with a Coke, lay down on my bottom bunk, and waited to die.

Looking back now, I don't think I really wanted my life to end. I really wanted attention. I just felt so unseen, so alone, and in so much pain and despair, I couldn't bear it.

I vaguely remember being half-carried down the stairs to the school infirmary. After a night of spectacular vomiting, I awoke to the warm, friendly face of Mrs. Wysong hovering over me. (Besides being the elderly woman my mother had rented our Traverse City house from two summers ago, she was also our dorm mother.)

"Oh, honey," she said so gently to me. "If you promise not to do this again, we won't call your mother."

What? I thought, There's a way Whitney could *know* about this? But if you *don't* tell her, she *won't* know.

"Mrs. Wysong?" I said. "I don't promise."

A faculty member must have called my parents, told them what had happened, told them I was expelled. I was told to pack my things, that I'd be leaving the next day and I was not invited to return. I felt so sad, so full of regret that I couldn't make it work there, and knew at the same time I couldn't have done it differently. I wasn't looking forward to my long flight home. I had no idea what ignominy awaited me when I got home. What punishment would Jack contrive?

The next morning I was told to bring down my suitcases, that my mother had arrived. *My mother had arrived?* My mother *had come to see me, take me home?* My mother wouldn't come *out of her room* to see me. I couldn't conceive that she'd come all the way across the country. And she came alone. She didn't just send Jack.

It was a silent flight home, Whitney sitting, staring out the window most of the trip. It was so hard to grasp that she had come or what that meant. I was so glad to be with her; I kept waiting for her to say something. I wanted to know why she had thought it important to come. Was she worried about me? Was she wondering why? I couldn't ask. I didn't feel I had permission to ask. Back again in the Hollywood Hills, it appeared that no one — not my father, my mother, or Jack — felt comfortable addressing the incident with me. So my brother Dick was summoned home from his day job at the newspaper and assigned the task of getting me to explain to *him* why I was so sad. I don't know what Dick asked me or how I answered. All I remember is later, sitting with him and my parents in their bedroom (which was strange since we were so rarely allowed in). "Don't send her to a psychiatrist," Dick said to them. "Just *talk* to her."

A few days later, they sent me to a psychiatrist. After the one session, he told my parents, "She's a perfectly normal sixteen-year-old girl."

He even got my age wrong.

No one ever mentioned my suicide attempt again.

CHAPTER 3

Kicked out of Interlochen, living back at home and being perfectly normal, I finished out the last two months of my senior year at Hollywood High, failing to distinguish myself in anything. I didn't have many friends there anymore; Tory and John had graduated the year before. I was restless, listless, lonely, irritable, and discontented. I wore my Interlochen uniform to school, navy corduroy knickers with navy long socks and a white shirt. Trust me, *no one else* dressed like that at Hollywood High. I spent much of my after-school time alone in my bedroom reading Keats and Shelley, writing bleak, artless, rhymeless poetry. When I wasn't writing I was at Wallach's Music City at Sunset and Vine, sitting in a sound booth, listening to the Vivaldi *Gloria* and singing along in Latin loudly, hoping someone might wander by and wonder, "Who is that *fantastic* singer?" I felt rudderless and untethered. I slid back into play production and tried to make a place for myself.

It was the spring of 1965, and for the past several months the deployment of U.S. troops to Southeast Asia had continued to escalate. The Vietnam War was on everybody's minds; boys in my class were getting drafted left and right. At the time, being drafted meant the infantry, and being shipped off to Vietnam, which instantly conjured up nightmarish visions of sloshing around a faraway rice paddy while being shot at by armed villager insurgents. So, my brother Dick enlisted in the air force and crossed his fingers that his journalism experience would help him land a safe post on a base newspaper. It did. After basic training, he got a job in the information office at the Suffolk County Air Force base in Long Island.

With Dick gone and Brian out on his own, I was now at home alone with Whitney and Jack, where a different sort of trouble was brewing. As *Hazel* entered season five, the writers had feisty Hazel and the Baxters' young son, Harold, now living with Mr. B's younger brother and sister, and in an even odder plot twist, sending corporate lawyer Mr. B and his Missy B off-camera — way off-camera — to Saudi Arabia.

Poor Whitney had been fired from a series she despised — one of the more ironic forms of showbiz indignity. Even more humiliating — for all her attempts to be seen as young and vibrant — they'd been replaced by a younger cast, ostensibly to appeal to a more youthful viewing audience.

Right around this time I was at home alone one evening when the doorbell rang. There stood our former tenant, Harvey, the focus of so many of my teenaged romantic fantasies, looking good and as tousled and rumpled as ever. I hadn't seen him in a couple of years. He was looking for his agent, Jack. But there was just me.

Now, at eighteen, I was no longer the same little girl who mooned after Harvey when he lived with us, but he still made my heart leap. His business with Jack must not have been so pressing because he said to me, "C'mon. Wanna go for a ride?"

"Okay," I said, unable to even consider another answer, as if I'd just been sitting there wondering when someone would come roaring up to find me. I hopped on the back of his motorcycle and wrapped my arms around his waist. I don't think I'd been on a motorcycle before. The wind made my eyes tear as we sped off along the

Hollywood Freeway and rode to his apartment about ten miles away in Highland Park.

Where we had sex.

I shouldn't have been surprised but I was. I mean, what else *should* I have expected? Conversation? I wasn't wanting sex but I suppose I'd wanted *something* . . . something romantic or sweet, hopefully gentle. But it wasn't. When I'd lost my virginity the year before, I'd felt detached, unemotional, almost indifferent, but I wasn't humiliated. It wasn't too dissimilar with Barry. I wasn't hurt; he was kind and I appreciated his tenderness. But this felt like cold, aggressive, mean sex. It was so confusing. I couldn't figure out what I'd done that it had turned out so badly.

Afterward, Harvey took me home. As he dropped me off in front of my house, his parting words were, "Tell Jack Fields that I just fucked him." Then he roared off. I stood there, dumbly, in the street.

What? This was about Jack? I'm just a stand-in for *Jack?*

I never told anyone except Tory.

Even I knew I was floundering. Once I graduated high school, I halfheartedly started taking classes at Los Angeles City

80

College. I was quasi-interested in my literature class but, in truth, I was so done with
school. I got a job, my first job, $30 a week
as an usher at the new Cinerama Dome in
Hollywood. My responsibilities were mindless: ripping tickets in half, shining a flash-
light so moviegoers wouldn't stumble in the
dark, and, of course, there was the concession stand. As far as I could see, this movie
theater was new and innovative only in their
huge wide screen and how they produced
popcorn — they didn't. Unlike other theaters, where the smell of corn popping lured
you to the concession counter even before
you rushed to save your seat, the Dome
folks had the popcorn trucked in in huge
plastic bags, prepopped! We had a popcorn
room. Another hapless usher and I would
stand in the small room and upend massive
bags of popcorn onto the bare concrete
floor so were standing in it. We'd unfold the
rectangular boxes, scoop them full of the
popcorn around our shoes, fold the tabs,
stack the full boxes, and transport said
boxes to the concession stand, where they'd
sit under a heat lamp until purchased.
Mmm. Would you like a Coke with that?

I started spending time with a guy named
Rick whom I knew from the Hollywood
High theater department. Rick and everyone

else seemed to think he was the king of the drama class. He had the arrogance and posturing of a seasoned performer, although he couldn't have been more than a year or so older than I. He was short, had floppy, dark blond hair, and might have been handsome except for the air of dissipation that made him seem older than he was. Rick lived in a typical sixties-era teenager's idea of a perfectly acceptable apartment: a long, narrow, one-car garage, minus the car, with a stained mattress at one end, a hot plate for making coffee, and candles stuck in wine bottles everywhere to supply flickering, spooky mood lighting for the endless pot and Red Mountain wine gatherings. One afternoon Brian and a guy named Bob Bush showed up at Rick's place. Bob had also been part of the Hollywood High theater crowd, but he was two years older than I so our paths had never crossed.

Back in high school, Bob was a bit of a hybrid — part popular kid, part tough guy, part drama geek. He had slicked-back hair and wore tight black jeans, tight white T-shirts, and pointy-toed black boots. If Rick looked a little bit like James Cagney, I'd describe the young Bob Bush as a sturdier, more sultry, five-foot-ten Tom Cruise. He had dark hair and distinguishing eyebrows that he'd arch to punctuate a sentence. Bob lived in a commune of sorts, a group house that everyone called the Snake Pit, where kids from Hollywood High would go and do drugs. When Brian cut school, he'd go hang out at the Snake Pit and he always told me he didn't want me going up there, which of course only increased its allure.

The way Bob tells the story is that Rick had two girlfriends — me and a girl named Donna. One day after we'd all been hanging out together, Bob said to him, "Hey, man. You can't have both of these chicks. You've got to make a decision. I want one of them," and somehow he got me. This was the free love era, so I guess that's how guys found their mates. I didn't seem to have had any say in the matter but must not have minded. I think I was glad to be chosen by someone. It helped that Brian liked Bob; it gave him the seal of approval. Bob was very easygoing and made me laugh with his sharp wit and funny observations. It helped that he also understood the trials of coming from a dysfunctional family.

Born and raised in Hollywood, Bob's father was like a shady character out of a Damon Runyon short story, only the not-funny, real-life version. He was a professional gambler who ran floating games around Los Angeles. He was also an alcoholic, the kind who'd have a few drinks and get verbally and physically abusive. When Bob was sixteen, he and his mother couldn't take it anymore and found their own apartment farther east, near Los Angeles City College. I remember Bob telling me about the day when his father showed up at their new place, unannounced, and Bob let him know just how unwelcome he was by picking him up and throwing him down the stairs.

Bob never asked me out on a date. This was the '60s. *Nobody* dated. Plus neither of us had any money. We just walked. Everywhere. We'd literally walk for hours. What I liked most of all was walking in residential neighborhoods where I could look in windows. I couldn't get enough of watching families together. I especially liked seeing mothers and fathers with children, seeing them sit and laugh together, especially touching each other . . . it was just enthralling.

Bob started bagging groceries at the Ralphs supermarket on Sunset Boulevard. If we pieced our two tiny paychecks together, we could just barely manage to make the rent on a cheap apartment. So, in 1966 we found a small place for $70 a month on a narrow, dead-end lane, at 10000 Honey Drive, #10, just off little Laurel Canyon Boulevard. I moved out of my mother's Whitley Terrace house and moved in with Bob.

In the mid-sixties, rustic, woodsy Laurel Canyon was where everyone — musicians, artists, *everyone* — lived. Some even called it the "birthplace of the hippie generation." Our neighbors included Sonny and Cher, Stephen Stills, David Crosby, Joni Mitchell, members of The Mamas & The Papas. Jim Morrison lived behind the Laurel Canyon Country Store. Frank Zappa and his family's house was just off of Mulholland Drive. Jimi Hendrix stayed at a log cabin down the hill from our apartment. We were in the happening place! But while they might have lived real close and breathed in the same canyon air, we never saw any of those folks.

Whitney and Jack weren't happy about my being with Bob. For some reason, they thought we should be married. (Like that had worked out so well for young Whitney!) Living together in those days was just not done, and they liked things done their way. Once Jack showed up at our apartment and suggested Bob move out or he'd break both of his legs. But when threats of bodily harm didn't do the trick, more extensive measures were taken. Somehow Jack got my father, Tom, to pull some strings with the air force, and big brother Dick was again brought home from his post on Long Island, arriving like the cavalry to save his errant sister. Jack and Whitney had me in temporary custody and wanted me to get married, goddammit! Dick strolled into our family summit meeting in full uniform and announced, "Why get married? Why don't they just keep living together and see how it goes?" Then he left to get on with his forty-eight-hour fun pass away from the military — and Bob and I continued to live together unchallenged for another six months.

The fact that everyone said that the complex we lived in had originally been a whorehouse — and that our unit used to be occupied by the madam — made our new home very enticing. Our corner unit was just a bedroom, a kitchen, and a bathroom. But it was a big circular-shaped corner unit, with windows that looked down on the street so the madam could spot police cars. I used them for the same purpose. Every one of our neighbors was a character: the guy downstairs was a magician and always seemed to burst in when we'd just smoked a couple of joints, then he'd entertain us by doing tricks with flash paper and blow our minds.

Bob knew a guy named Larry, who was our drug dealer. We were very low-level druggies and only got weed from him and Dexamyl by the bagful. Ah, Dexamyl . . . it was essentially a dreamy combination of dextroamphetamine (speed) cut with amobarbital (a downer) in a time-release spansule. I loved staying awake for days, not eating, thinking I was brilliant, feeling the surge of the amphetamine as I talked about changing the world with Free Love, No Nukes, Legalize Marijuana — all the bumper sticker slogans. I lived for Larry arriving with the big plastic bag that didn't last long enough. I had a gradual realization that I was downing a lot of them every day although at no time did I ever feel dependent. I counted taking twenty-six one day and had a mini-moment of clarity, wondering, What are you *doing?* Clarity didn't last long. I shrugged it off. "Who cares?"

At some point, I got a job as a cashier at the Ontra Cafeteria on Beverly Drive in Beverly Hills. Another mindless job but perfect for someone who was stoned a fair amount of the time. Customers would serve themselves, then slide their trays along the counter to my register, I'd add up the dishes, then hit a small bell — *ping!* — that would summon a runner to carry their tray to the table for them. Many a time I knocked the bell into their applesauce.

In our apartment, we glued red, yellow, and green tissue paper on the windowpanes to make it look like stained glass, listened to music nonstop on Bob's amazing stereo system, and dried kilos and kilos of marijuana in the oven. We heard that you could get high smoking bananas or "mellow yellow" — it had something to do with extracting a supposedly psychoactive substance called bananadine, so I followed what I thought were all the steps: scraping the whitish, pasty residue from the banana peel, spreading the paste out on a cookie sheet, and baking it until it turned into a fine black powder. Then I scraped up some powder, rolled it up in a joint, smoked it, and waited.

What happened? Absolutely nothing. It was horrible. Someone told me later I was supposed to have *boiled* the stuff before I baked it, but I defy anyone to tell me that would have gotten me high. I'd have tried it, though.

What *was* effective and required less effort but was even more *disgusting* was the old Vicks inhaler cotton. I'd hammer open the Vicks plastic tubing, extracting the two-inch length of dense cotton saturated with propylhexedrine, a stimulant. I'd cut the cotton into small cubes and swallow them, gagging constantly, determined not to throw them up. God knows, I didn't want to spoil a good high. The recollection of trying to choke that cotton down has totally eclipsed any memory of what the high was like. Today, I can barely look at a Q-tip.

We were so broke. Even with our little jobs we lived like paupers — just enough money to buy some pills or pot. Finally, I was able to pull the money together to buy an old Borgward Isabella, a clunky German two-door sedan, from Jack's secretary for $100. That was more than it was worth, but I *loved* that car. Walking was cool, but driving was just so much better. We got to visit friends in the *Valley!* It had an iffy clutch and the engine wouldn't always turn over, so some-times I'd take the bus to work, but I didn't mind. I was still a car owner. When the clutch went out altogether, it started gather-ing tickets, so we'd roll it up or down little Laurel Canyon a few feet every couple of days; I didn't want it to be pegged as an abandoned vehicle and get impounded. Of course, one day we forgot. My car was towed away and the cost was $100 to get it back, and who had that much money? Good-bye, Borgward. Oh, well.

Bob ran in the same crowd at Hollywood High as a lead guitarist and singer named Lowell George, who was in Frank Zappa's Mothers of Invention band and went on to form Little Feat, a rock and blues band. Occasionally we'd go over to Lowell's place and a bunch of his musician friends would be there and Lowell would reach for his slide guitar or Fender Stratocaster. Bob would pull out his harmonica. I'd sing harmony, play the spoons or tambourine, and we'd make music for hours and hours because we could. It was great. It was crazy. I was eighteen, having fun, loving the music, loving the freedom and autonomy. Anything was possible.

Bob and I were out with our dealer, Larry, one evening and we wound up at his girl-friend Shirley's apartment at the Shoreham Towers above Sunset Boulevard. She had a beautiful place. She had furniture, not just crates or bricks and boards. There was a great view, white shag carpets, white sofas, white chairs, and lots of mirrors. Shirley was not a hippie; she lived a much ritzier lifestyle than any of our other friends. She was a working girl, a high-class hooker. Shirley, in my memory of her, stood apart

90

because of her long legs, long flowing golden hair, and equally long, flowing diaphanous gowns.

Shirley was checking me out pretty thoroughly. She lit a joint, draped herself over the arm of her luxurious sofa, and told me (I think she purred) that I too could have a nice place like she did. She handed me the joint and said that I could come work for her. She said I could do better than the stupid Ontra Cafeteria. I'd be good working with her. She could teach me.

Oh. I'd be good? Shirley thinks I could be *good*? I could be marketable? Through the pot I was trying to decide if this were good work opportunity.

It was about this time that the cocaine came out. Larry offered me a line of white powder on a paper. "Have you tried this before?"

"Of *course*." Duh. Well, I'd certainly heard of cocaine.

"Cool. Try this."

Often wrong but never in doubt, I awkwardly leaned toward his outstretched hand, trying to figure my timing, and inadvertently snorted out onto the paper, sending a small cloud of cocaine powder up his shirtsleeve. It was around this time that Shirley withdrew her job offer. Which, I realized, I was seriously considering.

Unbelievably, cocaine never crossed my path again.

The following week, armed with the appreciation that my skills were wasted at the cafeteria, I found another job. A real job. A job that required me to think. I moved into a new, highly injudicious profession for me — I became an eighteen-year-old premiums adjuster at Washington Mutual. How I made it through their vetting process and got hired is lost to history. I had waist-length blond hair and looked about twelve.

I loved being in an office playing secretary. I loved typing. I loved filing. I loved having a desk and a stapler. I loved answering the phone "Premiums adjuster, Miss Baxter." I worked hard and considered myself a good employee, even though I didn't understand the first thing about insurance. I talked to lots of customers, most of whom were remarkably patient and friendly, but I doubt I was ever of any service to anybody.

After being employed there for a few weeks, I was on my way to work one Monday morning, after an entire weekend spent on acid. A bunch of us had been up all night and my friends were driving me to work in their beat-up red VW van that we called the Jellybean. Having a job that demanded more responsibility than counting plates, I had the maturity and foresight to be concerned about my condition. How in the world was I going to stay awake all day?

"Here, take some of these," a helpful buddy said, and handed me a jewelry box filled with pills, all different kinds and colors, none of them labeled. Maybe taking a handful of them wasn't the best idea.

I'm sitting at my adjuster's desk and staring at the file cabinets across the room. I know I have to get from *here* to *there*. But the cabinets have taken on a life of their own, keep shifting positions, vibrating and leaning sideways. When I finally get up from my desk to walk across the room, past my coworkers, my steps are measured and determined, and I am trying to tilt at the same angle as the tilting file cabinets. I am leaning very far to one side, as if on the deck of a listing ship.

The next thing I remember is waking up in the coffee break room, my arm draped over the shoulder of a coworker who was trying to rouse me by walking me around the room. Eventually my boss called me into his office and asked me for an explanation.

"Well you know, my grandmother died and I just stayed up all night," I told him in my best Shirley Temple voice. "I didn't know *how* I was going to stay awake so a friend of mine gave me this diet pill and I've never taken *anything* like that before and I had *such a big reaction!*"

My boss didn't deliberate. He said, "You're fired."

I was the only one making any money at the time. Without my paycheck, we couldn't afford the rent, as cheap as it was; Bob and I had to move out of Honey Drive. What a heartbreak. We loved that place. His mother, Melba, offered us the second bedroom in her small apartment but said her landlord would want us to be legally husband and wife before he could let us move in there. I suppose I loved Bob. We had a good time together. He was kind and he made me laugh. Why not get married?

So, on June 23, 1966, Bob and I asked two friends, Robin and Mike Steckler — that's it, just our two friends, no Bob's mother, no Whitney, no Jack, no one who, just months before, had been exhorting us to tie the knot — to meet us at a small Unitarian church in North Hollywood and we got married. It was not a dressy occasion; I think I wore a cotton sleeveless dress with a floral print. I'm not sure if we did anything to celebrate this momentous event. We might have gone to Der Wienerschnitzel.

■ ■ ■ ■

Our reason for getting married was so flimsy that our new status shouldn't have changed anything, but in a lot of ways it did. I missed the freewheeling camaraderie of Laurel Canyon and Honey Drive. Now we were living in a two-bedroom apartment at least an hour's walk from Hollywood and our friends, *with a mother-in-law.* I liked her a lot . . . she was very different from my mother. Melba was very loving, very attentive, sharp, and no-nonsense. She was also very kind to me. Whitney was a great cook guided by *Gourmet* magazine, but she never had the time to teach me anything. Melba was the one who showed me how to cook and plan a meal. Every time I make a light, flaky piecrust today, I can hear her patiently talking to me in her kitchen. "One part Crisco to three parts flour . . ." "Don't overwork the dough, dear. That makes the crust tough."

Just after we moved in with his mom, Bob and I got together with Rick and Donna and a few other friends late one night at the Villa Valentino, a famous courtyard complex of historic Italianate apartments on Highland Avenue. We were drinking, lying around, smoking joints, listening to music,

95

just like we used to in the canyon, and digging the romantic setting, when all of a sudden someone yelled, "It's the cops!" Within seconds we all sprinted out of the apartment, up the long driveway, and to the street. There in the pitch-black night, we were met by several police officers. Apparently, a neighbor had complained about the noise and the marijuana smoke billowing out the windows. (Remember, this was the mid-'60s. Marijuana use was still considered a heinous crime and people were tossed in jail for possession of tiny amounts.) "Are you the kids from the Villa Valentino apartments?" the cops inquired, blasting their flashlights into our eyes. Adamantly, we assured them that we were just taking in the night air.

Not buying our story, they herded us back into the apartment. Loudly and insistently protesting they had the wrong kids, that we'd never seen this room before, we were lined up against a wall and frisked like on the cop shows. In a momentary lull, I quietly asked the closest officer, "Um . . . could you please hand me my glasses on the end table over there, please?" He smiled broadly and handed them to me. Donna, the friskee to my left, gave me such a kick! I'd just placed us inside the apartment.

Next thing I knew, we were handcuffed, and Donna and I were loaded into the backseat of a police car. We came down off the pot high on the silent drive to the Sybil Brand Institute for Women, then the women's jail in Los Angeles. We were pretty humorless as they formally processed us and gave us paper dresses and paper shoes to put on. It may have been a June night, but it was awfully cold in the jail, so they gave us sweaters. We were held for a short time in a fairly clean room with benches so narrow they defied our lying down on them, but we were able to muster some laughs by playing games with the buttons we tore off the sweaters. When I was finally put in a cell, alone, I think, all the cell doors closed automatically with a vehement clang, which seemed to reverberate throughout the whole jail building. At which point I began to cry. And cry. It took me that long to appreciate where I was and how much trouble I was in.

The next afternoon, when I was finally allowed to make a call, I dialed my parents' number. Whitney answered on what I could tell was the poolside phone. I disguised my voice and asked for Jack. "It's one of your girls," said Whitney flatly, and passed the phone to my stepfather. He laughed when I tearfully told him my tale of woe.

Now, I was afraid of Jack, I deeply resented his violence against us, I hated how he sexualized me, I felt he'd taken our mother away, and I didn't trust his motives. But the sorry truth was that he was all I had to turn to. I hated to admit it, but I could count on him.

Late that night, Jack came downtown to bail me out; Bob was sprung by his mother a few days later. My arrest warrant read, "Possession of narcotics, to wit: Marijuana." The charges were eventually dismissed because, despite my glasses faux pas, the police couldn't prove we were the miscreants in the apartment. A couple of days later, Bob and I celebrated our two-week wedding anniversary.

Just as my first marriage was getting off to a bang-up start, Whitney's second was winding to a close. This didn't necessarily come out of the blue. She and Jack would have epic fights. One occurred about two years earlier over the quality of their seats at the world premiere of Stanley Kramer's much-anticipated film *Ship of Fools.* I could hear Whitney yelling at Jack and I think she threw a jar of cold cream. She was miffed that they'd be sitting up in the balcony where no one would see them. *Hazel* had ended on a downward spiral for her. She had reason to want to appear to be a happening actress — and apparently you aren't happening if you're sitting in the balcony. She told him that she wasn't going.

Jack's trump card? Me. He said, "Fine, I'll take *her*."

I was not unaware that I was being used. And where the hell I got an appropriate dress is beyond me. But I imagine Whitney felt wretched later on when she found out that she could have been seen at the lavish after-party at the Beverly Wilshire Hotel. There was drinking and dancing and somehow they got a huge model ocean liner and floated it in the swimming pool.

Years later I asked Jack what it was — the marathon shouting matches, how my mother blamed him for her flagging career, their apparent lack of chemistry — that finally convinced them both to call it quits. Jack's response was so odd I can still picture it today. He stuck out one of his very polished, almost glossy, black lace-up shoes, and said, "Look at these shoes. Aren't these nice shoes? Aren't these shiny shoes? Don't they look pretty? They look comfortable, don't they?"

He paused for a couple of beats, then asked me, "Can you tell where they pinch?"

CHAPTER 4

So, there I was: nineteen, a new, young wife, living with a new, young husband and his mother in her apartment. Hmm. In October of 1966 I found out I was pregnant with my first child, something I was even less prepared for than being a premiums adjuster. I guess no one checked my references to find out why my insurance career ended so abruptly, because soon I was taking the bus downtown every day to Pershing Square to my new job in the tax department of the Price Waterhouse accounting firm.

Before all their records and information were computerized, attorneys at the firm would come to the "Vault" to requisition the personal files of their specific clients. The Vault was a tiny, closetlike room, crammed to the gills with all the very sensitive, confidential dossiers of Price Waterhouse clients. It was overseen by a small, no-nonsense woman named Hertha and me. Many a new lawyer would do a double take when they came to the service window, because there's me — a wide-eyed, earnest, pregnant, big-busted, barely disguised hippie who still looked about twelve years old but eager to wait on them. The only recollections I have of that period are all those male attorneys standing at the window leering at me as I delivered their documents, and then me reading those same secret files at lunchtime, trying not to drop Thousand Island dressing on all the tax data. It is their good fortune I have the financial understanding of a milk shake.

As for home, the idea of sharing a small place with young newlyweds *and* an infant was probably more than Bob's mother bargained for, so we decided it was time to pack up our boxes and move again. We found a charming little one-bedroom bungalow in back of an apartment building on Oxford Street, just east of Western Avenue, in a slightly dodgy section of midtown Los Angeles. One day a friend of Bob's who worked in the mail room at KCET, the local public television station, told him he could get him a job there. Soon Bob was in a starter position at KCET, sorting letters and delivering packages in the hopes of working his way up into television production. It was the kind of entry-level opportunity that sometimes kick-starts Hollywood careers, so we were excited.

Meanwhile, Whitney had a new man in her life. His name was Allan Manings. He was a successful forty-three-year-old screenwriter and playwright from New York who shared Whitney's passion for the dramatic arts. Back in the '50s, he was working on *The Imogene Coca Show* when his agent told him he'd been blacklisted. The Canadian film director and producer Norman Jewison offered Allan work if he'd come to Canada. So, in 1957 Allan moved to Toronto. Seven years later, he returned to Hollywood and immediately started writing for hit shows like *McHale's Navy* and *Leave It to Beaver.*

Years later, I would hear about the cinematic way he and Whitney met. They were dancing with different partners at a party thrown by mutual friends when Joan, the woman dancing with Allan, tapped the shoulder of the man dancing with Whitney and said, "May I cut in?" Then Joan pushed Allan into Whitney's arms and rumba-ed off with the other guy. Whitney always believed the partner switch had been prearranged — she was separated from Jack, Allan was separated from his first wife. By the end of the evening Allan was smitten enough to ask for my mother's phone number and handed her his address book. I imagine she wanted to make sure she left a lasting impression, because she took Allan's address book and in green ink scribbled out her name and number in huge flourishing script as if she were signing an autograph. It covered two pages, obscuring about eight of Allan's other entries. "You ruined my address book," Allan told her forlornly.

A couple of days later, Whitney flew off to Mexico to attempt a prearranged reconciliation with Jack. It must not have been a success, because she called Allan as soon as she got back. By May of 1967, when I was going into labor with my first child, they were deep enough into a relationship that when Bob called Whitney in the middle of the night to tell her to come to the hospital, she was with Allan. Whitney told me she had wanted her bearded, pipe-smoking new boyfriend to get out of bed and come along with her, but Allan, ever the more reasonable one, begged off. "Does she really want a stranger there?" because he hadn't even been introduced to the family yet.

Theodore Justin Bush (known as Teddy until he was fourteen) weighed 7.5 pounds and had Bob's animated eyebrows with the blond hair and blue eyes of a Baxter. He was a good baby, as most first babies are. I didn't know much about mothering. Okay, scratch that: I didn't know *anything* about mothering . . . never having seen it done. It took me quite a while to feel any connection to Teddy, which worried me. I had long thought there was something wrong with me, that perhaps I had a limited ability to love. I liked him fine, but he seemed to require more attention than our two cats and that kind of threw me too. But slowly he grew on me. I came to look forward to his baths, particularly. Sometimes he'd get all red and angry when I'd wash his hair, hating the water on his head. He hated being changed even more, crying so hard, eyes squeezed shut, toothless little mouth agape. Then he'd pee! And pee right into his own mouth! I'd be gasping with laughter, he'd be gasping for breath, sputtering and madder than before. We were a great pair.

I loved nursing especially because it was quiet sit-down time. I could brew a nice cup of strong instant coffee, grab my tattered copy of Leon Uris's *Exodus* and my pack of Raleighs. Then I'd blissfully rock, nurse, drink coffee, and smoke for the next hour. I learned to drag out the calming ritual long after he'd fallen asleep. (Regrettably, I smoked my way through my first two children. I had no idea that I was contributing to their many years' struggle with bronchial problems.)

A most surprising and incongruous thing happened: Whitney came to our little house and helped me out! She typically didn't fit into my life that way. She had always told me she wasn't interested in doing that. Long before I'd even had children, she'd said vehemently that she was not going to babysit. I don't think she was at all happy about my having made her a grandmother at forty-one. But there she was, washing diapers on my old-fashioned hand-crank wringer washer, standing at the sink sudsing and rinsing dirty dishes, heading off to the market to buy us groceries. I would have never asked her to come, which meant she must have just come. It was very touching to me then — and now. It was a onetime occurrence; she never helped out with any of my other children when they were little. But that's okay. She did it for a first-time mom trying to get her bearings, and that made all the difference.

My mother wasn't the only unexpected visitor. Occasionally Jack would call, asking me if he could come by, say hi to Teddy, and bring me a burger for lunch. Jack and I had never been especially close, and he was no longer a part of our family since the divorce, so I was grateful for his thoughtfulness. He came only during the day, when Bob was at work. I wasn't working and my husband's minimum-wage mail room job didn't bring much money at all. That hamburger and cardboard container of French fries he'd bring over meant a lot to me — especially because sometimes I'd find a $50 bill slipped between the wrapping paper and the top bun.

One time instead of the burger and fries he brought me a gift-wrapped box. I opened the lid and inside found a beautiful, very expensive, diaphanous aqua peignoir with magenta trim. Well, *this* was unusual. I remember picking it up, seeing how transparent it was, and feeling uneasy. Old apprehension returned.

"Thank you very much, Jack. This is nice," I told him politely and put it back in the box.

"I'd like you to try it on," he said.

Uh-oh. Flashbacks to the old days of bathing suits and his friends. I just slid my arms through the peignoir sleeves and pulled it on over my T-shirt and jeans, then slipped it right off. "This is really beautiful, Jack. Thanks so much."

"I can't tell what it looks like over your

clothes," he complained lightly.

"Jack. You know, I don't feel comfortable doing that."

He said, "Well, if I can't have the mother, I'll take the daughter." That just defied a response but I managed to hustle him out of the house. I don't remember what I did with the negligee so Bob didn't see it. Jack's behavior was creepy and confusing. Yes, he'd always back away whenever I rebuffed him, but why was I even *having* to rebuff him? I didn't want to alienate him, but I hated how he came on to me.

For much of Teddy's early infancy, Bob and I had been talking about moving to Canada to become landed immigrants. It sounded like a great adventure, a way to be off on our own, away from threat of the draft and Jack. Back in 1872, the Canadian government passed the Dominion Lands Act, which essentially offered 160 acres of undeveloped land in the prairie provinces for free to male farmers who agreed to cultivate 40 acres and build a permanent dwelling within three years. The property we would be gifted was located in Canada's Northwest Territory near — and this is the part we found incredibly cool — the Peace River. Why we thought we were up to the task is anyone's guess. Sometimes I look back and think I had the IQ of a landfill. I didn't know anything about *anything*. I was a California baby and had always been pretty comfortable and lacked for nothing. But, having the arrogance and hubris of youth, we considered ourselves sharp and resourceful and capable of facing whatever lay in our path. We got some books on farming, land management, and log cabin building, sold whatever we could, gave away the rest, and on December 28, 1967, flew with seven-month-old Teddy and a dog to Vancouver, British Columbia.

Part of our plan was to meet up with my brother Brian, who, months earlier, in order to escape the draft had hitchhiked with his pregnant girlfriend Bonnie to a farm in a small town in western Canada called Wetaskiwin. Until we got there, Bonnie was employed as a housekeeper and Brian was working at the farm castrating pigs he said were as large as sofas. Brian, exhibiting symptoms of the same strain of hubris that we suffered from, had already drawn up a schematic drawing for building an A-frame house that we could make out of the lodgepole pine trees we'd read were abundant in the Peace River area.

Then we discovered that the land parcel coming to us was in a section of Canadian prairie where the ground is in permafrost for seven or eight months out of the year. That meant it wasn't soft enough to cultivate for over half of the year. It didn't take us long to realize we were in over our heads. We were stumped. Our only choice was to join Brian and Bonnie, who had just moved to Red Deer, a town in central Alberta, about a two-hour drive from Edmonton.

Our stay in Red Deer lasted five months. Brian and Bonnie lived in a *basement* pretending to be an apartment. In a corner of the largest room was a massive furnace with big low, round pipes that went up in all directions into the apartments above. Its lights and buttons would flicker at all hours; a red glow and constant grumbling made the furnace seem like a malevolent character in a children's storybook. The apartment entrance opened into the furnace room so you'd have to duck under an obstacle course of pipes to get to the other rooms.

We had a small eat-in kitchen, which was the center of our lives there. Bob and I slept just off the kitchen in the living room, on a foldout couch. Teddy slept in a crib at our feet. Even when it was bitter cold outside, the moist heat of the furnace made the pale green walls of our tiny kitchen and living room sweat. Whatever slivers of natural light spilled into our apartment came from a window that required me to stand on my tiptoes if I wanted to look out. Still, my line of vision was barely even with the frozen ground.

We were flat broke. The food we'd eat — we'd buy ten loaves of bread for a dollar and cheap, cheap, cheap ground pork — was often of such poor quality that it gave us food poisoning.

Though life in that cramped, damp apartment might sound like something out of Dickens's London, it didn't feel like that all the time. It was a special period in our lives where everything, even adversity, was fresh and exciting; we were living not quite off the grid, but at least not part of the Establishment. We solved our problems as they arose and felt like we were all on a wonderful adventure. What can I say? We were so very young.

Because we didn't know anyone in Red Deer, we were our own cozy social circle. There were all-night cribbage and canasta sessions, broken up by bouts of brainstorming, or talking about where our lives would go. Sometimes Bonnie would play the guitar and we'd sing folk songs — Buffy Sainte-Marie, Joan Baez. (A couple of times back in Los Angeles, Bonnie and I performed at open mike nights at music clubs. Our voices meshed well together and I could do a mean harmony in those days.) In the morning, Brian and Bob would get up and walk in the icy chill to their entry-level positions at Alberta State Hospital. Bonnie and I would stay home and take care of Teddy and do the housework.

Washing and drying diapers in a climate as frigid as Red Deer's was different from doing laundry in Southern California. Like every good hippie mother, I eschewed Huggies (not that I could have afforded them anyway), so Teddy's diapers were the big, gauzy cloth variety, the kind you fasten at the corners with safety pins. To wash them, I'd throw them in our wringer washer (yes, again with a wringer washer), feed them through the rollers, pressing out as much water as I could, then I'd run outside into the freezing air and hang them on the clothesline. When the weather is so dry and frosty, it completely takes the moisture out of the clothes and actually sanitizes them. They'd be stiff as a board and smell great when it was time to collect them. I'd carry in a thin stack of rigid, clean diapers and lean them up against a wall. When they dried, they'd collapse on the floor, at which point I would fold them and put them away.

When Bonnie had her baby, Tommy, in January shortly after we arrived, between the two of us we took over the entire clothesline system set aside for the whole apartment.

As spring came, the ground was thawed and yet it was still insanely cold during the day. We had all struggled with bronchial congestion in our damp sweaty abode, but little Teddy was particularly challenged by the elements. One night Bob and I were asleep on the foldout bed and we awoke to the sound of our son's wet raspy breathing, even more labored than usual. His temperature was high enough that we called a cab and rushed him off to the hospital, where he was instantly put into an ice bath. The diagnosis was pneumonitis, or a combination of pneumonia and bronchitis. He was hospitalized for four days, in and out of an oxygen tent. I remember the sheets on his little crib were very rough and they scratched and reddened his already thin, dry skin, but the nurses were kind, attentive, and supportive; I became an instant fan of socialized medicine.

I don't recall if Teddy getting pneumonitis is what finally broke us, but it was certainly a major factor. We'd all been sick just too often.

In April of 1968 I called someone —
maybe it was Jack, maybe Whitney — and
asked to be wired enough money to bring
me and my little family back home. Brian,
Bonnie, and Tommy came back shortly after
us. Our days as landed immigrants were officially over. We made no impact on Canada,
but I felt severely dented by the great
Northwest. I didn't think I'd ever be warm
again.

Jack came through for us. When Bob,
Teddy, and I arrived back in Los Angeles,
he had rented half of a duplex for us right
across the street from the North Hollywood
police station in the San Fernando Valley.
Partially furnished, it was pretty and had
roses growing on trellises in the front yard.
In fact, it was so nice that we couldn't afford to stay beyond the two months' rent
Jack had paid. It was hard to leave . . . this
was by far the prettiest place we'd ever lived.

That meant another move. This time we
were on the second floor of a two-story
apartment building on Hinds Street, also in
the Valley. The upside was that it was a
clean, airy one-bedroom and we had a
modern-ish kitchen; it was the first time I
had a nice stove and refrigerator since I
moved out of Jack and Whitney's house. The
downside was that we lived directly in the

flight path of a small public airport then called the Hollywood-Burbank Airport. The roar of the jets was so low and loud, the dishes would rattle. When I looked out the kitchen window it appeared as if those huge planes were going to fly right into our apartment; it took weeks before I didn't feel the need to drop to the floor as they approached.

We'd been back from Canada for about five months when Whitney called me with an announcement: she and her boyfriend Allan were getting married. I was surprised. Not that I'd given it a lot of thought, but it hadn't occurred to me that she'd ever marry again. Her previous marriages had been bitter disappointments; I couldn't see how this would be much different. Allan must have been very persistent in his pursuit of her. One day he said, "We should get married. We're good together," and my mother apparently agreed. I hadn't even met him yet. But hey, it was a party to go to. Plus they acknowledged Bob and me as a couple.

Earlier in the year, Allan had landed a staff writing gig on the hugely popular TV variety comedy series *Rowan & Martin's Laugh-In,* and Whitney's career had taken another left turn. Her guest star roles had begun to dwindle, so she started cohosting a late afternoon talk show called *Boutique* on the local CBS affiliate. The series gave her the opportunity to hold forth on all sorts of topics — men, fashion, interior decorating. But she also saw it as a way to shake off Missy B from *Hazel* and show the world how smart and opinionated she was, that she was nothing like her wishy-washy fictional counterpart.

Whitney was so determined to make the talk show work that on the day before her wedding, when many brides-to-be might be attending to the last-minute details of the event, she could be found in a booth at the Villa Capri restaurant, giving an interview to a local newspaper about *Boutique.* Even the reporter seemed stunned by her focus on her show.

On August 24, 1968, my brothers, their wives, and Bob and I gathered at the Hollywood house of Allan's best friend, Dr. Mel Avedon. Allan and Whitney stepped into the room; Whitney was wearing a lovely chic white suit. A hush fell over the small group of guests and a Unitarian minister began conducting a humanistic, not very religious ceremony. My brothers and I watched our mother get married for the third time and met our new stepfather, all in the same day. My mother had waited fifteen months after

Teddy was born to introduce us to Allan. What could she possibly have been waiting for? Was her hesitation about us or about him?

In Whitney's case, the old saying "The third time is the charm" actually seemed to hold true. For all his purported imperious ferocity at the writers' table, Allan was pretty much a lamb with my mother. One of the things I always found engaging about them as a couple was that when they fought, it couldn't last long. Sometimes I'd call and I'd hear that familiar tight sound in her voice that indicated there was tension between them at the moment. Then I'd hear Allan making a comment in the background, she'd say a few words back, as would he, at which point she'd just start laughing. Allan was so funny he could do something no one else could: break through my mother's anger. It was a marvel of their relationship.

I can't remember what kind of job Bob had at the time, but I do know that between rent, food, and diapers, there wasn't much left in his paycheck to cover drugs or alcohol. If anything, we had beer, which I thought was disgusting, so I rarely drank at all during this time. On occasion friends would share some pot with us but, except

116

for occasional acid trips, my pill-taking days were pretty much over. Getting married had cut our ties with Larry the drug dealer and Canada had taken care of most other contacts. In November, just as I turned twenty-one, I found out I was pregnant again because, oh yes . . . no money for birth control pills, either. Teddy was one and a half and climbing everywhere. I was sure he was going to fly headfirst down the apartment stairs. How do people care for two children at once? Whose idea was *this?*

With our family expanding, I had to figure out a way to bring in some extra cash. Not having gained a lot of confidence in the office arena, I thought I should try a less formal approach to commerce: Tupperware parties! I could get into the business with the help of my stepmother, Ginger. Ginger was the most hardworking, positive woman I've ever known. Anyone else with that quick a smile and direct eye contact would have made me flinch, but she was 100 percent authentic. She cared, she listened, she was a go-getter. These traits served her so well that in just two years she'd gone from being simply a Tupperware dealer to being one of their top managers.

As soon as I told her I was interested, she arranged to take me to one of the big Tupperware meetings at the distributorship she worked through in the San Fernando Valley. Hundreds of women attend these to announce their staggering sales figures, receive support, and get leadership counsel. I was given one of their sales kits, a suitcase filled with about $200 worth of the company's signature plastic products, catalogs, hostess gifts, and a few sample prizes. I'd been to some of Ginger's Tupperware parties when I was younger and had marveled at the cool sales tactics she'd employed. She had a lovely style of self-deprecating humor as she put the women through the party games and presented her products, laughter being a very important element in her techniques. So when Ginger gave me a few of her party dates to help launch me, I considered myself pretty prepared. Kind of the same way I went to Canada. To be honest, I wasn't bad when it came to talking about Tupperware. I had used and loved the products for years (Ginger and my father had given me and Bob a starter set as a wedding gift and we were often given hostess gifts on holidays), and I thought of the presentation as an acting exercise, like the kind I did in high school drama class: I'd try to be warm and chatty and look people in the eye and tell funny stories, mostly stolen from hearing them at company meetings (and embellished by me). I felt they liked me.

I remember cracking up a group once. There was a sandwich-sized plastic container that had a little divider you slid down to separate different foods. I told them, "This is great for nuts and candy or meats and cheese." Then I'd waited a few beats and said, "Soup *and* nuts? Do not try this. This does not work!" Oh my, my . . . the laughter! (I figured they didn't get out much.)

But I couldn't pressure anybody. The *party* part I liked; the selling part I could manage; booking the *next* party I found excruciating. The Tupperware trainers would tell us, "This is the way you get them to agree to a party: Ask them, 'What's better for you? Thursday or Saturday?' " The best I could muster would be to mumble to a prospective hostess, "Um, you wouldn't want to book a Tupperware party, would you?" And they'd agree with me straightaway that no they wouldn't. And that would be that.

Ginger really wanted me to succeed, she really tried to give me every opportunity. But I was a distracted pregnant twenty-one-year-old with a toddler at home and driving a little blue '54 Ford that was always breaking down, which required my being rescued all the time. I was game, though, and did lots of parties all over town; I even did one on a small sailboat in the marina with a tiny galley and a low ceiling. I set up my wares on a low table and did my presentation tilted, with my ear to one shoulder because I couldn't stand straight, and heartily made my soup and nuts joke. I was afraid someone with another boat *would* book from this party.

But no bookings means no sales and eventually I just got too discouraged. I think I made about $600 for the one year I was selling. The man who helped us do our taxes thought my poor sales figures so unlikely that he suggested I was hiding income. Whatever plastic housewares samples were left in my kit I just put in my own kitchen and quietly closed the cupboard on my Tupperware sales career.

With no income from my end and another baby on the way, we needed to find a cheaper place to live, which meant moving yet again. We found a three-bedroom house in North Hollywood that on paper sounded fabulous:

"Large, white, free-standing house, lots of light, long living-room/den, with fireplace, roomy master bedroom, spacious eat-in kitchen with appliances included, big yard on a corner lot, long driveway, separate rear buildings, no houses close by . . . lots of privacy. $77 a month."

Wow! A dream come true, yes? In reality it was what was left of a phased-out, condemned chicken farm and not really fit for occupation. The floors sloped; nothing in the once white house was level. The appliances were filthy and antique, the linoleum was peeled and spotty. There was a swamp under the kitchen floor. True, the rooms were large, except for two smaller bedrooms, which could barely contain one twin bed each. The "lawn," front and back, was a stretch of dry, beige scrub, accented here and there with tumbleweeds and one wayward tree that offered little in shade or relief. But there was an unfenced acre of dirt and weeds in the back where Teddy could run and play, if supervised; just beyond, a sparkling new housing development could be seen, which stood in stark contrast to our ramshackle abode. We took it. Everyone called it the Chicken Ranch.

We were on Ethel Avenue, just north of Saticoy Street, along which ran several blocks of salvage yards. We were next door to an airplane seat factory and there was a crazy biker gang that lived across the street in a house as dismal as ours. The only thing

121

that set us apart were the upside-down automobiles on their front lawn. Those separate buildings in the rear of our house were little chicken shacks, crappy little sheds that we actually rented out, as if they were darling guest cottages, to folks even less discerning than we were.

My second child, Eva Whitney Bush, was born on August 6, 1969. I loved her name, I thought it was musical. I'm sure I included *Whitney* as an oblique way of laying claim to my mother.

Eva was the prettiest baby. She had big big big blue eyes, eyes so big she could have been a Keane painting. Eva was fussier than Teddy. Thank goodness she had a winning smile and bubbly personality. But two children felt exponentially more difficult than one.

On the way to the hospital when I was in labor with Eva, Bob and I had stopped off and bought a Kawasaki motorcycle so that he could make the ten-mile drive to a job he loved — selling remainders and art books at Pickwick Bookstore in Hollywood where my brother Brian worked. One morning two weeks later, a couple of hours after he'd left for work, I got a phone call.

"This is Valley Doctor's Hospital. Could

you please come in and identify your husband?"

Bob was on his way to work when the driver in front of him slammed on the brakes. He flew into the car, dislocating his shoulder and crushing his tibia and fibula between the bike and their bumper. Life as I knew it became trying in a different way. Poor Bob was in lots of pain and fully dependent on me, which must have been hideous for him, Eva was needing the attention any one-month-old requires, and Teddy, once doted on as an only child, was wondering why he couldn't get my attention anymore. I remember feeling so overwhelmed. So terribly tired. I had few reserves when it came to caring for Eva. She suffered from colic, crying much of the time, and seemed to defy comforting. I remember walking with her, rocking her, singing to her, petting her, then finally crying and shaking her in my frustration. I was horrified that I'd done that and it only made her cry harder. I experienced her continuous sobbing as a personal reprimand. What was wrong with *me* that I couldn't comfort *her?* I felt too ill equipped to handle it all.

After Bob was back on his feet and healing, Jack suggested that perhaps we could rent out the tiniest bedroom to one of his clients because he knew we were hurting for money. Grateful for any relief, we agreed and invited Susan to move into the back bedroom. Susan was a lovely young actress, pregnant, smart, and unattached. We all became good friends and learned to function pretty well as an expanded family. Even after her son Christopher was born, we worked okay together; the house just got noisier.

Life resumed and friends would come over for evenings of music and talk. Bob was wise and very funny and was quite an attraction to many young creative types. They'd come, sit, get high, and talk about a wide range of topics. I seem to remember they half-jokingly called him the Buddha. It was amusing to watch but I don't recall being part of much of it.

Slowly my thoughts turned to the world that existed beyond life on the Chicken Ranch. I was feeling the burden of tedium, the weight of responsibility, the sameness of my life. For a while, I toyed with the idea of trying out for the cast of *Hair*. Jack had taken us to see James Rado and Gerome Ragni's revolutionary American tribal love-rock musical when it was being performed in L.A. for the first time at the Aquarius Theater in Hollywood, and it was the most out-there, sexually stimulating thing I'd ever seen. Ben Vereen as the politically militant character, Hud, climbed out into the audience, bare-chested and in torn jeans, and walked on the backs of our seats bellowing out "Colored Spade." I went out immediately and bought the original cast recording and learned all the songs. I told Bob I wanted to audition when they were ready to recast at the Aquarius; he told me that he didn't want me to.

The fun was definitely over. I remember leaving the house at times and feeling jealous that Susan was there alone with Bob. I think I was making up a problem to distract from the depth of my own sadness. I was feeling so hopeless about what my life had become: taking care of two young children, living in this ramshackle house. It wasn't Bob's fault; he was a good guy. Things weren't horrible with him. But I was filled with discontent. I didn't see any future for us. I wanted my life to change. Maybe I could act?

I suppose if my parents had had a lumber store, I'd have started selling plywood. But my mother was an actress, my new stepfather was a screenwriter, and my ex-stepfather was a theatrical agent. Maybe Jack could get me a job. I never really wanted to be an actress. But what else was I going to do? I didn't have any better ideas.

CHAPTER 5

You know the saying "Better the devil you know than the devil you don't"? When it came to entrées into show business, Jack was the devil I knew. I could have gone to my mother and asked her about acting — but I didn't know her well enough. It was Jack whom I called and asked, "Can you send me out on jobs? I need to make some money." He was able to set up several auditions for me, including one to play a prospective marriage partner for a lonely teenager in a dark comedy called *Harold and Maude* that was going to be directed by Hal Ashby. I didn't get it, but the film became wildly popular and over time developed a cult following. I had that nagging feeling of having missed a very important boat, like *National Velvet,* but there was nothing to be done.

Eventually I landed a small guest role on a CBS medical drama series called *The In-*

terns. You could call it the *Grey's Anatomy* of its day. On my episode of *The Interns* I was a wide-eyed candy striper, while thirty-year-old Martin Sheen played a politician. I was thrilled!

While I consider this my first real job, technically speaking I'd already had the tiniest bit of on-camera experience. When I was about seventeen, Jack pulled some strings and got me a onetime appearance on a semi-reality series called *Day in Court.* As I understood the way that show worked, a team of writers would find a real legal case, fictionalize it slightly, and convert the court transcripts into teleplay form; then it was taped and broadcast live. Real attorneys would argue their case in front of a real judge, but the witnesses and defendants were actors. I played an abducted teenage girl and the case that was being tried concerned whether I had been kidnapped or gone willingly across the state line.

My *Day in Court* turned out to be particularly memorable. In the middle of taping I was being cross-examined by one of the lawyers, per the script — again, not an actor but a working attorney — when he accidentally dropped his unstapled script, sending sheets of white paper flying everywhere. As he scrambled to pick up the

128

pages, he kept throwing questions at me. Questions I'd never heard before. I'd love to say I suddenly adapted to acting in front of the cameras, tossing my memorized dialogue out the window, and just improvising some pithy responses. However, my character rapidly changed from simply being a flustered stammering teenager into someone so nervous and terrified by the unexpected questions, she would happily have confessed to any number of crimes just to make it all stop! If those tapes had survived, I doubt I'd have a career today.

Doing *The Interns,* though, was one step closer to ending my marriage. I quickly initiated an affair with an actor I'd just met on the set. Confronting Bob about our problems and attempting to discuss them as an equal partner simply never occurred to me. I seem to have learned that when you wanted to get out of a relationship, you did something to make it impossible to be together anymore — like having an affair. It wasn't as if I was even attracted to the guy I took up with. As calculated as it sounds, I walked onto the set of *The Interns* and thought, "Who's it going to be?" I decided on a sweet, older guy. He never knew he was just part of a passive-aggressive plot to facilitate my freedom.

When we started filming, I'd tell my husband I had an earlier studio call than I really had and stop off at the actor's house on the way in to work. Or stop in on the way home. Although the affair lasted only a short time, the lies and deception required to maintain it immediately began to weigh heavily on me. I was confused and hating myself. I needed to get away even if it was just for a weekend. Since Jack had a luxury trailer out in Palm Springs, only a two-hour drive from Los Angeles, I gave him a call and asked if I could borrow it for a few nights.

First he said yes. Then, before I could pack an overnight bag, he called back and said he'd forgotten that he and a casting director friend were taking their girlfriends there for a double-date weekend.

"You're welcome to come! It's a very big trailer! There's a small little back room!" Jack said.

"Never mind," I told him, not wanting to even imagine what it would be like to be there with them and their women.

A little while later, Jack called again. "My girlfriend can't come. So I'm not going. Now it will just be the other two. You're still welcome to join them."

Now I was supposed to spend the weekend

with a couple who were hoping to have the trailer to themselves? Why would I *want* to? "No thanks," I told him.

About a half hour later, the phone rang and it was Jack with yet another update.

"My friend's girl can't come. It will just be the two of you. I think you should go," he said.

Oh. So this was just a long drawn-out charade about him setting me up with the casting guy? That's right . . . this is what Jack *did*. I'd heard that he often provided women for men in high places. I hadn't expected to be one of them.

"Jack. I don't want to do this."

"You aren't very ambitious, are you?" he replied. Then, referring to the rickety Dodge station wagon with push-button transmission that Jack had recently helped Bob and me buy, he added, "You need new tires on your car, don't you?"

"I don't need new tires that much," I said.

I wanted to tell him not to pimp for me, but I didn't have the courage. I replayed that line over and over in my head for many weeks afterward.

Maybe he thought he was being helpful, in his way. But he wasn't just my agent; he had raised me for ten years and this was very confusing. For all the things that went on between us — the peignoir, setting me up with the casting guy — I was never able to tell Jack how creepy it felt. I harbored a lingering ill will and deep lack of trust in him personally at the same time I handed him my so-called career. For many years, I walked that thin line of agent-father, never certain just who I was dealing with.

Once I had *The Interns* on my professional résumé, Jack had something to build on when it came to my nascent career. I went from *The Interns,* to the set of *The Young Lawyers,* an ABC series set in Boston. Lee J. Cobb played the gruff but dedicated mentor with a group of earnest young law student protégés. I wasn't in any scenes with Cobb and never met him, but I do recall sitting in the makeup room my first day of work and seeing a wig form on the counter with Cobb's hairpiece pinned to it. The receding hairline, wavy forelock, and color were so distinctive; it was as if Lee J. Cobb's disembodied head were sitting on the counter.

When I finished my guest spot on that show, I was set to begin work on a pilot called *Young Love,* a spin-off of *The Doris Day Show* produced by Arwin Productions, Day's own company. In it, I played Doris's niece, April Toliver-Clark, one half of a cash-strapped newlywed couple trying to make their way in the world. Michael Burns was my graduate student husband, Peter.

This show was produced by Abner "Abby" Singer, a name that meant little to me at the time but has stayed in my mind because of a legendary habit he had: Abby was always reluctant to quit for the day. Whenever he was asked if he was satisfied with the final take, Abby would say "Yes, but let's do just one more." So, on many a show over the years, as filming wound down for the day, someone might call out, "Okay, this is 'the Abby Singer' " — or the penultimate shot. The *ultimate* was the martini shot.

So I was on a roll: in less than a month I'd gone from know-nothing guest star to the lead role in a possible series of my own.

As Jack told me at the time, in cheerleader agent mode, "They're in line for you!" I was on my way. I was getting offers. I was earning money. (I was having an affair. Aargh.) Was this typical Hollywood? It was a very heady experience. Of course, *I'm* thinking this is just what happens when someone decides to become an actor . . . they actually get to start acting. (They don't necessarily start having an affair.) It took me years to really appreciate how much was a combination of luck, good agenting, and the calling in of favors by Jack X Fields.

Then, one day when I was at work, Bob found my diaphragm case in the bathroom and opened it. It was empty.

When I got home, he confronted me about it — "Are you having an affair?" he asked me point-blank — and I lied, because that's what I did. Now, on some level that I didn't want to acknowledge, all of my actions were designed to bring about this sad moment. At some point I must have told him the truth because I remember that we went to see a marriage counselor. Bob wanted us to stay together. I remember crying and feeling devastated at what I'd brought about, but the sad thing was that in my mind I'd already left; I was looking for another life for me, Ted, and Eva. And it was important for me to say I never left Bob for another man. I never left anyone *for* anyone else. I left for myself.

Our relationship staggered to an end, becoming increasingly painful and volatile. On the morning of February 9, 1971, Bob and I had been up much of the night arguing. We were still in bed when he got terribly angry and at one point started choking me. I wasn't really afraid; I couldn't believe he'd actually hurt me. Bob had never touched me violently before. But obviously my infidelity was so extraordinarily hurtful, I think he felt he had no other way to get my attention — he didn't want to lose his little family.

Bob put a pillow over my face and was muttering angrily about the Doris Day pilot I was then preparing to shoot. As he hissed, "They won't want a one-eyed April" (now he was going to *blind* me?), there was a strange rumbling sound. We instantly froze. Being natives of Los Angeles, we had no trouble recognizing powerful seismic activity. Later on, we'd find out that the Sylmar earthquake, as the media named it, after the section of the city where the epicenter was located, measured 6.6 on the Richter scale. And we were only eleven miles away from Sylmar.

The old farmhouse started shuddering in waves. It was made of wood and so old that the floorboards were rolling. The floor in front of the fireplace sagged and some bricks from the chimney crashed down. I jumped up and ran to Teddy and Eva's bedroom to make sure they were okay. We sat on Teddy's bed and looked into the kitchen. It was like something out of a horror movie. The cabinet doors were open and dishes, glasses, bottles, and cans of food were literally shooting out of the cupboards. That apocalyptic image of the flying food in my kitchen is the last thing I remember of Bob's and my life together. Within a week, I'd packed up the kids and moved to Whitney and Allan's new home in Trousdale Estates. We stayed there for two or three days. Then Whitney helped me find a small house in North Hollywood.

I couldn't have gotten this little yellow two-bedroom tract house without her help. The rent was $400 a month, over five times the rent of the farmhouse, but then it was a real house in a real neighborhood, and I was walking tall when I finally took over paying the rent myself. It was a far cry from the Chicken Ranch. I recall curdling with shame when the owners would come there on rent day. Invariably we wouldn't have the $77 and I was desperate to avoid the landlady. She was in her seventies and heavy set with a wide, rolling gait. She'd prowl around through the weeds, peering into windows, and screeching, "Murdith! Murdith? You in there?" I'd be lying on the floor under the windows, in the kitchen, on linoleum so thin the plywood showed through, praying for the grace of a few extra days. They must have hated us.

For some, acting is about finding an outlet

for their creative passions, making their fantasies come true. For me it was strictly about paying the bills. I was twenty-four and a newly single mom with two young kids. I knew that I had to keep the jobs coming. I was a total amateur, so the only thing I felt I had to offer was that I arrived on a set prepared and ready to learn. I kept my mouth shut, listened carefully to whatever direction I was given, and took mental notes on whatever anyone did around me.

In the case of *Young Love,* it wasn't just anyone. It was Doris Day, and what I learned from this beloved megastar was what it means to be a consummate professional. I had been a huge fan of hers when I was much younger, singing "Que Sera, Sera" in her style as best as I could and learning all the words to *Pajama Game.* I loved singing, "There once was a wo-man, who loved a maa-aan. She was the one he slew the dragon foo-oor." But I'd never seen her series. By the time I began working with her, *The Doris Day Show* was midway through its five-year run.

One rule of actorly etiquette I learned from her had to do with the reverse shot. Usually, after the master shot (in which everyone is on camera) of a two-person scene is filmed, singles are filmed with each actor delivering her part of the dialogue to the other actor, who stands just off-camera. That footage is then cut together to create a back-and-forth. But on *The Young Lawyers,* when any of my young scene partners finished shooting their portion of the dialogue, they'd just sort of disappear. I'd then play the scene with the script supervisor or dialogue coach standing beside the camera. I didn't know that not sticking around to say your lines off-camera for the benefit of your fellow actor was almost unheard of. I thought, Oh, this is acting. I do my single shot alone. You do your single shot alone. But Doris never left. And when she stayed and cooed her lines off-camera for me, it made all the difference in the world. I had someone there relating to what I was saying, not just reading lines. Such a better system.

Doris Day was classy. She was also orange. Back in the '50s and early '60s, when she starred in those legendary romantic comedies and musicals like *Pillow Talk,* her appeal was all about being bouncy and squeaky clean, the blonde with the megawatt smile. Now nearing fifty, she'd adjusted her image to good-natured, sporty sun worshipper, and in an effort to always appear tan and fabulous, she used some kind of terra cotta–hued makeup. However, it wouldn't look right to cut from her (color of adobe) to me (normal flesh tone) and back to her (color of adobe). We'd both look funny, but she'd look worse. They remedied that by making me tanner.

The first morning I was going to work with Doris, I sat down in the makeup chair and was told, "Get ready, we're going to ruddy you up, honey!" And they did, until Doris and I almost matched. There was less difference in our coloring now, but on camera, Doris always looked just a little bit tanner, just *that much* healthier than anyone else around! It struck me as odd but interesting, and an early lesson in the technical instruction on just what makeup could achieve.

Sometimes, I would learn, being the first name on the call sheet manifested less charitable impressions. When I shot a guest role on a lawyer series called *The D.A.,* I found myself acting opposite Robert Conrad, at that time a big television star from his role as the wisecracking gunslinger James West on *The Wild Wild West.* My part on the episode was that of a hippie who for some reason was in a swimming hole, supposedly nude. It was wintertime and we shot this outdoor scene on the Universal back lot, where there was a big pond. They tried to heat it up, but the water was still so numbingly cold that by the time they finally got the footage they needed, I was chilled to the marrow and shaking so hard I couldn't stop. As soon as I stepped out of the water, the costumer wrapped me in a quilted piano blanket and, pointing toward a limousine parked nearby, said, "Go get in the car, go get in the car!"

Happily! I ran to it, leapt in, and no sooner had I settled myself into the backseat when the door flew open and Robert Conrad's head popped in.

"Hey," he barked. "This is my car."

Damn. Hippies got *no* respect.

As it turned out, none of the networks was interested in picking up *Young Love.* Back before I'd shot the pilot, Jack told me that if the spin-off didn't work, there was yet another series that was ready to cast me, and if *that* fell through, there was yet another one after that. So no matter what happened, I was guaranteed a show. Okay, that sounds great; I'm on a roll! But they didn't happen. Each one fell through. Another lesson. Unless I am standing on the set with a script and someone is yelling "Action!" *I don't have the job.*

So now I'm an *unemployed* young single mother with time on her hands and no one to tell her what to do. Teddy was about three and a half, Eva about one and a half, and when we weren't reading stories, much of their playtime was spent romping with the many neighbor children. I was by far the youngest mom around, certainly the least mature, and most likely to be out there playing with the children. I remember washing dishes one day, watching the kids out the kitchen window. It overlooked the driveway and I could see about six little ones, Teddy and Eva among them, hustling about with water balloons. I hooted out the window at them; they jumped in surprise and heaved a couple of filled balloons at me in retaliation, which exploded on the window screen, soaking my shirt and face. I roared and leapt out the back door, chased them around, then grabbed the garden hose they'd been using. They fled up the drive, laughing and screaming, ran all the way around the house and back into the kitchen, confident they were safe. I raced after them into the kitchen, hose bent in half so no water could come out, where we had a standoff. They had one more balloon. I had the hose. They threw the balloon. I unbent the hose and began squirting them. We were all shrieking! I don't think any of us could believe I'd actually hose them in the house but it was the most freeing, reckless, fantastic thing I'd ever done. My house was damp for weeks but I was the Wyatt Earp of the neighborhood.

The kids would see their dad periodically. After our divorce, Bob's fortunes took a sharp downward turn. I would have loved it if he could have taken the kids during my occasional jobs, but for a while he was basically living out of his truck. I opted for leaving the children with a sweet neighbor family with six children when I worked. It was difficult for Bob and the kids to spend time together. I know the kids missed him but I was ill prepared to know how to make it easier for them or him. When my mother and father divorced, Whitney rarely spoke to Tom. When he came to pick us up she'd have Jack or one of us kids answer the door and my father *never* came in the house. It was all fairly antiseptic. I actually believe my mother added a canopy to our front doorstep on Whitley Terrace so in case of rain there would still be no need to invite my father in. I basically learned, when you divorce them, you kill them. I didn't question it. It seemed to work for everyone. I never heard my father complain. I accepted those were the rules of divorce. I myself followed those same guidelines. I had *feelings* about it, but I certainly never examined them.

In the early '70s, hippie characters were becoming popular on mainstream television and I was casting-perfect with my long blond hair, big eyes, and soft voice. If a casting director needed to find someone to wear a headband and a dress made from an Indian-print bedspread, it wasn't exactly a stretch to imagine me in the part. I was an all-purpose hippie. On an episode of *The Partridge Family* called "Where Do Mermaids Go?" I played Jenny, a backpack- and sleeping-bag-toting hippie girl who appears to be penniless but is secretly . . . a benevolent heiress. In predictable sitcom style, Jenny teaches the Partridges how difficult it is when people are interested in you only for your money. (As if they didn't know.) Lessons are learned all around. Roll end credits.

In doing this show, I reconnected with and started dating David Cassidy, the star of *The Partridge Family.* We might have met before the show but I'm not sure; I'd been hearing his name for years because his mother, Evelyn Ward, and her new husband,

Elliot Silverstein, were friends with Whitney and Jack. I felt like David and I had a history together.

David was a perfect teen idol and could ignite hysteria by entering a room, so we rarely went anywhere in public. When my brother Dick heard that David and I were an item, he drily asked, "Do you know how many twelve-year-olds wish they could trade places with you?"

Cassidy was a very sweet guy and we laughed a lot together. It was a lark for me while it lasted. I wasn't interested in a serious relationship, but I found David very touching. I can't tell you exactly how we ended, but I think it had to do with him flying around the country, performing at sold-out concerts, and my reading about him being with other women. He was three years younger than I and doing what came with his rock star territory, which was fine. There was just nothing for me there.

In the meantime, I was making my feature film debut in the horror sequel *Ben.* The idea behind *Ben* was to capitalize on the surprisingly successful *Willard,* a weird little drama about a young man who cultivates a rat army that eventually turns on him. The sequel concerned another frail, lonely protagonist — this time a little boy — whose only friend is a rat he names Ben. Sadly, the boy's pet is evil and possesses telepathic powers that allow him to rally swarms of other rats to assist him in taking control of Los Angeles, as rats are wont to do, I imagine. Some film executive heard a pitch about rats taking over Los Angeles and thought he had a hit on his hands. In the end, the film is mostly remembered because Michael Jackson sang the theme song; not only was *Ben* his first number one song as a solo artist, it was nominated for an Oscar and won a Golden Globe. Not bad for a love song about a rat. To fans of the genre, *Ben* was too hokey to capture much of the creeping fear generated by its predecessor. But I loved making it.

In one of my favorite scenes, the little boy discovers that the Board of Health is out to destroy Ben and he heads down into an underground sewer to warn him. My character, the boy's older sister, follows him into the darkness and is attacked by a mob of rats.

In retrospect, the special effects used in this scene seemed hilariously low-tech, sort of the grand-scale version of something you'd see in an elementary school play today. The special effects guys had boxes full of stuffed rats in varying sizes and colors. Some looked phony, others were real taxidermied rats. They fastened them to me with varying lengths of string so when I moved, the rats would swing around somewhat. For the big rodent-swarm moment, I was supposed to crouch down and look into the opening of a pseudo-sewage pipe, facing the camera. The sewer, dressed to look revoltingly filthy and solicit "eews" from the audience when I fall in it, was just peat moss and bits of fake garbage. On *"Action!"* a bunch of real live rats were released down the pipe toward me and at a given point the camera found me being attacked by rats, all of them looking very threatening and disgusting. I screamed, thrashing about wildly in terror, which meant my little tethered vermin passengers were thrashing wildly, too. Ah, we could taste the Oscar.

The other exciting part about *Ben* was that I was paid $5,000 for my week of work. That was the most money I'd ever made! I was going to be moving into a larger house in Sherman Oaks, which was great but was lacking in some major essentials. With my big paycheck, I went out and in one day bought a washing machine, a dryer, a television set, and a freezer. I was the appliance queen!

When it came to jobs, I never worried

about career advancement, I just wanted to get paid. My mother always seemed to feel she needed to subscribe to whatever Hollywood's rules were — predominantly, in the '50s and '60s, always be young and beautiful and happy. I felt the pressure wore her down, brought her disappointment, and made her bitter. It's an uphill battle; who can always be young, beautiful, and happy? I think I tried to be the anti-Whitney. Sure, I always tried to look my best, but I think my rebellion focused on the honesty. I'm sure I startled more than one casting director when I'd walk into an audition room, stick out my hand, and say, "Hello, my name is Meredith Baxter. I'm twenty-four and I have two children." This was probably more for me than for them. I wanted to remember who I was. Also I didn't want to start some fantasy about myself that I'd have to live up to the rest of my life.

I was so excited no matter what work Jack found for me. During a lull when I wasn't getting hired for anything, Jack arranged for me to work for director Milton Katselas, who would go on to become a very famous director and popular acting coach in Hollywood. Katselas was in preproduction on the Screen Gems lot for the movie version of the Broadway play *Butterflies Are Free,* about the relationship between an overly protected young blind man and the pretty, aimless young girl next door who befriends him. Katselas was screen-testing actors for the male lead, and they needed someone to play the flighty airhead neighbor girl opposite the various guys trying out. I got hired for $50 a week to rehearse and test with these actors.

What a terrific gift this turned out to be. I got to work with this amazing director, who had studied acting with Lee Strasberg and apprenticed with Elia Kazan. He'd work for days with a new actor, helping him find his strengths so that he'd be his very best in the screen test. I got to spend downtime alone with Milton, going to lunch or dinner, talking about which actor we favored and why, talking about the importance of listening, discussing how to find what a character wanted. He was equally helpful in guiding me to be as alive and vibrant as possible so as to enhance each young man's performance; I came to understand that good acting is also performing a service. Milton lit a fire under me about acting that until now had been barely smoldering. Yes, I decided, I think this is what I want to do, not just to support my family but to really pursue it as a craft.

I'd been working with Milton for a couple of weeks when for some reason, a different light went on . . . "Oh oh oh, *I* have the part!!" For a couple of days I was so excited. This was *great* because I'd worked so *hard.* Then that light blinked out. I'm sure I'd been told, but somehow I never grasped the fact that Goldie Hawn had been cast in the part months before and I was just standing in for her for the screen tests because *she didn't do those.* I felt so stupid, afraid I'd made a fool of myself in front of Milton by acting so chatty and confident, when I was really just a nobody. I'd gone and lost a part I wasn't even up for. *Sigh.* But, here's the great thing: About fifteen years later, when I was appearing in the comedy *Vanities* at the then Westwood Playhouse in Los Angeles, Milton was called in as a secret undercover director to save our show. The show was in deep doo-doo, there was dissension among the three women in the cast, we were all going to walk if they didn't replace the original director, *and* at the same time the show was in preparation to tape from the stage for HBO, one of the first productions to do this. So the theater managers brought Milton Katselas into the chaos (by that time he was a heavyweight director) as our stealth (for political reasons) savior. He was great and as happy to see me as I, him. He indeed saved our show with grace, gentility, and humor.

For all my disappointment and unfounded surprise at not being cast in *Butterflies Are Free,* there was a reason for me to have been at Screen Gems. As I was leaving one afternoon, about to get into my car, I was approached by the legendary casting director Renée Valente. She asked me if I'd be interested in reading a script for a new sitcom called *Bridget Loves Bernie,* about a wealthy Irish Catholic girl who marries a working-class Jewish cabdriver. Was she kidding? Was I *interested?* Were we doing business in the parking lot?

I never even auditioned for the part of Bridget; they just offered it to me. Now, *that* had never happened to me before. For years I'd always assumed that I got the part because someone had seen me hanging around Screen Gems for weeks or that someone had seen my screen test footage. But as it turns out, Fred Silverman, then a young vice president of programming at CBS, remembered me from the Doris Day *Young Love* pilot. I figure he told the *Bridget Loves Bernie* casting department, "Get me that orange girl!"

CHAPTER 6

The media always claimed that *Bridget Loves Bernie* was inspired by *Abie's Irish Rose*, Anne Nichols's popular Broadway stage play and radio series about the romance between a wealthy Irish Catholic girl and a working-class Jewish boy. Shakespeare's *Romeo and Juliet* could have been credited as well. Bernard Slade, who wrote and produced *Bridget*, told me that it was his own personal story. The premise of *Bridget Loves Bernie* involves star-crossed lovers whose parents object to their union. In it, I played Irish Catholic elementary schoolteacher Bridget Theresa Mary Colleen Fitzgerald (daughter of upper-crust, town-house-living New Yorkers Walter and Amy Fitzgerald), who meets and instantly falls for Jewish cabdriver and aspiring playwright Bernie Steinberg (the son of blue-collar, Lower East Side delicatessen owners Sam and Sophie Steinberg). The couple's decision to marry in a civil ceremony happens so quickly that neither family can intervene, but each clan is equally convinced of the unsuitability of its child's choice in mate. Bridget and Bernie, intoxicated with each other, are merely amused by their parents' religious intolerance. Bickering made up the comedy and the conflict, but love won out by the end of every episode.

I met then thirty-two-year-old David Birney, who was cast as Bernie, at the initial table reading. On the first day of work David and I had lunch on the patio in front of the stage on the Screen Gems lot. At the end of the week's shooting, the company flew us to Manhattan for a few days to shoot the exterior street scenes. David and I ate a romantic candlelit French provincial dinner at Le Champignon, and by the end of our time in New York, we were sleeping together.

Having never been to New York before, I had arrived early, with one day to play in the city before starting work. I'd never spent time alone before. I'd lived at home, then with just Bob, then with Bob and two little ones, then just me with the little ones. Now I had one bright, cold spring day all to myself. CBS had put us up at the Essex House, right on Central Park South, and first thing in the morning I ran over to the park. I climbed out onto some large boulders in one of the ponds and watched the ducks. I'd splurged and bought my first camera just for this trip and sat there taking pictures of ducks or of my bare feet on the rocks, which cast long morning shadows into the water. The whole concept of this huge mass of parkland in the middle of a city was dizzying and incomprehensible to me. As an unworldly twenty-five-year-old, I'd always thought of New York as an endless slab of concrete, yet I sat in a lush oasis with the spectacular skyline barely visible through the treetops. I remember lazing there in the sun, feeling new and very full, very centered, very happy in my life. I had a job. I loved living as a single woman. I loved spending my days playing with my kids and reading. I felt like I was getting stronger; I was self-supporting, starting to feel a little confidence. And then I got involved with David.

I think early on I'd decided that *the answer* (to success? happiness? driving?) was having a man at the wheel. Jack had always been firmly at the wheel, strong and decisive, which is why I think Whitney chose him. So there was David, a majorly charming guy and very attractive: dark-haired, intense, lithe, and graceful. And he paid attention to me. But I was most attracted to how erudite he seemed to be; he had so much confidence, he had opinions, he'd traveled, he *knew* things. He listened to Bach and Mozart and quoted passages from Yeats and Shakespeare. Okay, I thought that was a little pompous and if I'd gone to college I probably wouldn't have been so impressed, but at the same time I was dazzled; this was so outside my experience. He had a good education: on a scholarship at Dartmouth he graduated with honors in English literature and then later got his master's in theater arts from UCLA. When he was drafted into the Vietnam War, he had the good fortune to be assigned to the Second U.S. Army Showmobile and spent most of his tour singing and dancing in the Army Special Services variety show; there was no danger on the horizon for him.

After receiving an honorable discharge, he went to New York and paid his dues in the classic, serious actor, way. He worked for legendary theater producer Joe Papp's New York Shakespeare Festival, then moved on to make his Broadway debut in playwright Ron Cowen's *Summertree.* He worked with the Lincoln Center repertory group and played Mark Elliot in the soap opera *Love*

Is a Many-Splendored Thing. Along the way, he amassed an impressive collection of commendations: the Clarence Derwent Award, the Barter Theatre Award, and the Theatre World Award, but it was his work on the soap opera that brought him the greatest popularity up to this point. I think this galled him; he'd have much preferred that it come from his theater work.

David was just coming off a critically acclaimed stage turn in George Bernard Shaw's *Major Barbara* at the Mark Taper Forum in Los Angeles when he was cast in *Bridget Loves Bernie.* Jack had even told me he'd heard great things about "this David Birney," that he was someone to pay attention to.

So I did. I was very aware that I was working with quite an accomplished actor. I, on the other hand, was still unsteady on my feet. I might have had some natural instincts, but I wasn't always sure how to make the most of a line reading, time an entrance, or use the camera to my advantage. David would often correct me, suggest a different line reading or another position in front of the camera. He was so knowledgeable. You cannot imagine how heady it was that this golden boy of the theater world was interested in *me.*

Perhaps six months later, about a week before *Bridget Loves Bernie* aired, CBS sent us both back to New York to do publicity and suddenly there we were, the costars of a new series, fielding reporters' questions about the show and being ferried around Manhattan in a limousine. One night David and I were off to see a play. When our limo pulled up in front of the theater, a guy named Broadway Dave, one of those local characters who hangs out along the Great White Way hoping to spot celebrities, ran over to our car. Before our driver could get out, Broadway Dave opened our door, stuck his head in, checked us out, and then turned to the crowd. *"It's NOBODY!"* he howled with disappointment, and slammed the door shut. I *was* a nobody and was pleased to be recognized, but David was a known entity in New York, so this must have been ego bruising.

But when *Bridget Loves Bernie* debuted on Saturday night at 8:30 p.m. on September 16, 1972, everything changed very quickly. It got big ratings right out of the gate, eventually becoming the fifth most watched show in America. At that time, before the world of hundreds of channels and more diffuse ratings numbers we live in today, that meant a lot of people — tens of millions, numbers you only see shows like *American Idol* getting now — were tuning in. Of course, we had something of a boost in the fact that CBS scheduled us in the slot between two of its biggest shows, *All in the Family* and *The Mary Tyler Moore Show.* Nothing against our series, but a program about cleaning carpets would have done well in that spot.

Another factor in our success was that the series generated a lot of press, much of it having to do with the show's subject of interfaith marriage, but also about what was going on with David and me behind the scenes. Let's face it: two young, attractive actors playing an embattled couple whose love knows no bounds, while having a real-life affair away from the cameras, is a time-honored media hook, and somehow the story got out. Our relationship seemed to garner some attention. In early September, a good ten days before the show aired, a photo of the two of us seated and lightly holding hands appeared as a one-page Fall Preview ministory in *TV Guide.*

Three weeks later, roughly two weeks after the premiere, we were upgraded, with a shot of just our heads, shown in intimate profile as we smiled happily at each other, plastered on the cover of that same publication. (I thought David looked great; all I could see of me was my overbite.) I was already smitten with David at the time but I had no idea how he felt about me. Thinking back on the photo of me and David "lightly holding hands" makes me wonder what he thought of that. He rarely, if ever, allowed any public display of affection. Walking on the street he'd always pull his hand away if I tried to grasp it. I came to interpret that as his not wanting me to have any claim on him, to not *assume* we were "a couple." Even after we'd been married many years, I still had that same feeling. Because, if we were a couple, well, that closed off other possibilities, didn't it? So how that hand holding in the photo came to be is a puzzle; it must have caused him some discomfort.

Years later my stepfather Allan would tell me an anecdote about my mother's reaction to the pilot episode of *Bridget Loves Bernie*. Just before they fade out of the very last scene, when Bridget and Bernie kiss, David moved close to me, gently cupped my cheek and part of my forehead with his hand, then tilted my head over to one side so I was completely obscured and only his face filled the screen.

I was too green to get what was going on. To me, I was just getting kissed on camera.

I didn't yet understand what the camera saw. But Whitney knew. Allan told me she turned to him and groaned, "That fucking *actor.*"

The truth was, I liked making *Bridget Loves Bernie.* I liked the process. I liked going to work five days a week. There was much laughter among all the actors. The show was where I began my lifelong habit of making friends with the hair and makeup department. Like David, the rest of our fabulous cast were all seasoned professionals and I was so new to the game that I felt like a pretender. I had a hard time finding my rightful place in the mix. It was the folks in the hair, makeup, and wardrobe departments whom I felt most comfortable with; they talked to me, I felt welcomed there. But on the set, I was uncomfortable with the attention we as actors would get from the folks in these departments. Although it was part of their job to check us thoroughly before a shot because it was required that we look the *best that we could,* it still felt like overexercised vanity to be looking at myself so many times a day.

I was lucky to work with the great character actors we had in our cast. There was no one who didn't adore David Doyle, who

159

played Bridget's father on the series and later would become known as Bosley on *Charlie's Angels.* He made us laugh all the time. And I loved working with Audra Lindley — later of *Three's Company* fame as Mrs. Roper — who was my mother; and the great Bibi Osterwald and Harold J. Stone, who played Bernie's parents, were always sweet to me. In fact, the only member of the ensemble I didn't spend much time with was an older actor named Ned Glass, who played Bernie's wise, funny Uncle Moe Plotnick. Ned was darling, but he was also a client of Jack's; I thought that if Ned disapproved of anything I did, he'd tell Jack and then I'd be in trouble for . . . something. One great thing about all of them was, because of their years in the business, they knew the score. They were grateful to be on a seemingly successful television series at their age. Whether or not they liked the show never really mattered. They just showed up and did their job.

The order for the first season of *Bridget Loves Bernie* was for twenty-four episodes. Because I was a lead on the series, that often meant twelve-hour days and coming home dog tired. It also meant figuring out how to establish a stable home environment for my children. I was able to have the production company hire my old friend Robin Steckler, who was now also divorced and had two young kids, to be my stand-in. Robin and kids moved into my four-bedroom house on Stone Canyon in Sherman Oaks and we hired a housekeeper to take care of Robin's children, Aimee and Jason, who were six and four, as well as Teddy and Eva, who were then five and three. In retrospect, in many ways I was replicating for my kids the same household structure that I found so lonely as the child of an acting mother. That said, I did try to keep my eye on my maternal responsibilities. By this point David and I were a pretty steady couple during the day but at night we'd sleep at our own houses so as not to confuse the children.

I knew what being taken care of by an endless stream of changing faces was like. For continuity's sake, Robin and I tried to find just one suitable nanny, but looking after four preschoolers was a tall order and it felt like we were always training someone new or some nanny was throwing up her hands and turning in her resignation. During breaks at work I'd call home from the set to see how things were going. In those days, remember, there weren't cell phones. I'd use a stage phone, a big rotary-dial phone that was mounted on the wall. Right before the cameras rolled, a big warning bell alarm would sound, and the power to the telephone line would be shut off, rendering the phones inoperable.

Once I was making one of my regular "How are the kids; what's going on?" calls to the latest housekeeper, Barbara from Barbados. I was talking to her when I heard someone from the crew say, "All right. We're ready for the first team." I think I wasn't in that scene, but the loud warning bell sounded so I hissed to Barbara, "Oh, I've got to go. They're shooting," and the phone went dead. What I found out later, after I returned home to a shell-shocked house-keeper, was that Barbara had called the police, fearing for my safety! In my haste, it didn't occur to me to explain the studio phone situation to Barbara.

Our one-level house had four bedrooms, though it was by no means palatial. There was no yard, but it had a nice big kitchen/family room with a fireplace that was pretty much the center for us all. We had a picnic bench kitchen table, which handily seated four manic children and two weary moth-ers. The master suite was right off the fam-ily room. Three bedrooms opened onto a long hallway. The kids were divided up; one room bunked the girls, the other the boys. I took the small bedroom at the end of the hall and shared a bathroom with the kids. My room was cozy and had a window to the street. I tacked an Indian-print bedspread to the ceiling, creating a canopy, and made the room into my own little nest. I'm kind of hard put to explain why I didn't take the master suite. I was paying a larger portion of the rent, but I didn't feel comfortable taking that much space. So that was Robin's room for the year we all lived together. After they moved out, I eased myself into the suite comfortably.

Teddy was ensconced in kindergarten at a little neighborhood school down the street, and I'd try to get to school functions whenever possible. Once I stuck my head into a PTA meeting and I was shooed away with, "This is a meeting for parents, dear." Humph. I was twenty-five.

When the show took off, CBS amped up its publicity assault. David, seeing an opportunity, came up with an idea for a photo op. Why not fly us and a photographer up to Bear Valley, a ski resort located between Lake Tahoe and Yosemite, and do an article on Bernie teaching Bridget how to ski? What a great way to get free snow time and a little PR as well. Wildly enough, CBS agreed. But there was one hitch. David was an accomplished self-taught skier. I'd never skied a day in my life. To remedy the situation, it was decided that I'd take a couple of intensive private skiing lessons as soon as we arrived. I have never been much of a sportif but I was game. Watching David ski so gracefully, seemingly effortlessly, at first gave me the confidence that I'd be right behind him by the end of the day. (Does *Canada* or *Tupperware* come to mind?) So he *whooshed* off to enjoy himself, all lean and athletic in his ski outfit, while I, looking like the Michelin man in my rented puffy snow clothes (*whose* idea was it to belt my parka?), fastened brittle boards to my feet and clumsily duck-walked my way to my instructor and my first ski lift.

To this day I can't figure out why the instructor did this . . . maybe he didn't understand what *can't ski* means. Maybe he couldn't bear my unwillingness to actually lean down the hill in the direction he wanted me to go. Maybe he didn't like his student sniveling in fear. After lunch, we wound up on one of the higher peaks in the resort, marked with a black diamond for "special!" Instead of the wide-open and smooth terrains I'd faced earlier in the day, this was narrow and had large bumps; it looked like many skiers before me had just been buried where they fell. Although I'm sure the teacher was shouting instructions at me as I hurtled off into space, I couldn't hear him over my own screams. Halfway down the slope, I handily sunk the tips of my skis into the topmost side of what I later learned was a mogul and flew ass over teakettle, wrenching my left knee, which didn't want to bend that way.

The next thing I knew, the ski patrol was bringing me down the hill in a bucket sled. I remember being frightfully cold and feeling my lips go numb as I started to go into shock. From the ski resort I was taken by ambulance down to the nearest town, where they found I'd damaged some ligaments in my knee, and then they sent me back to Los Angeles in a hip-high cast. So much for the shots of Bridget and Bernie cavorting happily in the snow. David told me later that he'd had to pack up my clothes and things at the resort and bring them home for me. He said it felt like I was dead. For some reason, I found that touching. I thought it showed he cared for me.

Here's a lesson that CBS learned: Even if the leads of your series are young and healthy, your show still needs proper insurance coverage. Okay, I'd already had the one skiing mishap, but the lesson was reconfirmed roughly midway through the filming of *BLB,* our shorthand name for the series. One night I was at Alice's Restaurant on the Malibu Pier, having dinner with David and an actor friend of ours named Oliver Clark. We had a great time, but later that night I was kept awake by the worst stomachache ever. I was sure I had food poisoning. I felt somewhat better in the morning and went to work. Midday, the pain started up again; I was in such pain that sweat began pouring down my face; I could barely stand up to play my scene. By early evening the pain had subsided once more and I was actually on my way out to eat again with David and Oliver and I told them about what had happened. Oliver was very concerned and really pushed for me to go to the hospital.

It seemed like an overreaction to me because, after all, *I was better.* However, Oliver's persistence won out and when we got to the hospital, it didn't take long for the emergency room doctor to determine that I was in the middle of an appendicitis attack. I was taken into surgery with dispatch to have my appendix removed. I remember Teddy and Eva were brought to visit me at the hospital but they were too small to be allowed upstairs. The best we could do was wave to one another from the window. They looked so small from the second floor. Teddy had burst into tears when I came home in my skiing accident leg cast and had been afraid to come near me. But not even being *allowed* to be in the same room with each other was harder. They didn't understand.

This is where our show was in trouble. They had not insured me. And they had to shut down production for a week while I recovered from my appendectomy. Taking advantage of this little downtime, David took me, while I was so tender, to the seaside resort town of La Jolla, to an on-the-beach hotel. I'd not been there before and found it extraordinarily beautiful. The only thing I could do was lie in the sand, so we did that, loving the sun. David said he was going off for a run and would be back soon and he sprinted off. I was lying there on my back, kind of like an upended turtle — still weak from the surgery and in so much pain that I couldn't turn over without help. I was stuck on the sand, faceup, unable to move, anxiously charting the sun's progress until David returned from his long (and I thought later, selfish) run. I was burned and blistered but didn't have the words to say anything to him. I didn't know how to ask him to consider me.

The physical travails of *BLB*'s star was nothing, however, compared to the storm of controversy that brewed when our show went on the air. Interfaith marriage may have been a lightning rod topic in the early '70s, but I think no one could have predicted the hullaballoo a lightweight little ethnic comedy would create. Early on, Jewish groups, typically with Conservative and Orthodox religious leaders, began complaining that the show didn't just stereotype Jews but also made marriage between Jews and Christians appear too easy, too attractive. To be fair, many Irish Catholics weren't too keen on the show, either. But their objections didn't come close to the uproar in Jewish communities: there were campaigns to get people to write protest letters to sponsors like Procter & Gamble, and one rabbi attempted to negotiate with CBS to get *Bridget Loves Bernie* taken off the air permanently. Compared to television these days, intermarriage seems like such a harmless plot device. However, Bernie's parents running Steinbergs' delicatessen and constantly making jokes about matzo ball soup and gefilte fish jokes only fueled the turning-Jews-into-cartoon-characters argument.

In order to respond to the criticism, the

show's writing staff began to soften the scripts, which were never what you'd call edgy in the first place. Something as innocuous as Bernie saying, "I don't like my mother's cooking" would be examined, then reexamined, then rewritten, then reexamined, and then cut out entirely so as not to be seen as casting aspersions on Jewish cuisine or mothers! That kind of caution — self-censorship, really — only led to idealizing characters. Bernie became perfectly bland, Bridget became blandly perfect, and when that happens, nobody comes off as human. As the show went on, I began to wish that Bridget had a clubfoot or was maybe a kleptomaniac, some kind of detail that would allow me to bring contours to the character. I was learning what Whitney discovered from her *Hazel* experience: nice, cute, perfect isn't very interesting to play.

On the other hand, I was happy to have a regular job and to be taking home a paycheck. I was slowly getting established in television and it gave my iffy confidence a much-needed boost. But David was very serious about acting in all its permutations, so the change in the quality of the scripts drove him around the bend. He was *always* trashing *BLB* both to me and to the press. He thought the story lines were simple minded and in dire need of a substance infusion beyond plots such as "Shall we get a puppy?" or "Shall we get a water bed?" He probably wasn't wrong, but his feelings seemed to take him overboard.

Late one night we were standing out in the short driveway in front of a house he was renting in Beverly Glen, talking about the show. Now, I may have grown up around this world, but the truth back then was, I wasn't really invested in it beyond my immediate job; I had no fantasies built up around what it was or what it meant. David, though, had very lofty perceptions, and on this night he was going on and on, gathering steam about what television was, what it wasn't, and what it *should* be. A perfectly intelligent wish, granted, but what he was saying seemed to me to be so disconnected from the kind of show we were doing that his anger seemed misplaced, even crazy. We were making *Bridget Loves Bernie,* for crying out loud. It wasn't *Masterpiece Theater.*

Finally I said, "David! It's just *television!*"

And he knocked me down. It was so sudden and unexpected, I couldn't tell you which hand hit me, or even how hard. I do recall thinking, "I'd better not get up because he's going to hit me again." I don't

170

think I was hurt much. I just lay there, flat, staring at his shoes. At the time, he always wore Florsheim zippered stack-heeled boots. Tonight he wore the black ones. Will I remember this night when he wears them again? I wondered. I could hear cars whip down the canyon of Beverly Glen. Did they see us? Did they think they were experiencing a Kitty Genovese moment? I considered staying on the ground, pretending I was dead, but that was improbable; I wasn't hit that hard.

I didn't understand. It was just a conversation. But for some reason he felt that I was undercutting his dreams or the work he was trying to do or somehow minimizing him. I wish I could have said to him, "You putz! Why is *hitting me* your response? Is there only room for *your* feelings?" But instead, the following morning, I went back to his house and apologized for being insensitive. And he graciously accepted my apology. I figured he'd gone to college, I hadn't; he must be right. His anger reflected a passionate opinion about something, an emotional investment. I didn't seem to have passionate opinions about many things. I think he had no patience with my uninformed opinion and he was just protecting his passions. I'd try to be smarter next time.

I assumed that his volatility had a lot to do with his childhood. Born in Washington, D.C., but raised in Cleveland, Ohio, David was the eldest of four boys. His father, Edwin, was an FBI agent. Years later, David would always tell our kids, "What happens in this house, stays in this house," and I think that attitude had a lot to do with growing up with a privacy-obsessed dad.

This was the man that David just revered. I think he wanted to *be* him. Edwin was smart, had a great mind, wrote interesting letters, but when I met him, later on, I found him to be a cold motherfucker. Ed terrified me. He was a big man, around six feet and broad across the shoulders, and to David, who was very small as a child, he must have seemed even larger. Ed appeared to have more bulk than muscle and he had an air of menace about him that probably served him well in the FBI. David's mother, Jeanne McGee, once told me a story about being sick and how she couldn't come downstairs because she was in so much pain. So when she needed something, she'd have to pound on the floor with her cane, hoping Ed would hear and come upstairs to see what she needed because he never checked on her otherwise. One day, her pounding elicited no response. Finally she had to phone one of David's brothers and say, "Can you call your father and tell him that I need a glass of milk to take my medicine?" A little while later, Jeanne said, Ed wordlessly walked into the room, plunked the milk on the nightstand, and made his exit without so much as a "Can I get you anything else?" or "Are you okay?"

I experienced a lot of Ed in David. Jeanne had a little girl from an earlier marriage, about six years older than David, who suffered immeasurably at Ed's hands. Little Betty Jeanne, as Jeanne told me, wasn't allowed to eat at the table with the boys or use the door as an entrance to the house, just one of the windows, and Jeanne felt powerless in the relationship and had little voice to combat Ed's decisions. Her best solution was, after a few years of this treatment, to send Betty Jeanne away to live with another family. These stories and Ed's behavior often came back to me years later, after David and I were married and had children of our own.

As the television season wound to a close in the spring of 1973, the religious furor around *Bridget Loves Bernie* continued spinning out of control. Groups were picketing CBS headquarters in Manhattan, and one of our associate producers was carrying a gun because he'd been getting death threats. Two members of the Jewish Defense League showed up on the doorstep of my Stone Canyon house and told my housekeeper that they wanted to talk to me about changing the show. When my housekeeper told them, "She's not here, she's on a plane coming back from New York," they wanted to know what flight I was on so they could meet me at the airport. They never returned, but it didn't make me feel particularly comfortable that they knew where I lived.

Meanwhile, CBS was trying to do some damage control. There was no official second season pickup, but new producers had been hired to provide a less controversial spin if the series continued. There was talk of cutting Bridget and Bernie's families loose and focusing more on the trials of a young married couple adjusting to life as a pair.

Thankfully, I knew nothing of this at the time. I was off on an adventure. As soon as we went on hiatus, I was cast in a stage version of *Butterflies Are Free* in Addison, Texas, a town about twenty minutes from Dallas. John Spencer, who would go on to play White House Chief of Staff Leo McGarry on *The West Wing,* was the blind mama's boy, and this time, I got to be Jill

Tanner, the dingy next-door neighbor, the Goldie Hawn role I longed for just two years earlier. Redemption!

I was thrilled beyond words to have this work. I'd never done a play outside of Hollywood High before and I worked prodigiously to get my lines down before rehearsal started, some weeks down the road. Then I started to come down with something: I was having difficulty swallowing. Eventually I lost my appetite, stopped eating, and began losing weight. I could detect the lump in my throat that was making even swallowing saliva painful. This sucked! I just get my first stage part and I get cancer? I was way too young for this. I consulted an internist, who gave me the requisite liquid barium test (yech!), but he saw no lump or obstruction at all. Afterward, in his questioning me, he asked if I were anxious about anything . . . anything at all?

Duh! Hello? A play! Standing in front of hundreds of people — sometimes wearing only a bra and panties — trying not to goof up my lines and look foolish. The doctor's simple question was magical. By day's end, I still had my anxiety, but my throat was back to normal.

I can still recall the lurch in my stomach I felt when a Dallas-based reporter told me that CBS announced that *Bridget Loves Bernie* wouldn't be coming back in the fall. Whatever reservations I had about the series, I was still really disappointed. The five-year contract that I signed had always brought me a measure of security. In my head, I could calculate out the revenue stream that would support my kids and me until Teddy was nine and Eva was seven. So much for that plan.

CBS did what it could to make it appear as if they were not caving under pressure. Data was released citing the number of complaint letters regarding our show (it turned out to be fewer than two hundred) to the outpouring of letters from viewers who objected to the abortion episodes on Bea Arthur's *Maude* (more than six thousand). They told newspaper columnists that *Bridget Loves Bernie* was underperforming, pointing to the drop-off in viewers between *All in the Family* and *The Mary Tyler Moore Show*. Whatever. To this day, *Bridget Loves Bernie* remains the highest-rated show ever to be canceled by a network.

In all fairness, CBS put a real winner in our time slot: *M*A*S*H,* the TV adaptation of Robert Altman's 1970 darkly funny feature film about Korean War medics, an award-winning series that ran for almost

176

eleven years and still runs in syndication.

I didn't understand why they'd pretend that there was any other reason we went off the air but this: a small but articulate group of detractors didn't like the message of our series and CBS blinked.

CHAPTER 7

Any actor will tell you that each job feels like it's their last. I hadn't even been an actor that long, but that's how I felt after the series was canceled and *Butterflies Are Free* closed. Fortunately, I landed a nice role in my first made-for-TV movie, a mystery called *The Cat Lady*. In it, I played Rena, a salesgirl at a head shop who turns out to be . . . *the reincarnation of a murderous Egyptian cat-headed priestess. Woooooo.* When I first read the script, I politely pointed out that with gender in the title it wasn't hard to figure out which character was transforming into a cat and killing everybody. When I received the next draft, the title had been changed to the more mysterious, asexual *Cat Creature.*

These days, if people think of made-for-television movies, they might assume they fit into one of three different categories: issue-oriented stories ripped screaming from the headlines, disease-of-the-week tearjerkers, or women-in-peril melodramas. But in the early '70s, sci-fi and horror TV movies were also popular, and they drew notable talent. One reason *The Cat Creature* worked was that it was directed by the great Curtis Harrington, who was responsible for several classic "Grande Dame Guignol" movies like *What's the Matter with Helen?* and *Whoever Slew Auntie Roo?,* aging-starlet chillers in the manner of *Whatever Happened to Baby Jane?* Something I might be cast in today, for example.

Curtis had one foot in mainstream Hollywood and another in experimental and occult films. Because of this he managed to persuade established movie actors to appear in what was essentially a small-screen reworking of Val Lewton's 1942 horror classic, *Cat People.* The Academy Award–winning actress Gale Sondergaard played one of Rena's first victims. David Hedison, John Carradine, the venerable Stuart Whitman, Kent Smith (who starred in the original *Cat People*), and Keye Luke (who played Number One Son in the Charlie Chan movies) were also part of the cast. I think the network was looking for a name, but Curtis Harrington fought for and eventually succeeded in convincing the network to cast me as the lead. He also somehow managed to secure the original costume that Elizabeth Taylor wore in *Cleopatra* for the scene when I turn into the bloodthirsty Egyptian cat-goddess. At the time I was a size 6, but they still had to let the gown out to squeeze me into it because Liz Taylor was a tiny thing! And it weighed about 70,000 pounds because it was embroidered with real gold! Really! I coughed and popped off a few gold bugle beads. I watched the equivalent of my salary disappear through the floorboards.

The entire experience of making *The Cat Creature* was fun, but one of my most vivid memories of the production happened way off-screen. After *Bridget Loves Bernie* was axed, David landed a starring role in the feature film adaptation of Alistair MacLean's *Caravan to Vaccares,* which was filming in the south of France. As soon as I wrapped *The Cat Creature,* I was going to go join him. But first I had to get a passport, and in between the shooting schedule and taking care of the kids, the only time for running that errand was on my brief lunch break and there was no time to change out of my thick, wavy, shoulder-length red wig and feline-green contact lenses, which is what most cat-goddesses wear. So I went as I was into the U.S. Passport office at the

180

Federal Building in West Los Angeles and presented myself at the counter.

I filled out my questionnaire, handed it to the civil servant in charge of processing my passport, and he looked at the part that read, "Blue eyes, blond hair," looked up at me, looked back at the form, then looked back at me, and finally said, "I'm sorry. Are you this person?" "Why, yes I am," I said adamantly, then marched off to have my photo taken. So not only did I go to Europe with a passport in which I looked totally like someone else, which could never happen today, it was also a particularly *unattractive* someone else. I might have looked better with a fake nose and eyebrows. Passports have to be renewed only once every ten years, but believe me, as soon as I found the time I renewed it so at least I wouldn't have to explain to any border police what I'd done with the *real* Meredith Baxter, assuming there was one.

Arles and Les Beaux in the south of France were stunning and amazing. It was hard to take in that there were places that had such coffee and croissants, were so romantically beautiful, and existed just air-hours away yet instead we spend our time in Los Angeles. I loved the food. I hated the bullfight. I felt uncomfortable with David

181

but figured it was just me.

Not long after I returned from France, I started work on another movie of the week, this one about a young woman and man, both adopted in infancy, who are in search of their birth parents. It was originally called *My Mother's Eyes, My Father's Smile,* but by the time it aired, in March 1974, the name had been changed to *The Stranger Who Looks Like Me.* Considering my background, the title could have been *Are You My Mother?* a popular children's book I read to my kids. I probably didn't do myself any favors psychologically when the director, Larry Peerce, told me he was still looking for someone to play my real mother, and I suggested Whitney. Larry, who knew my mother slightly, instantly agreed it would be a brilliant piece of stunt casting.

I'm not sure what was going through my head. It's not as if I ever thought that acting alongside her would be fun. But I might have assumed it would be interesting or powerful to have the woman who basically ignored me throughout my childhood play someone who never really knew her daughter. Maybe I hoped she'd understand how I'd experienced those early years and beg my forgiveness. Maybe I figured that I could handle it because in the three-plus weeks it would take to shoot *Stranger,* only one long scene would be between me and my mother. Maybe I had an agenda.

I loved working with my colead, Beau Bridges, whose character assisted mine on her quest and at the same time sought out his own natural parents. But the shoot turned out to be draining. The roller-coaster ride began on the first morning, when Larry Peerce, who had directed the critically acclaimed big-screen adaptation of Philip Roth's *Goodbye, Columbus,* announced that we would be improvising our dialogue during key scenes. I hadn't done much ad-libbing since *Day in Court,* and we remember how well that turned out. In the end, *Stranger* would contain an exchange where a group of adoptees (my character included) argue angrily for the right to know the details of their personal history — the names of their biological parents and where they lived, as well as the reasons behind their being given up for adoption — while another group defends parents' rights to remain anonymous. It was like a debating team free-for-all. The pro-adoptees and the pro-parents argued from their own position, each actor speaking his or her own un-scripted words. The result was mayhem, powerful and tempestuous, and the scene ran for almost five minutes.

As for the time I spent with Whitney on the set in the house where we were filming, it wore me out emotionally. I was spinning inside the whole day we filmed our big scene, the one the entire movie built toward: the moment where my character shows up and asks her real mother, "Why didn't you keep me?" The exchange was so loaded for me, as of course I knew it would be. This scene was *the reason* I wanted to do the movie. In this scene I could ask the pointed questions I'd always wanted to ask, albeit with not quite the right words, though they would serve. In my *mind* I'd confronted Whitney repeatedly, but never in reality.

Usually we rehearsed a scene several times but I only wanted to run through the lines. I didn't want to use up the emotional fuel I was stoking. Besides, Larry was going for the ad-libbing thing. Well, I'll give him ad-lib. So I am there, ready to shoot the master, I'm toeing my mark and wired, the camera is favoring me while I face Whitney, whose back is to the camera. She has the first line and when she speaks I am primed to spit out, *"Where were you all my liiiiife?"* dripping with decades of vitriol, anguish, and loneliness for everyone to see. And then what? What did I expect? Everyone would hate

184

her? They'd throw things at her?

There are delays while the crew adjusts lights, puts a new battery in the camera, and I just stand there . . . staying tight, staying ready, looking down, not ready to see Whitney's eyes. By the time Larry finally quiets the set to start shooting, I realize in a panic, *I'm dry.* I've lost it; my edge, my ammo is gone. I'd been too focused on it, it took too long, and now it's gone. Larry whispers "Action" to Whitney, and she doesn't say *her* lines . . . she starts talking about my real brothers! "You saw the pictures on my mantel?" she said. "Dick is there, Brian is there. You're not there. I didn't want you there." Indeed, she'd brought framed photos of Dick and Brian and actually put them on the shelf above the fireplace on the set, where I could see them.

It was just too on the nose for me. I couldn't get out my lines or any words to save my life. Midway through the shot, I was so wound up and in distress that I turned and ran out the front door crying, and apparently Whitney ran out the back.

She'd come intending to pull a stronger performance out of me by capitalizing on my real feelings of abandonment.

Whitney and I eventually calmed ourselves

down, came back to the house, and completed the scene. It was everything that was required on the page, but I don't know if it ever approached the heights of brilliant drama I'd imagined when I arrived on the set that morning. And it's probably just as well it didn't. Acting is not therapy. A movie set is not the place to work out familial angst.

Years later now, I wonder that my mother decided she could address my feelings in such a public yet indirect way as she did that day, yet never again. Not that I ever brought it up with her. I never felt I had permission; I was far too afraid of her. But I'm grateful she took that chance. She was helping me, not that I realized it then. This took another twenty years of grief and reflection. I'd come loaded for bear, ready to deliver some snarky "news," make sure she understood I was not acting. But she didn't need to be told. She knew and was playing on those same raw feelings to excite a better, deeper performance from me, *for* me. For the movie.

Even though *Bridget Loves Bernie* was over, David and I stayed a high-profile couple in the eyes of the media. Whenever we did press, there was always a sentence or two that included a fairy-tale retelling of how we met, fell in love, and stayed together after our series ended. Typically, the reporter would throw in a question about marriage plans — as in, did we have any? The truth was that we both felt skittish about making our relationship official. David's previous marriage — to a coed he'd met at Dartmouth — was, as I understood it, brief, had ended badly, and left him with unresolved feelings about ever getting married again. He also struggled — and he was always very open about this both to me and in interviews — with whether or not he was ready to commit to raising Teddy and Eva. It wasn't just that they weren't his, I just never got the feeling he was wild about kids, period, although he had said many times that a prerequisite to getting married would be my promise to have another child with him. I was only twenty-six at the time and just getting a career off the ground. I wasn't real confident I wanted a third child. *I* was on the fence about getting into another marriage anyway. I'd been through too many fathers with Whitney and I didn't want to put Teddy and Eva through the same upheaval.

This isn't to say that we weren't talking about it. One night we were sitting together in front of the fireplace at my house in Stone Canyon, and David was talking about his work and how he had to make a certain amount of money if we were going to get married. As it happened, my career had moved on pretty steadily since *Bridget Loves Bernie* ended: I'd starred in two TV movies and done several guest spots.

So I assured him, "I'll . . . I'll be working, too."

David sighed, shook his head wearily, and said, "What *you* make doesn't count. It's what *I* make." He put no value on any contribution I could make; only what he did was important. He told me that he'd made "promises to himself," meaning, I think, about the amount and quality of work he would do in a lifetime. David pointed out that I'd made no such promises, which I think he interpreted as my having no pride or commitment to my work, which rendered it valueless and superfluous. He had a facility for erasing me with relatively few words. I knew being with him required that I be real small, not take up too much space; well, that was familiar. I didn't like it but because he was smart and spoke with educated confidence and because I was primed to disappear on cue, I acquiesced.

In early 1973, not long after our dispiriting fireside chat, something happened — who knows what the last straw was? — and I walked away from the relationship. I'd just had enough of David's snarky comments, his preening self-importance, being constantly made to feel bad about myself. I had gotten a part in a TV movie that was filming in Palm Springs, and right before I left Los Angeles, I broke up with him. I was so thrilled that I had summoned up the courage to call it quits that I called up David's friend Oliver, who had a many-years-long love-hate relationship with David because David was also verbally abusive to him, and I said, "Oliver, I did it. I DID IT. I'm OUT of there!" He was so happy for me. I felt free. I felt strong and alive and wonderful. I felt like me again. It was short-lived.

I got to Palm Springs, settled into my hotel room, and went to the production office to check on rewrites, get a shooting schedule, pick up my per diem. That night the calls from David started coming. He wasn't angry; he was wooing me back. I'd have none of it. I had made a decision I'd been terrified to make and I didn't want to talk to him. I couldn't be very articulate — even over the phone he still scared me. I just said, "I don't want to do this. I don't want to do this." The calls kept coming and my response never changed. The next day, he showed up at my hotel. What? *What?* He just drove all the way down here from Los Angeles? For *me?* I couldn't believe he did that. I couldn't believe I mattered that much to him. I must have been wrong about him. I didn't have any defenses in the face of what I saw as a grand gesture. It was kind of like Whitney coming to get me at Interlochen. He wanted to be with me so much that he was just going to come get me. For the rest of the weekend, he was sweet and solicitous and funny, all of the things that he could be when he felt like it.

I had no birth control with me: I'd been a single girl when I packed for Palm Springs. David and I prowled a nearby pharmacy looking for something familiar but we were leery of someone yelling out, "Hey, there's Bridget and Bernie buying some Emko foam," so we abandoned that pursuit and spent a couple of cozy days together. My fate was sealed. Somehow I'd managed to leave David, reconcile with him, and get pregnant in less time than it takes to make a ninety-minute TV movie.

I don't remember being proposed to, but immediately, as soon as I found out I was going to have a baby, marriage was in the mix. I wasn't thinking about having an abortion, and there was no way I'd have a baby on my own. In a reversal of conventional bride and groom roles, David took over and mapped out every single wedding detail — he chose the date (April 10, 1974), where our church ceremony would be conducted (New York's Madison Avenue Presbyterian Church), and the location of the reception (The Player's Club, right across from Gramercy Park).

The next month, in early April, David and I flew to New York to get ready for the event, staying at David's wonderful, high-ceilinged apartment on West Seventy-seventh Street and West End that he had kept when he moved out to Los Angeles for the series. One day, while David was out taking care of loose ends at the church, I was getting ready to leave for a job interview some blocks away, but I was feeling so low. I was a month pregnant and a week away from my wedding, Teddy and Eva were flying in with the nanny the next day, and I missed them terribly. I started crying. And then I couldn't stop and proceeded to have a mini-breakdown. All the thoughts I'd been fighting not to think, all the feelings I'd been trying to keep pushed down came flooding up and I was sobbing and sobbing so hard, I could hardly stand. I was next to the front door, hands spread on the wall to keep me upright. I knew, right then, I acknowledged to myself that I was making a terrible mistake, that this was going to be a horrible, punitive marriage, but I didn't know what else to do. I didn't think I knew enough to be a good mother on my own and David seemed to agree with me. I thought this was the only thing to do, that it would be a good thing for my children. I knew I'd have no voice in anything and I would probably always feel powerless, empty like I did then. I finally stopped crying and as I dried my eyes and left for my interview, I made the decision to *not know* what I knew and I told no one. Who was there to tell?

David is Irish, so he decided that the ring he wanted me to wear would be a specially designed claddagh, a charming traditional Irish wedding ring that features two hands holding a heart. Only two or three days before the wedding, David went to his jeweler and was told that my ring wouldn't be ready in time. That evening we were eating at the Irish Pavilion, one of David's favorite restaurants. As our waitress served our food we noticed she was wearing a claddagh ring. We told her our sad story and she told us her happy one. Her boyfriend,

Seamus, had given her the ring just a few days earlier. When David offered her $30 for the ring, I remember her worrying that, "Oh, Seamus will be so upset." David was pretty convincing but I think she was won over by the idea of being such a heroine and saving our wedding day. I wore Seamus's ring for the next fifteen years.

While our wedding was to be attended by several of David's New York friends, his mother and one of his three brothers, Joe and Peppy Stern, and his best man, Oliver Clark, I hadn't invited any guests. I had no friends who could afford to fly to New York and I knew no one who lived there; Jack, my ex-stepfather and still my agent, would be in attendance, and Whitney. She was my only family member who'd be present. I asked her to be my maid of honor since there were no other candidates. The day before the wedding she took me to lunch at The Pierre. Afterward we were standing on the street and just as we were about to part, Whitney turned to me and said, "You know, you don't have to do this." I looked at her standing there, looking beautiful in her white St. John suit, concern filling her face. I was aware of the bustling of cabs, the bright sun, and the screech of tires all around us. I had a sense that it was too late for anything, including my mother's advice and changing my mind. Pregnant on the eve of my wedding, I had no better ideas; I was too small; I felt bereft of choices. I told her, "Yes, I do."

Twenty hours later I walked down the aisle in an off-white dress I'd bought for twenty-seven dollars. My hair, still long at the time, was down. I'd planned to wear a small floral wreath in my hair that Whitney brought for me, but David didn't like it. He was always sensitive about his height — he's about five-ten, I'm five-seven. He thought my floral wreath made him look short.

Right before our wedding I was offered a high-visibility role as William Holden's daughter in a big Hollywood disaster movie, *The Towering Inferno,* and I turned it down because the shooting schedule overlapped with the honeymoon we'd planned. But we didn't go on a honeymoon. Work intervened — for David. He was offered the lead role in a production of Shakespeare's *Romeo and Juliet* at the American Shakespeare Festival Theater in Stratford, Connecticut, and he needed to rehearse.

Being married changed our lives in a myriad of ways. For one thing, David and I bought a big four-bedroom redwood house together on a cul-de-sac in Santa Monica Canyon and for the first time all four of us lived together as a family. I didn't want our household to be like the one I grew up in: a collection of strangers who lived under the same roof but sequestered by themselves in their own rooms. I wanted to protect my children from the bleak isolation that characterized my childhood and create a place of warm, loving cohesiveness. I didn't want them to live in a house where there was a "Jack" or a "Whitney" or an "Allan." I wanted there to be a "Mommy" and a "Daddy." Period.

I was so determined to make this happen and so fixated on the goal of a happy home, though, that my approach lacked sensitivity. My future child would be calling David "Daddy," and I wanted Teddy and Eva to call David "Daddy," too. That they already had a perfectly serviceable father outside our home was an impediment I paid little attention to — I was forging my family, dammit! I realized later calling David "Daddy" made them feel terribly disloyal to Bob. I remember poor Teddy telling me years afterward that he didn't ever want his father to know that he enjoyed anything in his new home — and that he didn't want David or me to know if he had a good time with Bob. He was desperate to protect feelings on both sides and was often defeated in his attempts. David would ply them with questions about what they did while with Bob and then heap criticism on whatever activity they named, whatever meal they had. I would sometimes participate because I thought it pleased David, backed him up.

In some ways, our new life was a rude awakening for Teddy and Eva, because my ideas about child rearing were less restrictive than David's. Suddenly there were lots of rules regarding how much television they could watch and how to behave at the dinner table. David had never spent much time around children before, but he sure knew what behavior he wanted to see. David and I took the kids to dinner one night at the Sea Lion restaurant in Malibu. Eva ordered a shrimp salad and when it arrived at our table, I thought it might be a problem because it was ridiculously huge and she was about five. She could only eat a little and David was furious. What was confusing was that his anger came so fast and out of nowhere. I remember him threatening her, saying that he was going to pour a bowl of chowder over her head if she didn't clean her plate. Perhaps he was mad that his authority had been flouted . . . she *didn't* eat it all as he'd demanded but *didn't* eclipsed *couldn't*. David hadn't spent any time around kids and he wasn't interested in hearing that that there was no way a five-year-old could have eaten such a large portion. The evening ended with Eva crying all the way to the car and David sort of throwing her in the backseat. I didn't intervene. I was afraid of the suddenness and ferocity of his rage. And part of me wondered if maybe he was right; perhaps children were supposed to do exactly what their parents said, that their explanations were just excuses. And I often felt just like one of the children.

Somewhere along the line I decided it was easier to live with whatever rules David laid down than to fight them. Someone had to know what was right. He always seemed sure, so he made the decisions. He wanted his way even when it had nothing to do with him. Take my hyphenated name, Baxter-Birney. For the sake of my career, it would have made more sense for me to continue using my maiden name. I *wanted* to keep using my own name. However, if David and I were at someone's house or out somewhere and he had to introduce me, he'd pause as if he didn't know my name, then say in a tone dripping with sarcasm, "What am I supposed to call you? Who *are* you?

Who do you want to *be?*" and then he'd laugh, like look at this idiot woman I'm with, as if wanting to keep my name was a stupid, mindless thing. I expect he felt it was a rejection of him but he never said that; he just humiliated me. After a while it felt like it wasn't worth the harassing and the jokes made at my expense. I told myself it could be a good thing; if it would make David happy, it was a small thing to do. I needed to *choose* to change it, not because I was bullied. So I went through the legal process of becoming Meredith Baxter-Birney. I showed him the official affidavit as a surprise. He seemed unimpressed, like I was late to the show.

On December 5, 1974, I gave birth to our daughter Kathleen Jeanne Birney, whom we called Kate. I had a saddle block when both Teddy and Eva were born, which requires numbing the mother in all the requisite areas from the waist down. David had done some research and decided he didn't want his child to be born with drugs in her system, so he had me do natural childbirth. No drugs. Which, let me say, is a *stupid* fucking way to have a child! With so many modern techniques and all the safety measures at hand, I feel there is no reason, short of some man's whim, to forgo the relief drugs offer and endure the horrendous discomfort. Obviously childbirth has been around longer than drugs but it might have died out altogether if it weren't for drugs. That's my feeling.

Now there were five of us. And here's where David did something inspired. In order to pay tribute to our first Christmas together as a family, he went out in mid-December and bought an enormous tree, maybe ten or twelve feet tall (we have very high ceilings in our redwood living room). David wanted it to be a surprise, so he hid the towering evergreen behind the garage so the kids wouldn't see it. I was in the kitchen a few days later, watching Ted playing out in the yard, and I saw Teddy wander behind the garage, where he was sure to see the tree. I told David and that night he made an announcement after dinner. He said, "Kids, I gotta tell you about something" — and I'm paraphrasing this, of course — "whenever a new family comes together, very often Santa Claus will bless that family with their own special, magnificent tree. Now I don't know if it's going to happen to us because it always comes as a surprise. In fact, it might not happen, but I just want you to know that it's kind of exciting that we might get that blessing." As David spun his tale, I remember watching Teddy, and he was *beside* himself with excitement. He was leaping up and down saying, "It's us! It's us! I saw the tree! It's us!" It was beautiful. It was a brilliant story, and its message — that we were united as a family — was so timely and openhearted.

It was like the letters David would write when any one of the kids would lose a tooth: he'd make up these intricate stories customized for the individual child. They were works of art, really, written in a semicalligraphic style with intricate illustrations in the margins, and David would sign them Almalda the Tooth Fairy. He also wrote equally elaborate Santa letters to the children with ornate designs; they were glorious! He put so much work into them that it ultimately became too unwieldy and the ritual eventually ended. Sometimes, particularly after one of David's inexplicable rages or his punishing one of the kids for an insignificant infraction, I'd try to find some congruity between the rager and the creator of Almalda; I just didn't understand how they could coexist.

In the early part of 1975, just after Kate was born, a small but exciting job opportunity came my way: a small role in

Alan J. Pakula's *All the President's Men,* the feature adaptation of Bob Woodward and Carl Bernstein's book about how they broke the Watergate story. One of the peripheral characters, Hugh W. Sloan Jr., was the treasurer of the Committee to Re-elect the President, Richard M. Nixon's 1972 campaign committee, and I was cast as Debbie, his loyal wife, who answers the door when Bernstein and Woodward — played by Robert Redford and Dustin Hoffman — come to interview him. (Stephen Collins played my husband, Sloan.)

Until then, my brief career had been mainly in television, where the tempo was very fast-paced; time was money; on an average TV movie we could shoot eight to ten pages of script a day. So it was unfathomable to me to be working in Washington, D.C., on a feature film that had such a big budget that it might do only two pages a day. There was a lot of sitting around, waiting to work — much more so than in television. I recall people just sitting in clusters playing cards, sleeping, or talking; I mainly sat and read and tried to eavesdrop on Pakula, Redford, and Hoffman discussing and arguing about upcoming scenes.

I was still carrying around some post-Kate baby weight, but Debbie Sloan was supposed to be pregnant, so they just padded me up. I had only two little scenes, but the most operative one was when Woodward and Bernstein come to our door. The camera picks me up coming out of the living room, takes me to a doorway, and then follows me down an entryway to the front door and you see my back as I open the door, revealing the two reporters standing there. Such a simple shot, you say? Ha!

It almost defeated me. They wanted to frame the shot so that when I opened the door the back of my head was in the center, revealing Redford on one side, and Hoffman on the other. That meant the door had to stop on a particular mark so that it formed the right side of the frame. But my back was to the camera, and I couldn't look down to see how far I was supposed to open the door. It's not as if I could just magically figure it all out while the camera was rolling. They were looking for precision and I was a novice and not producing that for them. I was in a panic trying to make it right. I'd already blown it several times before they broke for lunch. So, on the break, I worked by myself on the darkened set, over and over again, walking along the entry to my mark counting the steps and opening the door just so, trying to get a good sense of exactly the right amount of space between my shoulder and the door (honest, hitting your mark is a major part of acting), and by the time we started up again I was pretty confident I had it right. Everyone reassembled on the set, I got in position, they called action, the camera followed me down the hall, I opened the door to perfection, but *Oh my God, Robert Redford and Dustin Hoffman* are at my door and standing in the wrong places! They had switched positions just to mess with me! They were successful. I blew it again. I felt like I'd be a newcomer *forever.*

They were both really very nice and patient. I was especially nervous and self-conscious around Redford. I passed by him on the set once after lunch while he was taking a bite out of something and I flippantly said, "Oh, eating again?" Why did I say *thaaaaat?* I wanted to stab myself in the head with my plastic fork.

As I was getting acting jobs, opportunities for my mother were drying up. This is what happens in the friendly, loyal movie business as one gets older. Being shrewd, talented, and resourceful, she moved on to creating a sitcom that she could star in. Whitney always felt that there was a series in her, that the obstacles she faced as a single parent raising children were fodder for great social comedy. So she pitched an idea to her husband, Allan, about a divorced woman raising a teenager on her own in Indianapolis, and her hope was that she and I would star as mother and daughter. For the next five or six years Allan shopped the premise around with the piquant working title of *38 . . . 18 . . . And . . .*, meant to suggest both age and a woman's measurements. Mostly Allan heard a lot of nos. By the mid-'70s, though, he was a writer-producer on Norman Lear's popular Chicago-based sitcom, *Good Times.* Allan ran the idea past Norman, who commissioned him to write a pilot script.

By the time *38 . . . 18 . . . And . . .* made it through Lear's famously soul-crushing development process of notes and rewrites and polishes, it had become *One Day at a Time,* a half-hour comedy-drama about Ann Romano, a divorced woman in her thirties hoping to reclaim her independence while raising two teenage daughters, Julie and Barbara Cooper. Not only did this mean that Whitney, who was pushing fifty, was now too old to play the character based on herself, but to heap insult upon injury, Norman Lear refused to let her audition, not even as a courtesy. Theater actress and former child star Bonnie Franklin was cast, and the role put her on the map. As disappointed and irked as my mother was, when *One Day at a Time* premiered in December of 1975, Whitney got out there and did press for it, bringing attention to and wringing whatever glory she could out of her "Created by Whitney Blake and Allan Manings" credit. Given that the series eventually ran on CBS for eight highly successful seasons, that was eight years of being reminded of what could have been. That must have felt like a constant painful reprimand for her.

Watching Whitney struggle was a perpetual reminder for me to appreciate the work that came my way — even when it was a freaky, wrong headed TV movie like *Bittersweet Love,* which David retitled *Bittersweet Turkey.* I starred as a young woman who meets a man (played by Scott Hylands), falls in love, gets married, then, after discovering she's with child, finds out that her husband is also her half brother. Oops! Headlining in an incest movie — and a bad one at that — isn't what made this experience memorable. It was the genuinely talented, seasoned actors who were featured in the cast as well: the amazing Celeste Holm, Robert Lansing, and Robert Alda.

And the actress cast in the role of both my and my husband-sibling's mother was Hollywood icon Lana Turner.

Working with her was exciting and peculiar. It was dispiriting that, given that Ms. Turner had been a larger-than-life star for decades, she turned in a crazily hammy performance and it was pretty clear she was drinking through most of her scenes. There was one scene where I walked into the foyer of a very grand house with a circular stairway, at the top of which is Turner, who's supposed to greet me from the landing. But she would be slurring her words and so the director kept yelling, "Cut." We'd start again, and Lana would come out and do the same thing. And then she'd apologize profusely. She was holding a paper cup in her hand during most of the takes and I was wondering what she would do if they made her put it down. They didn't, so we just had a very long day. I vowed to myself never to behave so unprofessionally.

CHAPTER 8

In 1975, Fred Silverman, then the head of programming at ABC, was trying to figure out how to fix a series he felt had promise, a one-hour TV drama called *The Best Years*. It had been inspired by PBS's groundbreaking weekly documentary series *An American Family,* and everything about the project had a special shimmer. The script — about the daily struggles of a normal, middle-class, married couple living with their three children in suburban Pasadena — was written by the esteemed Jay Presson Allen. Award-winning film and theater director Mike Nichols had come on as executive producer and assembled a prestige cast including noted stage actors Sada Thompson and James Broderick (Matthew's dad) as the parents and Gary Frank and young Kristy McNichol as two of the three children. Execs at ABC, it was reported, had emerged *weeping* from the pilot screening.

(This was a good sign?)

There was some difficulty, however, with the casting of Kate and Doug Lawrence's eldest daughter, Nancy Lawrence Maitland, a newly divorced single mom, played in the six-part miniseries by an actress named Elayne Heilveil. When *Family* went to the full series, Heilveil bowed out of the show and Jane Actman replaced her. But Fred Silverman still felt that the balance in the casting was slightly off; he wanted someone older in the role of Nancy when it started up production at Fox Studios in its first official season as a series. Without consulting anyone — not even Carol and Nigel Mc-Keand, the executive producers who were assigned to run the day-to-day production — Silverman decided I was the one for the job.

Even though my little one, Kate, was not quite two at the time, I was very happy to have a steady gig again. She was a joy and a delight. She was strong, precocious, and smarter than me; I'd be hard put to find someone who made me laugh so much. Eva and Teddy were darling with her, let her trot after them into the pool or out into the neighboring bamboo to play. I loved having the quiet at-home stretch with her but being home full-time became difficult for me.

I had some help but never from David. He was good for playing with Kate in the pool or having her perform for admirers or putting on a good daddy show when an audience was around, but he was never a helpmate, even though he'd been so adamant about wanting his own child. It was clear he felt that child care was *my* job; he wouldn't do it but he had strong opinions about how I did it. Correcting me in front of the children and calling me names were his most reliable tactics, particularly when there were witnesses because he knew that enhanced my shame quotient. Consequently, I was more than ready for the relief of a soundstage when the *Family* offer came.

My first week on *Family* was spent reshooting scenes from episodes that had originally been filmed with Jane Actman. To save the production time, they only reshot my character Nancy's singles or angles that included Nancy. That meant that I had to replicate every position, gesture, or action that the previous Nancy had chosen so that I fit in the rest of the puzzle. And I had to say my lines with the *same intent and inflection* as the previous Nancy so that original reactions of the other characters would still seem responsive with *my* Nancy. Grrr. I stuck to my usual mode of working: I arrived on the set on time and prepared, kept quiet, and did my work, but it felt *horrible*. I had my head screwed on wrong and felt hobbled and uncreative. What about *my* interpretation of Nancy's lines, huh? My lack of humility and experience were showing. Toward the end of that week, during a brief break, I was on the living room set, brooding and resentful. Jim Broderick sat down with me on the sofa and we just stared up into the rafters, at the platforms and catwalks that crisscrossed the upper domain of the cavernous soundstage.

"See that door waaayyy up there?" said Jim, pointing at a tiny portal near the roof.

"Yes," I replied.

"You know what's up there?"

"No."

"That's where we keep *allll* the old Nancys."

It was the only reference anyone had made to my predicament. But Jimmy seemed to understand how difficult it was for me, so I developed an instant crush on him; he was darling, kind, and perceptive. He was also a beautiful actor, low-key and very present. I never felt like he was acting. His words just seemed to come as if he'd thought them up on the spot. I didn't think his fine, subtle work got enough credit; I figure no one could tell he was acting.

As casual as it was on the set, *Family* was a show with serious intentions. It tried to realistically address the uncertainties of everyday life; at a time when TV families lived an idealized, laugh-track existence, the Lawrence clan bickered, sulked, and were short-tempered with one another. And at the end of the day they hadn't always healed their rifts or retained their loving equilibrium.

Jim's character, the kindhearted Doug Lawrence, was an independent lawyer, while Sada Thompson's Kate was a housewife and the slightly stern center of the family. Gary Frank played the Lawrences' only son, Willie, who was very idealistic and had dropped out of high school to pursue a career as a writer. Buddy, the youngest daughter, who tended toward frank, thought-provoking declarations, was played by Kristy McNichol. My character, their eldest daughter, Nancy, was there, it seemed, to try everyone's patience at every turn. In the original miniseries a pregnant twenty-four-year-old Nancy catches her husband sleeping with her friend and they struggle to move beyond his infidelity issues. But by the time I came into the picture, Nancy had a young son, Timmy, and was living in her parents' back guest-house. She was married, divorced, and a single parent when far too young (hey, this could have been *my* story!), and many episodes focused on Nancy taking advantage of her parents' and siblings' willingness to double as free child care while she goes off on dates that often end the following morning.

The part of Nancy was everything that's fun to play: spiky, selfish, shortsighted. Because so many producers were invested in their characters' being likable, there weren't many regulars on shows at the time teeming with such unappealing personality traits as I got to display. I loved that the McKeands were willing to write Nancy so unattractive and so real. I'd have these great scenes where, say, Buddy would come into my house and sweetly ask, "Oh, Nancy, I don't know how to dance. Can *you* show me how to dance?" And instead of giving the expected positive answer, they'd let me totally dismiss her with an "Uh, no. Sorry . . ." I wasn't burdened with being a role model for young adults. I was allowed to play a totally normal albeit exceedingly self-centered young adult. And audiences got to see the consequences of such behavior — it didn't happen in a void. She never got away with much. Someone was always calling her out for her thoughtlessness, usually Momma Kate.

I didn't have to do any research for this part; it all came embarrassingly easy. I would read a scene in which Nancy totally takes advantage of someone, tramples all over their feelings, and folks would be all upset and retaliate and I'd be thinking, "So . . . what's the problem? She didn't *mean* to hurt them," as if intentions mattered. It is chastening to realize how much I identified with this self-absorbed girl. I too had married and divorced young, had been ill equipped to be a parent, and had flailed about looking for some guy; wasn't some guy supposed to carry me?

Kristy McNichol, at fourteen, was sweet and seemed to be very much at home in front of the camera. Since I didn't work with her all that often, I didn't get to know her very well and there was quite a disparity in our ages, so I probably wasn't that different from the show's Nancy. I wouldn't have showed her how to dance, either.

I do have one vivid memory of shooting a scene of Nancy and Buddy at a park, sitting in the swings. Kristy and I said our lines and I recall thinking, This is grueling; nothing is coming back from her. *I* emote, *I* give some feeling, and she simply sits there, twisting in the swing, limply delivering her lines. *I've* got to make it look like *something* is actually happening in this scene.

When I later watched the episode, I fully expected to see myself in the swing, trying to save the day. Instead, I saw magic happening that I could not see when we shot it. I could *see* Buddy's thoughts form, feel her hesitancy, and then her words would spill out in a natural, complex, beautifully nuanced presentation. To me it had looked like she was doing absolutely nothing but the camera picked up on it differently. I looked at her with renewed respect and made a note to self *not* to leap with my judgment so quickly. I had to allow that it was entirely possible that I didn't know what I was talking about. It didn't surprise me that *Family* became Kristy's launching pad to teen megastardom.

As for my TV mom, Sada, I thought she was great; she had a sweet sense of humor and a very close bond with Jimmy Broderick. I shied away from her because it felt like she had a little edge; I was always somewhat afraid of people being angry with me. She could make me laugh, although I didn't think she liked me a lot. I think she was impatient with me, maybe thought I lacked focus; since I was pretty immature, she was probably right.

One day when we were just back in production from a several-month-long hiatus, I was sitting in my open dressing room — in those days they were no-frills and the size of large toolsheds, square and windowless. Ours were all situated in a row alongside the stage. The big wardrobe trailer was parked right next to us and I could hear Sada, inside the trailer, wailing in frustration to our darling Irish costumer, Shirley Cunningham, "EVERY SINGLE ONE OF MY DRESSES HAS SHRUNK!! I cannot believe this has happened again!" I popped my head out of my room just in time to see a slightly stouter Sada march out of the trailer in disgust.

Before I signed on for the part of Nancy, David was clear he really didn't want me working all the time because of the children and insisted that the job was not an option unless I was in only half of the episodes. Although I didn't like being dictated to, I didn't like being away from the little ones for long hours either, so a lighter load wasn't a bad idea. I could do that. And out of the house was out of the house.

I never really thought David's motive was

about the best interests of the kids. That was always the banner he waved over me, but I felt it was because I was becoming known. I think he had a hard time as I started earning a higher profile. It seemed he felt it detracted from him. In my first season on *Family,* the entire cast was on the cover of *TV Guide,* which was great fun for me. It was the only magazine from the "industry" that came to our house, so the kids got to see it and I was really pleased. David didn't comment. When, perhaps a year later, I made the cover all by myself and Eva made a comment about how cool it was, David dismissed it with, "So, someone else will be on the cover next week." I had no illusions about being some big star. I understood the business was about promoting actors, ergo, promoting the shows, which promoted business. I never thought that being on a cover of something implied *anything about me,* although it seemed David thought I might think that, and he was the one to nip *that* in the bud. I started being careful to not talk about the show. I was afraid of sounding proud or pleased . . . I knew I would just draw fire and give him some reason to belittle me. I worked on getting smaller.

During the four seasons I was on *Family,*

David worked all the time, including on an NBC series based on Sidney Lumet's cop film *Serpico.* It must have crushed him when that series was canceled. I think he liked being identified with the heroic aspect of the character. He got to ride a motorcycle, and he'd grown a beard for the part since the real Serpico was bearded; it suited him and many people recognized him from that.

I brought that same sense of smallness to the fore anytime I was confronted with what I perceived as authority, be it my husband or my producers. One year during the contract negotiations, Jack, who was still my agent, said the *Family* producers refused to give me a raise. I had garnered a fair amount of attention and had been well received on the show and Jack had agreed that a small raise wasn't inappropriate. So I asked if instead they'd give me a car, as I knew this had been done in the past. I'm sure their sphincters tightened at that, envisioning pressure for some slinky European roadster. They asked me just what it was I wanted. I fixed them with my beady little mercenary eye and demanded a "little yellow Datsun station wagon" because I really needed one for driving my three kids to school before work. And they agreed!

Thank goodness a Datsun was really what I wanted. I didn't have enough self-esteem to ask for a fancier car and this suited my purposes. The producers may have thought I was a patsy but I was thrilled.

Between *Family,* David, and three kids, I didn't have much time left over for socializing. So something I loved, when it happened, was when, after dinner, David would pull out his guitar and play Irish folk songs and we'd all sing as I did the dishes and the kids and I would harmonize and they'd dance around the kitchen. We all loved the strong sense of family and togetherness these evenings afforded us. The suspension of tension was relished all the more sweetly because we never knew how long it would last.

We still saw a lot of Oliver Clark but David seemed to have many other friends I didn't really know. I had made one friend, Janet Taylor. She lived two blocks over from our house and I met her when Eva was six and in class with Janet's daughter, Mary. Janet and I were both pregnant when we met at the girls' school down the hill; she was due a few months after me and we spent many hours together, usually in her kitchen, talking about husbands, children, families, and babies. I'd never had someone to relate these experiences with before; my other pregnancies had happened in a vacuum with no one to really reflect back to me what it was like for them. This was a delicious connection; this was a girl *friend;* she was a pretty woman, tall, with long brown hair, sparkling eyes, and a great generous heart. As it turned out, David got along well with her husband, John, who was just the most fabulous, easygoing guy, so we became a foursome! *This was great!* This was a new experience for me. Neither of them was in the business, so I figured no competitive feelings would arise for David. We'd go out periodically as a group, or we'd go to each other's houses, just like regular people did. We even spent some time in New York together and I have to say, I *loved* having a sense of community. I loved the example set by a couple that had such a warm, loving relationship.

I was grateful just to have dinner with other people. So often David and I would be at dinner, out or at home, and we'd eat in silence. He rarely seemed to have anything to say to me and he seemed uninterested in anything I said to him. I'd be thrashing about in my head, trying to come up with some question I could ask that would elicit an answer that I hoped would then become a conversation, yes? Sometimes this tactic would backfire: if he just found me tiresome, then I would become the target. It could be excruciating. Having other folks, nice people, around was a great remedy.

An example of why the friendship meant so much to me was when I gave birth to Kate and David left town to go skiing for about a week. Almost immediately, I got a powerful case of the flu; I was so sick I couldn't stand up. I called for help, and Janet appeared on my doorstep at once and took Teddy, Eva, and my newborn baby to her house and cared for them until I was better. I didn't know there were people who did this for other people.

We'd all been friends for about two years and we were out one night at one of our regular restaurants. I believe there was some discussion going on about the Israeli-Palestinian conflict. Janet added her opinion about something, and David suddenly started shouting at her. He said something to the effect of, "That is the stupidest thing I've ever heard anyone say and I don't know why the fuck I bother spending time with you." He stood up and said, "This is the end. I don't ever want to do this again."

And he left. I followed David as he stormed out of the restaurant, asking, "What? What happened? I don't get it. What did she say that made you so mad?" I was used to David getting angry for no reason, but what was *that* about? I had no idea. These were *lovely* people, people we both *liked.* David didn't answer and we drove home in silence.

I continued to go over to Janet's because she had become such an integral part of my life. We'd talk about our little girls and their school; I'd talk about Teddy and our neighborhood children dynamics. Janet would talk about John's job or a trip they were taking, but we never brought up what happened. I'd never told her my difficulties with David and I didn't at this time either. I didn't tell her David was making snide remarks to me about still going over to see her, disparaging her character and how she was a waste of my time. Some part of me was hoping this would all pass, that Janet would miraculously be reinstated in David's good graces and we could go on as before, which I so desperately wanted. And I thought if I told her about him, she wouldn't want to reconnect, even if it were possible. Surprisingly, John and David did see each other once or twice after that, but then John called him and said, "I don't want to spend time with you if you don't want to spend time with my wife." All was lost for me at that point. I didn't know how to keep returning to her warm kitchen while this albatross was hanging on my neck. We were at a loss as to how to continue pretending there was no elephant in the room, so we sadly decided to end it "for now," limply leaving open the possibility of reconnecting. All my ties to the Taylors were severed. I felt strangled, with no words to say or anyone to say them to. I felt hopeless and desperately alone.

Sometimes I'd think about that evening and wonder what Janet could have possibly said that could have so ignited David's fury. It wasn't until years and years later, after David and I were divorced, that I got some clarity. Being resilient despite the problems of their parents, Eva and Mary had remained good friends all through high school and news of our divorce reached the Taylors. Janet called me. There had never been any animosity between us, but we hadn't exchanged a word in years. She said she had something to tell me about that evening some sixteen years or so ago.

When we met up, Janet explained that she hadn't told me anything about that night at the time for fear of hurting me. She thought

David and I had a good marriage and she didn't want to be a part of causing any problem. She hadn't even told her husband until he and David ceased their friendship. Apparently, on the day of our last dinner together, Janet had been at home alone when David appeared without announcement. He'd made a pass at her; when she rejected him he made a derisive comment and left. And that night we all had dinner together. Maybe he was covering up and saving face the only way he knew how. But oh, did he have to make a pass at my only friend?

Having an explanation was not much comfort, to be honest. It had been such a profound and inexplicable loss that now made sense when put in context because it wasn't the first time. I'd been sitting at David's desk in our bedroom on the phone some years before, talking with who knows who, and my eyes settled on a half-written letter, in David's handwriting, open on the desk. A line leapt out at me . . . "I should have married you instead of Meredith." What? *What?* It was addressed to Augusta, a woman David had spoken of frequently, whom he'd met while filming in England. When I confronted him, he hotly denied he was having an affair with her and reamed me for invading his privacy. I felt squashed and humiliated once again. He could shut me up and I would stay shut up. I felt like the verbal rug had been pulled out from under me. Somehow, I bought that I was wrong in this exchange and he seemed to come out clean while I was left hot, confused, in a blinding, unventable rage. It felt useless to say anything to him. I'd grown up with no voice and I'd married someone who allowed me no voice. This perpetuated the feelings of hopelessness and powerlessness and shame. I had a voice screaming in my head, sometimes at David but just as often at myself, thrashing myself for my cowardice and ineptitude. It undermined my being a mother because I had no confidence.

Teddy and Eva had an altercation one evening, as often happens with kids, upstairs in Ted's room, and I was in there, trying to sort things out quietly without drawing David's attention, when he bounded up the stairs and took over, berating me for not being the adult, giving all the power to the kids, and forcing him to be the bad guy. No resolution was reached with the kids and we all felt smacked and crappy, but it sure got quiet really fast, which must have been the objective because David seemed to feel much better.

Thank God for work. I think I would have lost my mind if I didn't have a place to go to feel valuable, where I could make a contribution, where people actually seemed to like me. Working, I could have ideas that wouldn't get shot down; I could make choices that weren't belittled. Working, I could discuss approaches to a scene, argue a character's point of view with give-and-take and not be humiliated if I made a wrong step or didn't understand something. I was funny, I was smart, I was present and felt in command of myself. All this left me when I headed home. So I was thrilled to keep the work coming in.

During one hiatus from *Family,* I landed the miniseries adaptation of Louisa May Alcott's *Little Women,* playing the eldest sister, Meg March. What a great cast: William Shatner, Susan Dey, William Schallert; Dorothy McGuire was the March sisters' beloved Marmee, and our aunt was played by the stunning Oscar-winning actress Greer Garson.

However, classic stories and stellar casts do not guarantee a successful movie, and this remake was no exception. Ultimately, I thought it was dull and uncompelling.

The most remarkable element in it to me was that the incredible Edith Head did the costumes: another Oscar-winning Hollywood legend in our midst. I was intimidated by her reputation as a stickler for period accuracy and the impressive history and temper of this tiny woman when I met her in the Universal wardrobe department. She looked just as she always had: short dark blunt-cut hair with bangs and thick oversized glasses. She had pulled several costumes for me from the Civil War costume archives and they were hung around the room on display. My heart sank as she watched me try them on. The style of the time was a pretty high neckline, sort of a crewneck shape, and the long full skirt had a fairly high waist, several inches above the navel. This was *not* a flattering look for the big-busted girl. Now, having already been working with fitters and looking at myself in wardrobe for a few years and having lived with this body for years more than that, I had a good sense of what suited me and how to fix what didn't. I needed more skin, more of a dip in the bodice, and not such a high waist, but wasn't this accurate for the period? I certainly wasn't about to start giving *Edith Head* pointers on how to make my wardrobe look better for *me*.

I just stood there miserably in one dress after another, afraid to say anything as she tapped a pencil and looked me up and down. "Okay," she said, "this is what we will do. We'll lengthen this" — showing me how she would drop the waistline slightly — "which will give you a longer line and pull you in here but drop *this* down just enough," showing how she would create a lacy faux V-line over the bodice that totally solved my bust problem! "Is that consistent with the period, though?" I asked. And she said in an overly theatrical way, "It's faaar more important that my women look faaabulous. And *who* will *know?*"

Family was a critical darling, and garnered two Emmy Awards for Kristy McNichol and one each for Sada Thompson and Gary Frank. Jim Broderick and I were both nominated but didn't win. Our show was a feather in the cap of its executive producer, Aaron Spelling, who at the time was mostly known for much lighter fare like *Charlie's Angels.* But *Family* never did well in the ratings; in 1980, after five seasons, ABC finally pulled the plug. Because I enjoyed the consistency and stability of being able to work regularly, I spent the hiatus before

Family's final year making an overheated, unwieldy, three-part, six-hour TV mini-series, a *Gone With the Wind* knock-off called *Beulah Land*. Based on a pair of Lonnie Coleman novels, *Beulah Land* told the story of Sarah Pennington Kendrick, a beautiful Southern belle (played by Lesley Ann Warren) who ends up the boss of her own sprawling plantation. I played Lauretta, Sarah's sort of slutty sister.

I always loved my hiatus projects, partly because it gave me a chance to get a break from David but also because I got to do a total about-face and be a wildly different character, meet new people, have great new experiences. *Beulah Land* was an exception because for the most part it was a pretty hideous experience. First of all, the shoot never seemed to end: we worked from January until Easter of 1979. We filmed in Natchez, Mississippi. It was unbelievably cold, and we were deluged with rain and rain and rain. There were mudslides along the Mississippi River and our sets were buried. Mud was up to our corsets (yes, another Civil War piece). Everything that could go wrong did. In the middle of stressful filming, our first director, Virgil Vogel, had a heart attack and we shut down for two weeks and went home until another director, Harry Falk, could be brought in. No one seemed to get along. Some of the African American actors in the cast protested the hackneyed way they perceived *Beulah Land* portrayed slaves and its obsession with interracial romance subplots. Actors were sick or having meltdowns and not emerging from their trailers. One of the production assistants, an active alcoholic, was so depressed and miserable that I dreaded knocking on his trailer door, fearful I'd find him hanging inside. I think someone made up T-shirts that read "Happiness is Natchez in the rearview mirror."

I didn't mind living for three months in the Ramada Inn on a hill over the banks of the Mississippi, except it was downwind from the paper factory, which produced odors unknown to anyone new to these parts. *Oh my God,* an unparalleled fetor emanated from that factory when the wind blew just so, and I'd have to stuff wet towels under my door and around the windows to hold off the stench. But the rank wind and the majestic, powerful Mississippi somehow coexisted, and my first action every morning was, through the closed window, to check out the river and count the vessels — see what kind of activity was going on: long freight barges, gambling steamships, private motorboats. The river itself had the buzz of a small metropolis.

Eventually, as I adapted to it, the smell faded to a mild irritant and I got on with nesting at the Ramada. I bought a little toaster oven and, because I'd just become a vegetarian, I baked potatoes with cheese or toasted rice cakes with cheese — just about anything with cheese. And I discovered the bar. Every night when the transportation van dropped me off after work, I'd head straight to the Ramada Inn bar and order two piña coladas or one piña colada and a brandy Alexander and trip off to my room and sip them while I watched my potato bake. It was better than television. I loved my evenings. I loved having alone time. I loved endless reading time. Except for my calls home every night, I talked to no one. My room was cozy and quiet and relaxing; I got a small buzz on (was it the cheese or the alcohol?) and I wasn't bothered by too much.

At the time, I wasn't much of a drinker and I stuck with the phoofy drinks that camouflaged the alcohol with lots of sugary calories. So, on *this* show it was the costumer telling *me* I was gaining weight. As it turned out, the style of dress from the years *Beulah Land* covered — 1827 to the postwar

Reconstruction — was very accommodating to my weight gain. I'd go to my trailer and say to the poor costumer in charge of lacing me into my corset, "Just yank 'em as tight as you can." The more she pulled, the more my waist pulled in, the more my bosoms heaved skyward. By the time we wrapped production, I could practically rest my chin on them.

A year or so after *Family* ended, David invited a writer-producer named Gary David Goldberg and his wife, Diana Meehan, over for dinner at our house. Gary was a guy on the rise. In recent years he'd worked on hot CBS sitcoms like *The Bob Newhart Show* and *Lou Grant,* and had made a name for himself in the industry as smart and witty. Around this time Gary had formed his own company, Ubu Productions, and was in the process of creating a series called *The Bureau.* He apparently was considering David for the lead and I think this dinner was the first time they were getting together.

I liked the process leading up to entertaining: straightening the house, coming up with a menu, drinking wine while puttering around the kitchen and cooking by myself, putting out the dishes, and setting the table. Maybe I just liked the *idea* of entertaining because the part I didn't care for was being with the guests. I didn't always know the guests but, in truth, it didn't really help if I did. I was pretty shy and shut down and although folks might have been warm to me, I don't know that I was able to reciprocate very much, so sure was I that I'd say something stupid that would draw criticism from David. And he would dismiss me in a manner that bespoke confidence that others shared his opinion, at which point I would just try to become invisible. So I'd serve the dinner and have absolutely no memory of the rest of the evening. Actually, I always thought I'd fallen asleep, although no one complained of my sinking into my soup. I have no recollection of most of those dinner parties — of what I served, of who was at my house, of what we talked about. That always perplexed me when I gave it any thought at all. Which I didn't, much.

No surprise that I didn't remember the actual dinner with Gary and Diana, but I do recall sitting in the living room with them after the meal while they discussed various projects with David. I couldn't say whether I participated in the conversation or not. They were warm and friendly when they departed and I thought nothing about them again. Until Gary called, saying that he was working on a comedy series about a couple of former hippies and their three conservative children. He thought I'd be perfect for the mother role. I didn't have to test for it. He was offering it to me.

What?

CHAPTER 9

Years later, Gary's wife, Diana, said that as they drove away from our house that night, Gary told her that he found the way David spoke to me so embarrassing that he didn't want to work with him. I couldn't remember anything David had said that stood out; I had no sense of that night being different from any other night.

Apparently, I also didn't remember Gary discussing over dinner the germ of what would eventually become *Family Ties.* The project Gary described at that time was a one-hour drama, not a sitcom. But the concept was the same. Gary's idea, largely drawn from his own life, was to create a show organized around a left-leaning married couple, Elyse and Steven Keaton, whose three children grow up to be surprisingly right-wing. All great pitches can be stripped down to the bare essentials and still seem to brim with possibilities. The pitch that Gary used to sell *Family Ties* to NBC came down to four simple words: "Hip parents, square kids."

Little Tina Yothers, a nine-year-old who'd been acting in commercials since she was three, was the first one cast. She played Jennifer, the youngest daughter. A young, energetic twenty-one-year-old Canadian actor named Michael J. Fox would assume the role of our eldest son, Alex. A dark-haired, pretty sixteen-year-old newcomer named Justine Bateman would play our daughter, Mallory. After I accepted the role of Elyse, I learned they were testing actors for the part of the husband, Steven. David started pressuring me to get Gary to meet with him.

This was so awkward on many levels. First of all, I had no influence on Gary; he was very much his own man. Why would he listen to me? Secondly, the thought of working all day with David and then going home to him, too, made me choke with apprehension. But I did as I was told. I was sure he'd find out if I didn't. I went to Gary's office like a good messenger, if not exactly a good pitchwoman.

"David would like to be considered for this."

"Hmmm, interesting idea," Gary said, distractedly. "We'll think about it." Then he sort of looked away and became very busy shuffling papers.

By the time I got home, David already heard they were testing actors he knew from New York. Why wasn't he among them? Hadn't I asked? I assured him I had; I'd done all I could.

After a couple of days, when he saw no invitation to audition was forthcoming, David sent me back to be more adamant: David *really* wants to test for this. It would be such great stunt casting!

This was horrifying to do. I was so ashamed. I felt like the cleaning woman demanding a corner office. As if!

And again, I got the same courteous, inconclusive "We'll see . . . ." Now, in fairness, this must have felt grotesque to David, too. I mean, hadn't Gary sat in our house and discussed the idea in front of *both* of us? Gary had come to see *him,* not me. From my childhood, I'm very sensitive to how hurtful being passed over is, and Gary's silence must have been hugely painful for David. However, it was hard to remain concerned for him when I was feeling so poorly used. I was overwhelmed with gratitude when Michael Gross secured the role of Steven Keaton and put an end to the awkward situation.

236

Michael was a tall, pale, gangly New York stage actor who had been appearing in the off-Broadway play *Bent* when his agent received a call to have him put a few scenes on tape as an initial try-out for *Family Ties*. The way the story has been told, it was Gary's daughter, Shana, who was responsible for Michael's getting cast. Apparently, Gary was reviewing a handful of audition tapes and when Michael's came on, Shana, then five, said, "I like him. He's funny!" Soon Michael was being flown out to Los Angeles to meet with a roomful of network executives. To this day he likes to joke that Shana still takes 10 percent of his residuals.

Michael and I met for the first time on day one of work, and we immediately became fast friends. I'm sure it's because I appealed to his New York sensibility when my first words to him were, "You need a tan."

As we shot the pilot, I thought we were an unlikely family. Dark-haired Justine bore no trace of a resemblance either to me or to Michael Gross. I figured her to be an incredibly beautiful child we found under a rock somewhere. Then there was little Tina, who was darling and so willing, but being so young, she had few stage instincts. She learned on the job.

As for Michael J. Fox, he was cast in the role of the Nixon-loving Alex after Matthew Broderick turned it down. Even after the pilot was in the can, and so well received that NBC immediately ordered thirteen episodes for the fall season, Gary had to go to bat for Michael Fox. The head of programming at NBC, Brandon Tartikoff, proclaimed Fox, at five-four and a half, too short ever to become a TV star and didn't want him to be part of the series. But Gary lobbied strenuously for him and prevailed.

I don't know if Michael Fox didn't drive at the time or if he didn't have an American driver's license, but at some point I offered to give him a ride to work. He was living in Brentwood, about five minutes from my house, so many mornings in the first months I'd drive to his place, pull into the alley behind his apartment building, and honk the horn. I hoped this would be his signal to come out and jump into my car. Except when I hit the horn, I'd hear a shower go on. I'd think, Fuck! and then I'd have to sit there and wait until this wet boy threw himself into my Mercedes; he would just air-dry as I sped to work.

I adored him. I thought Michael Fox was a darling kid although he wasn't *quite* young enough really to be my son. It was nice to see how grateful he was to be on the show; he was confident but not arrogant and seemed to be a really well-adjusted young man. One of the things I quickly became aware of was his ability to get the most out of a single line of dialogue. At thirty-five, I might have been the veteran in the cast, the only one with any real TV credentials, but Michael Fox was the first to figure out how to take a *Family Ties* joke, break it apart with pauses, and squeeze three laughs out of it instead of just one.

Gary and his staff of writers, Lloyd Garver, Michel Weithorn, Alan Uger, and Marc Lawrence, created a wonderfully complex Alex: very opinionated, arrogant, conservative, impulsive, romantic, idealistic, naïve — all fabulous traits upon which to build a character. And then, I think the writers fell in love with the Alex they created because in Fox's capable hands, he was comedy gold, good for the anticipatory chuckle and the follow-through laugh with every situation. They could think of a million setups into which to insert the brash, breezily confident Young Republican, and because his character was so well defined, the audience would be on the edge of their seats dying to see how they *knew* Alex would react. Once Gary, the staff, the NBC folks, and everyone else realized this, the writing, so to speak, was on the wall: the series' focus began to shift away from Elyse and Steven Keaton and home in on Alex.

I loved being on this show; I was so thankful to be working with such a creative cast and smart, funny writers. In the beginning I felt very positive and hopeful. The change came very slowly. On Monday mornings we'd assemble to read the new script, and sometime during the second season, it seemed that Elyse wasn't figuring very prominently in the stories. I didn't immediately recognize it as a trend. After all, there were five regular family members plus the neighbor boy, Skippy, who had to be kept alive during the span of the season. But as time went on, Elyse felt less like a lead and more like a supporting role. And no one ever came to me and said, "Meredith, I know you were hired as the star on the show but we're going in a different direction." A conversation wouldn't have changed the show's course or my ultimate feelings about it, but I sure would have appreciated the consideration.

Looking at it from a producer's perspective, I can see how it might have seemed like the only way to go for the series. Fox was sexy, young, and bursting with talent.

His fan base was large and growing. How could they *not* use him to his fullest? I had to fight feeling resentful toward Fox and the big shift that favored him. I was really fond of him and didn't want anything to get in the way of our personal relationship. I totally understood that this wasn't a situation he had manipulated. It just happened; it wasn't *his* fault.

I began to feel not just marginalized, but as if Elyse lacked a distinct character and voice of her own. It seemed that Steven and Elyse were becoming so interchangeable that once, as a joke, we tied our legs together and hobbled onto the set as one person. We felt it didn't matter which one of us said something as long as one half of the parental unit weighed in.

One thing about Elyse, though, was that no matter what happened, she loved her husband and kids. What I liked about the Keatons as a representative TV family was that when they disagreed about something, they'd talk it out. And when the fight was over, there was no lingering resentment. The love within the family was always palpable; there was a sense of mutual trust and respect, even for the youngest one. I could have used the Keatons' writers at my house.

At the Birney-you-can't-be-Baxter house,

I felt we were divided into two camps, and what united the kids and me was our fear of David. It got to the point that I'd hear his Porsche drive into the cul-de-sac and I'd immediately fly into action.

"Kids, get your stuff out of the front hall!"

"Whose book bag is this? Hang up your jacket and put this in your room!"

"Did you get your homework questions answered? Better have something to show to your dad . . . he's here!"

Now, I kept a fairly tidy house, I even had help to do it. But three active kids do contribute to a certain level of disorder and David seemed to take it as a personal affront. It could send him off the radar with anger.

Since I was rarely sure just what would set him off (was *I* a personal affront?), I would propel myself into a blur of straightening, cleaning, and cooking as soon as I heard his car. (Just recently, one of my daughters, grown and away from home for some time, reacted with a start when a Porsche drove up our street. That adrenaline rush of fear we'd *all* experienced was back in a shot.) Sometimes he'd come in and do nothing. Other times he'd just scan the kitchen with a distasteful look. Once, not liking what he saw, he opened up the silverware drawer and swept everything on the counter into it — a chopped onion, a knife, homework, pencils, coffee filters, a screwdriver, crumbs — and then slammed it shut. Then he said, "NOW it's clean!" He was the self-appointed ruler of our house and his slogan — always delivered shouting — was, "If something has to be done I have to do it. I'm the only one responsible here. You're all useless."

Ironically, David sort of became an odd ally for me around the show for a short time in an unexpected way. It had always seemed he resented my being in the show. Maybe he felt I'd taken something away from him. He never had anything good to say about it. I did everything I could to downplay it. I tried not to talk about my day at work. I'd usually hide the scripts because once he found one and flipped through it, then tossed it down saying, "You leave your children every day to do *this* piece of shit?" But at some point I must have said something to David about how disappointed I was by the way the show was changing because later I heard him talking on the phone with someone, discussing how I was being treated, sounding kind of indignant, and for once he sounded in my corner. My unhappiness seemed to allow him to be on my side, even if in some uncomfortable way it also delighted him.

Which was novel since we weren't a couple who delighted each other. I think he thought me inept, stupid, uninformed, a bad mother, and overweight. And he let me know this often. He was good at expressing himself. I could only assume he married me because he thought I'd be a good breeder. And I was.

I thought he was arrogant, vain, narcissistic, competitive, and mean. I never told him because I was afraid to express myself. I had no voice. I was afraid of him. I couldn't tell him anything I was feeling. I'd tried a few times but he maintained he wasn't my doctor and wasn't interested in what I *felt*. Perhaps if I ever had a thought I might share *that* with him. So I never bothered again. But I still thought he was smarter than me and seemed to have more rights than me. Somehow I'd given him all the power.

How do people like us stay together? We develop coping mechanisms. Initially mine was eating. David had complained about my weight for months. I actually went to a behavior modification clinic to see what I could do about those extra ten pounds. A seemingly teenage clinician chewed gum and flipped through a magazine as she lazily asked me what I was getting out of being fat. When it was posed like *that,* I got it immediately. I was getting heavier to keep him away from me, sexually. Making love could be unsatisfying or humiliating — or somewhere in between. I wasn't overly attracted to him and often tried to hide it by being the aggressor; perhaps he sensed that. I was grateful for the most expedient way through our encounters. When he would reciprocate, I could feel his lack of interest or enthusiasm in my satisfaction, which made me then even more unresponsive, at which point he'd mock me for my lukewarm reaction, shame me, call me names.

Running had become a useful outlet and coping mechanism in 1982, not long after *Family* was canceled; it was another way to get out of the house. Running was attractive because all it required was a pair of shoes, no equipment, no net, no ball, no partner. Running was also attractive because David was already into it, which I thought would make it easier for me, since he obviously liked it and couldn't easily object to *my* doing it. And Ted had been competing in track and cross-country in high school, so it was a family affair.

Despite my disappointment about watching my *Family Ties* character recede into the background, I appreciated having a place to be among the much happier *Family Ties* community. I think this is when I started to compartmentalize my life. No one at work knew about my home life except in the vaguest terms. I talked about David only in general and positively. It was important that I look happy. Oh, I talked about the kids, for sure; Kate even came to the set from school sometimes; but I didn't discuss stresses or conflicts with anyone, not even with Michael Gross, whose humor and confidence attracted me greatly and whom I came to love so much. He became my dearest friend but I never told him about the frictions with David.

And Michael Gross and I *always* got along! He was just so engaging — and so unlike most actors who'd come to Hollywood, get a taste of fame and money, and just go crazy. He was so unruffled by this, his first big paying gig. In the first year of the show, between scenes, he'd sit beneath one of the lights in the living room set and write letters to friends or darn his socks. For the first two years of the show, he didn't own a car and would often make the twenty-minute ride from his small West Hollywood apartment to Paramount Studios on his ten-speed bicycle. The guards at the lot wouldn't believe he was a regular on *Family Ties.* They'd always stop him at the front gate and say, "You're not on any show. You're on a bike!"

All of us got a kick out of making each other laugh on camera. And Michael would invariably succeed with me. Every Friday night we'd tape the show before a live studio audience. All the cameras would be clustered in front of one particular set, say, the kitchen, shooting the scene played out in front of them. Many a time, Michael and I would be situated just offstage, awaiting the red light that would cue our entrance into the kitchen. It was standard practice for us to just be chatting away about *nothing* while we're waiting, and of course, not *watching* for the light or *listening* for our cue. Consequently when Michael would interrupt me to hiss, "Go, go, go!" I would fly *unquestioningly* onto the stage, saying my line as I entered, and it would only be the sudden silence and the actors' blank faces that told me Michael had once more *purposefully* sent me out early. Oh, he'd still be safe in the wings, about to kill himself with laughing. I'd return to my waiting position, red-faced and flustered and plotting how I was going to pay him back, and the onstage actors would start up the scene again when Michael would say, "You missed it again. Go go go," and give me a little shove. And out I'd go. Again! Has there ever been such a dope as me? Thank goodness the audiences really seemed to like that sort of stuff, they enjoyed seeing how fond we all were, how much we savored mixing the fun with the task at hand.

I often tried that trick on Michael but wasn't very successful. I think all his years on the theatrical stage trained him to pay very close attention, and that guy knew his cues.

On an average week, I'd run about thirty-five miles total. But in the spring of 1982 I decided to run the New York City Marathon the following October, so I began upping my average. I'd get up very early in the morning, about 5 a.m., put on my shorts, shoes, and a T-shirt in the dark, and slip quietly out the front door. I'd been running with my neighbor Val, who lived just around the corner, and we'd decided to tackle the New York marathon together. We'd meet in front of her house and take off running, talking softly because the world was still asleep. I loved starting a run when the sky was still black. I loved watching daylight slowly creep into the sky and it would take on an apricot blush in front of me as I ran east, streaks of purple behind, and the day was *mine. I owned that day* when I could witness the sun coming up. And it was empowering for me to run and get stronger. I ran several 10Ks and I did okay. I didn't have a lot of speed but I could feel my endurance build. Some days I felt like I could run forever. So Val and I worked up a schedule to cover the three months of training we'd require and stuck to it religiously; it culminated in two 60-mile weeks, including two 20-mile runs.

I told everyone I was going to run the largest marathon in the world — except David. I was afraid all the training and staying in New York for a couple of days for the race wasn't going to go over well with him. I kept putting off telling him; I didn't want to deal with his attitude. The day I did tell him, I had just come back from a run and was watering the grass along our driveway. He'd come outside and I seized the opportunity to casually tell him I was *training* for the New York City Marathon. David was immediately indignant. What was everyone else supposed to do while I was off running? he asked. I explained to him the training schedule I had *been* keeping that he'd never noticed: when I was back home from running in the morning, I'd get the kids up and I'd make them breakfast if the nanny didn't have it ready. I'd shower in the kids' shower so as not to wake David. The nanny and I would split driving the kids to their respective schools, then I'd drive to Paramount for *Family Ties* rehearsal by 10 a.m. My running wasn't going to interfere with his life at all but David harangued me about it nonetheless, saying that I was selfish and not thinking of anyone else, but I didn't argue. And I didn't back down. In the end, his complaining stopped when he decided that he would run the marathon, too.

Being a part of the New York City Marathon was one of the most exciting things I've ever done. I'd worked so hard to be there that not even David's presence could dampen my excitement. On October 24, I joined more than 16,000 other entrants at the starting point on the Staten Island end of the Verrazano-Narrows bridge, and when we heard the sound of the starting gun we all took off.

David, being a faster runner, took off ahead of me and I never saw him again until after the finish. Val and I started out together but she got a sharp persistent side cramp and dropped back in the first five miles. I loved running in the sea of people. At the start, it was about 41 degrees and there was a light drizzle; many of us came prepared, wearing big green Hefty bags with arm and head holes cut out. One of the great things about this race in New York was that the citizens really come out in support of the runners. They hold their children up to see you and their babies' hands out to touch you as you run by; they offer drinks, orange wedges; they play music, they cheer and applaud and yell encouragement. They seem to really *know and appreciate* how big a commitment it is.

I was hitting the halfway point right at the punishing incline of the Queensboro Bridge, when I heard one of the race officials announce, "We have a winner! Alberto Salazar in 2:08:13!" And all I could think is, "*Anybody* can run for two hours. It's those of us out there for four and five hours who should get the kudos."

At around the nineteen-mile point, I really started to fade. I was overheating somewhat although the temperature never got much over about 46, which is perfect for me. I wasn't drinking enough water and my lower back was killing me. I'd slowed to a foot-dragging shuffle as the throng pushed through Harlem. I stopped to stretch out

251

my lower back and calves, wondering how I was going to continue, when a very large African American woman stepped off the sidewalk, came up to me, and briskly slapped me on the shoulder. "Honey," she said. "Don't you know *no one* walks in Harlem? Now you get movin'!" She meant business! Her slap was just what I needed. I slowly started up again, merging back into the runners.

The last three miles of the New York marathon takes you through Central Park. I wound up next to a guy wearing a green and white singlet and we just fell into synch together. We ran closely, picking up the pace, locked into each other's tempo; I felt the surge of his energy. My exhaustion lifted and I felt incredibly strong. As soon as we got within visual sight of the end near Tavern on the Green, my silent running partner leaned over, gave me a fast kiss, and just took off. I'd been carried but we'd not spoken at all. When I crossed the finish line, I couldn't believe it. I'd just run 26.2 miles in 4:08:30. As all the runners finished, officials wrapped us in shiny Mylar blankets to help maintain our body heat in the cold morning air. We looked like a bunch of baked potatoes milling around, searching for familiar faces. I was tired and I ached, to be sure, grateful not to be running anymore, but I didn't feel wiped out. I felt great! After having trained so hard, completing this race was a personal triumph for me. I was jubilant!

One Saturday in early December of *Family Ties*' first season, I was at home when I got a call from the riding stables up at Will Rogers Park in Pacific Palisades where my fourteen-year-old daughter, Eva, was taking lessons. She'd been thrown from her horse and couldn't move. We got her to Santa Monica Hospital, where X-rays showed she had crushed her third and fourth lumbar vertebrae.

She stayed in the hospital almost a week while the doctors tried to determine the best way to proceed without compromising her spinal cord. That Monday I had to go back to *Family Ties,* so David handled interviewing the doctors and surgeons, long-distance conferences with medical friends on the East Coast, and determining which surgical option they would pursue. David can be good in an emergency and he was very helpful here. I split my time between rehearsing, checking on Kate and Ted at home, and trying to be with Eva in the hospital. Her surgery was on Friday night, the show's tape night, and I was in anguish that I couldn't be with her.

My memory of that evening's performance is so blurry. Tom Hanks was playing Elyse's brother for the second time, so it had been a lively week. But I don't recall even being present while we taped. My memory was of fear and anxiety about Eva, forgetting speeches, trying not to cry, and calling the hospital during scenes I wasn't in. However, just the other day, I found that episode on-line and watched it, looking to see if the distress and agitation showed, expecting to see it laced through my performance. But I didn't. It wasn't perceptible. Now, I guess this is a good thing, that maybe I'm *so* professional that the show just went on and I rose to the occasion. But I felt a shock of concern that I didn't look as troubled as I know I'd felt. It took a moment to realize *this* was one of the results of compartmentalization; those feelings were shut down and they *did not exist* for that suspended period. That's how I lived so much of my life during those years.

Eva's surgery was complicated and difficult. Donor bone was combined with her bone to rebuild her spine and she was in a body cast for five months. It was just before Christmas, and David followed through with our original holiday plans and took Kate and Ted skiing in Park City. I felt just a bit abandoned but I don't think it was the wrong choice. Eva's recovery was a very tough time for her but I experienced much of it as a sweet time for the two of us since we were on our own. I remember reading stories and laughing together; I acquired a new respect for her and how hard she worked through the pain to regain her strength.

She was out of school for several months and kept up her studies through in-home tutoring. We realized we *really* didn't like her current school and spent hours poring through catalogs of possible boarding schools for her to attend in the fall. In the spring Eva was still in a body cast but able to travel and she and I went to visit a few schools, eventually choosing Kimball Union Academy in rural New Hampshire.

When I went there to visit Eva in the fall of '83 during Parents' Week, I found out that she was competing on the cross-country team and I was there for their first three-mile race. She got out of her cast back in May, before school had started, and she was much stronger, but cross-country was a surprising choice. Running had never been Eva's thing and I wasn't sure her back had healed sufficiently. It was a really hot morning and the girls took off down a path, running through the woods; I was worried that she wouldn't do well. My heart went out to her. I thought I had a part to play; I thought she could use some encouragement so I took off after her. I don't know what possessed me — I was wearing shorts, a silk blouse, and sandals and was carrying a big leather saddlebag purse — but I ran alongside her gasping out, saying, "You're looking good, honey! You can do it!" I think I had an overinflated sense of just how helpful I was being. Eva had several times waved me off but I was in motivating-mother mode and I just whacked my way through the underbrush alongside the race path. I'm sure Eva didn't appreciate it much — she was almost disqualified because of me — and I don't think she did any better than she would have had I left her alone. But I ran the whole three miles with her. In sandals. Carrying a huge purse.

Thinking back, this must have been so embarrassing for Eva. What? Her mother runs one marathon and now she's running through the woods like Natty Bumppo, thinking she's leading the way for the child who can't? I actually thought I was helping, making a bit of a spectacle, yes, but helping just the same. I think I wanted Eva to *experience me helping her,* as if I were desperate to make an impact. I think it was about being seen.

CHAPTER 10

For some time David had been talking
about wanting to have another child. Kate
was nine, Eva was fourteen, and Ted, sixteen. Honestly, I didn't want another child.
My life was so full, so busy. It was hard to
spend as much time as I wanted with the
children I already had. Over the months his
talking escalated to berating. David maintained I had no right to decide whether or
not he had another child. On a few nights,
when I'd been long asleep, David would
come in and wake me up with a tirade about
how selfish I was, how important being a
father was to him, how I was withholding
this from him. I'd sit up and try to participate, but I was too afraid to ever say what
my argument was, that I felt so lonely as a
mother; he gave me no help, just criticism; I
loved the children we had and they were
enough. It wasn't until the night he said, "If
I don't have one with you, I'll have one with

someone else," that I felt pushed to the wall. I just sobbed and asked was he leaving me? Did he already have someone else lined up? I was so exhausted, upset, and confused. Maybe I *didn't* have any rights here. I felt crazy and selfish. Was it *not* okay to consider what I wanted? I think I ultimately decided I had no choice. Oddly, I couldn't bear the idea of his leaving me. Love had nothing to do with it; I was convinced I'd be useless on my own; I wouldn't know how to parent the children, do *anything.* So *my* solution was to work my way into deciding that *I* wanted another child.

By March of 1984, I was pregnant. The second season of *Family Ties* had just wrapped, and though the ratings weren't great, we knew we were coming back for another season. So when I told the producers I was expecting, they decided that we'd return in April when I'd only be four months along and shoot an Elyse-is-pregnant episode that could kick off the third season in September. But as I started getting bigger and bigger I was concerned when my call to the set never came. Finally I put in a call to the *Family Ties* production office and said, "Guys! We've got to do this! Now! I'm getting huge!"

By the time the script was ready, it was

May. At four months along, I was much bigger than I had been in other pregnancies and was already wearing maternity clothes. The episode was supposed to be about Elyse not feeling quite up to par and then — *bingo!* — realizing, oh, she's pregnant. The problem *as I saw it* was that she'd have to be a chowderhead not to know she was pregnant. Hasn't she already had three children? Ah, well. Silly or not, that was our show.

We were midrehearsal on the soundstage when I got a call from my doctor. They'd done an alpha-fetoprotein test and found a sizable amount of protein in my blood, which was an ominous sign. The doctor said, "You either have a baby in trouble or twins. You've got to come in immediately for a sonogram." Of course, all I heard was "a baby in trouble," and that the child I was carrying could have spina bifida or brain damage and was sloughing off too much protein. I just said to the stage at large, "I'm going!" and drove as fast as I could from Paramount to the imaging center in Westwood. David met me there, and when they rolled the ultrasound conductor over my belly, one of the technicians said, "I see either two or three babies in there." Ohmygod. I was thirty-six, already the mother of three children, and I was having multiples. I burst into tears of gratitude that they were all right. Before we left that day it was determined there were only two . . . which felt more than sufficient.

I remember telling my kids about the upcoming babies. We showed them each the sonogram photo of the two little heads. Ted was low-key and feigned indifference, but was boy-excited; Eva was overjoyed with delight at the novelty of twins; Kate put her nine-year-old head down and wept. No more being the youngest for her!

And how did I feel? Okay, I had been bullied but then I had "decided" I could want another child. But could I want two? Like Eva, I was taken with the novelty of two, but I knew it would take so much. Of everything. Somehow I just leaned into faith that I'd be okay, faith that I'd not relied upon before. It all felt so much bigger than me, although, trust me, I got much bigger.

David figured our lives would never be the same (*now* he decides this?), so after I finished filming that one interim episode, we took a trip to Italy. There were many lovely aspects of the trip and we took in much of the beauty of Padua, Ravenna, Siena, and Venice. Because I'd been a vegetarian for a couple of years, my pediatrician was insistent that I eat copious amounts of extra protein to provide for the babies' needs. This was fun to do in Italian restaurants. They greet pregnant women warmly anyway but when I'd rub my swelling tummy and say, "Gemeli!" (twins!) they'd rush to seat me and get me anything I wanted. Twice a day I'd order two cups of yogurt in a large bowl and mix a fist-sized lump of protein powder into it. It was disgusting and could only be compared to eating wallpaper paste, but I'd dutifully clean my bowl, trying not to gag, and prayed my twins would someday thank me for their strong teeth and bones.

One night David and I were having a late (nonyogurt) dinner at Harry's Bar in Venice. It was loud and crowded and we were tossing about possible names for the babies. At this point we knew we were having fraternal twins — a boy and a girl — so David suggested Brendan for the boy, and maybe Elizabeth for the girl. I offered, "What about Lorca? I think it's pretty and musical?"

I was reading some of Federico García Lorca's poetry at the time and had been struck by the name. It seemed an innocent suggestion, but for some reason it enraged him. He told me there was nothing classical about Lorca, that it wasn't a queen's name, not even in the same genre as Elizabeth. *Lorca,* he continued, was a perfect example of how stupid, uninformed, and poorly educated I was. Then he got up and left the table.

I thought he'd gone to the bathroom or was cooling off outside or something. But he never came back. I didn't even realize that he'd left the restaurant until I paid the bill and discovered he'd taken his raincoat with him. I was pregnant with twins, it was late at night and pouring rain, and I could not remember the name of our hotel or where it was. I had to use landmarks to find my way back, crying all the way. I was blind with shame, humiliation, and self-loathing. What was wrong with *me* to just be left like that? I should never have suggested Lorca.

This is how toxic the situation was. Instead of feeling angry at David for his terrible behavior, I blamed myself. *I was someone to be left* kept running through my mind.

He was asleep by the time I found my way back to the hotel. The next morning I got up and left the hotel room very early. I think I left a note saying I was gone for the day. That was the best "Fuck you" I could muster. I had a great day. It was a very hot morning and it was exciting and daring to be off by myself. I got some coffee and a croissant outside of the hotel. Then I booked myself on a boat tour that went to the island of Torcello and I concentrated on the people and families around me, the seventh-century church and ruins. And, you know, it may seem like a tiny act of defiance on my part, but I felt really good, not quite so impotent. It was like I gave him the finger. Okay . . . a very little finger, but I asserted myself.

When I saw David back at our hotel at the end of the day, we both pretended nothing had happened, *as I knew we would.* We just resumed the trip and then flew home. No discussion. Nothing would change.

But I wanted things to be different in my house. I wanted to be a different person, for myself and for my children. I didn't know how to show up for them. I had this huge voice in my head that kept a running monologue of my ineptitudes and failures. I didn't need anyone else to undermine me; I could do it to myself. I felt acutely impotent when David would be agitated and target Eva. It felt as if David approached Eva the way his father had treated little Betty Jeanne, his half sister. David was always harsher with Eva than with the others; seemed to lay in wait to find fault with her. He'd be swift to jump on Ted or Kate or me as well and I felt just as inadequate to protect any of us.

Thinking back on those days, I'm heartsick at how abandoned my children must have felt. Yes, I can argue that I learned how to parent from watching my mother. But I had many years to look at that nonintervening method of parenting, see how it worked, and reject it; her way had crushed *me;* why would I choose to do the same thing to my children? However, unlike Whitney, I was at least *there,* I told myself; I couldn't stop what David was doing but I could at least be a witness — it wouldn't happen in a vacuum. But it *was* a choice because I chose between defending them or defending myself. I chose myself because I was so afraid of what he might do to me.

I think back to late one night in the second or third year of our marriage, when we were coming home from a party. I can't remember what had been said or done at the party or in the car that prompted my comment but I said, "I'm afraid we are going to be the modern-day Ed and Jeanne." I was referring to his parents and the sad repressive dynamic between them. He was a smart, cold tyrant with an iron fist around his family; she was a sweet but mousy, shutdown, manipulative martyr. Those were the dreadful roles I saw inescapably ahead for us and was naïve enough to say so.

He hit me. From behind the wheel of his Datsun Z, he backhanded me in the face as he drove, striking my big thick Gloria Steinem aviator glasses. The glasses broke against my face, cutting my left eye. The whole area swelled up immediately. David drove to nearby Santa Monica Hospital, where they took me right in because I was impressively bloody and swollen. Upon examination they said that the broken lens had sliced through the left lid into the cornea; the lid required stitches. A handsome young doctor asked how it happened as he prepared to sew me up. I was lying on the gurney in the examining room, the bright lights over my head. I could see David standing a few feet behind us. I closed my eyes. I didn't want to see David as I told the lie that would protect him.

I told the doctor we were on our way home from a party and I didn't have my seat belt on. David had stopped suddenly to avoid a car and I flew forward, hitting my face on the dashboard. It sounded simple and plausible and I have no reason to think he didn't believe it.

After I was stitched up they put a patch over my eye with instructions to keep it covered for a week to ten days to allow the cornea to heal. Then we drove home. There was no discussion, no argument, no recriminations, no apologies. There never were. We went home in silence.

The next morning, I was due to be part of an informal reading for *Family,* and I was ready to leave the house. David was sitting outside by the pool and I had to see him before I left, partly for the formality of saying good-bye but really more for permission to go. If he hadn't been there, I'd have jumped in my car and driven off. But he was there and I needed permission to leave. To be clear, he'd never demanded it; *I* thought I had to have it. He was in his short, green, terry-cloth bathrobe reading the paper in the sun when I walked out. He put the paper down and just looked up at me and said, "What are you going to say?" meaning about my eye. I replied that I'd probably tell the same story I had at the hospital, the same story I'd told the housekeeper and our children, which seemed to satisfy him, and he went back to his paper. Is dismissal the same as permission? I wasn't sure so I waited a few beats and then left.

Another woman would have walked away at this point. I felt such shame. I never wanted anyone to know what happened in my marriage; I didn't want anyone to know he thought so little of me. If *he* didn't care about me, if my *mother* didn't care about me, I must be a nothing. I had such self-hatred. I could pretend just fine in the outside world, but under the surface I was full of shame, fear, and unrealized anger. And if this were true, that I was a nothing, what could I possibly offer these incoming twins that would be different?

As a thirty-seven-year-old woman pregnant with twins, I fell into the "at risk" category of expectant mothers. My doctor put me on six weeks of bed rest, which really only meant that I had to stay home and take it easy. Consequently, I took a long leave of absence from *Family Ties* until about a month after the babies were born.

I'd been experiencing lots of false labor signs. False to the medical profession perhaps but as real as hell for me! I'd be timing contractions, calling in the troops, packing the bag, then racing to the hospital, where everything stopped. At home, I was agitated and in perpetual labor. At the hospital I was a small planet waiting impatiently to assume my new orbit. My twins — Mollie Elizabeth and Peter David Edwin Birney — were born on October 2, 1984.

They were breech, positioned butt to butt, so they were delivered by C-section. And of course, they were stunning! Mollie, at 6.8 pounds, was the heavier, and had a very healthy, peachy quality to her skin. My mother later described her as perfect as waxed fruit. Peter was more than a half pound lighter and much paler in complexion. I could see the blue veins throbbing on his little head and cheeks; he looked a bit . . . not quite done. If he were a biscuit I'd have put him back in the oven for about six minutes. Thank goodness we'd planned ahead and got a nanny. I found young Donna Holloran. She was from Indianapolis, was a huge *Family Ties* fan, had an infectious smile and endless energy. And damn . . . she loved babies and seemed to know everything one needed to know about them. Donna was there with us from day one and was a true godsend.

I'd had three children already but I was completely unprepared for two at once. Eva was away at boarding school, so the babies went in her room, in one large crib, divided with bumper pads. David and I would just look at them in there and say . . . *two?* I spent many of the wee hours hanging over the sides of the crib, half-awake, trying to pat, pat, pat them back to sleep simultaneously. The danger was that when I stopped, the lack of patting seemed to waken Mollie and she'd start squirming and an oh-my-goodness-please-don't-wake-Peter panic would spur me to pat her little back furiously until she nestled back to sleep.

I nursed all my kids and am glad I could. Nursing twins is a time-consuming but emotionally powerful event. They ate so much I could have used an extra row of breasts. I nursed them both at the same time, usually on the sofa in the den downstairs because I could sit with my feet propped up with a firm pillow along my left thigh. I always held them in the same position: I'd hold Peter on my right, cradled across me; Mollie would lie on the pillow, sort of under my arm as you'd hold a football, her little legs up behind me. My left hand would cup her golden head. Nursing was such a sweet time and she'd show her pleasure with a rhythmic thumping of her right foot back and forth, like a little pink metronome, *whack whack whack.* Peter would not break eye contact with me until he was asleep . . . he'd nurse with intensity as if I were going to cut him off any second and then *plunk* . . . you could almost hear him fall asleep. With little adjustment, I always had at least my left hand free to move them up to burp position over my shoulders, which I also did simultaneously. There was no way to avoid the usual spitting up on Mom, fore and aft; it just went with the territory. We went through clothes as if we owned Walmart.

I always thought having twins saved my life. Okay, a little dramatic, but in some ways it was true. Twins demand and require a lot of attention, and frankly, I think they were too much for David. Their room became a little sanctuary where Kate and I would often convene at night, just to talk about her day and play with the babies. David might come in but he didn't stay very often.

When I returned to work on *Family Ties,* I brought the twins and Donna with me. The producers built a beautiful nursery across from the soundstage so between scenes or during lunch there was a place I could visit my entourage of three. Often, Donna would appear on the stage while we were rehearsing, and I'd see her whispering and gesturing with Andrew McCullough, the stage manager. He'd check his watch, shake his head, and try to wave her off. Donna, with rising panic, would not be waved off and would turn her attention to me. I recognized

271

the look and, being a nursing mother, my breasts did too. Sorry Andrew, lunchtime; babies can't be waved off, scene break or not.

After lunch, as a rule, Donna would take the children back home, where she'd be with them until I returned after work. David may have taken those opportunities to spend time with the kids but I don't think he ever went out with them alone and never looked after them alone unless they were asleep for the night. Weekends David would play with them, often in the pool. When we went out we'd each carry them in backpacks, where they had a good vantage point of the world around them.

When they were working out the specifics of how the Keaton family would be expanded, I was asked, "Would Elyse prefer a single baby? Or twins?" I said, "Oh please! Don't make it twins!" I knew it was inevitable that Elyse would spend a lot of mom-and-baby time on the show. But if they gave her twins, there would be no such thing as a nonbaby-related moment for Elyse. I was so grateful when she only gave birth to Andy.

In season two, Judith Light did a wonderful turn as Steven's sexy production assistant who tries to seduce him. Hers was a powerful performance and it gave audiences a chance to see other dimensions of Steven Keaton, a married man whose vanity has been appealed to and feels the tug of attraction. It was a very compelling show and I admired that they trusted this sensitive topic in Michael Gross's hands. I, of course, saw this as an opportunity to suggest that in an act of parity Elyse could get a similarly tantalizing story line. I said to Gary, "What if an old boyfriend of Elyse's comes back in the picture and there's some spark between them, some kind of tension, so you get to see another side of *her*. It's a way you could explore her life before she was married." Gary was horrified. "But she's the *MOTHER!*" he bleated. And I thought, I see. *Well, that explains a lot.*

I interpreted it to mean that there was a sort of hallowed perception of who the mother character was and how far they'd let her go. Not far, it seemed. For instance, it was acceptable and right that Elyse might err in her commitment to her eldest and that that commitment might cause her to drive to another state to share his secret eighteenth birthday. However, it wasn't acceptable that Elyse, as *the mother,* might attract the interest of or be *interested in* another male, even in passing. I think I was hoping for further exploration of who Elyse was beyond the family, but the parental focus was kept very close to home.

Thanks to my colleagues on *Family Ties*, I did manage to have a lot of fun. For the most part, we enjoyed one another's company, and a free-for-all could always explode out of nowhere. One Thursday morning, around 1986, in season four, we were camera blocking as usual, introducing the camera operators to all the moves within the scenes, and little Brian Bonsall, who played five-year-old Andy, showed up on the set with a little squirt gun, which just tantalized the rest of us. Someone got the bright idea of sending a gofer to buy us all a bunch of larger water guns from a nearby store, and we had a good old-fashioned water gun fight. But apparently we were thinking small. While we were all laughing and spritzing each other, Michael Fox's assistant had gone out and purchased for him a Super Soaker water blaster, the kind that holds a large reservoir of water, and it became a him-against-us battle royale: *our* guns that needed constant refilling and emitted only pathetic little sprays of water against Michael, pumping his handle, Rambo-style with superb distance capacity, just drenching us. All camera blocking had come to a halt and there wasn't a dry actor in the house. Finally, amid the shrieking and running, the director, Sam Weisman, had to intervene. "Boys and girls, would you please cut it out?" he called over the sound system from the director's booth. Squirt, squirt, squirt. "Please . . . we need to get back to work." I think someone ran up to the booth to squirt him for being such a party pooper. It was just chaos. But very merry chaos and so much fun.

Michael Gross and I also had our own playtime rituals. On Friday nights before taping the show we'd go to the Paramount commissary for a light, preshow dinner. After dinner, we'd grab bowls of chocolate pudding, then take them to the back of the building and engage in a rousing game we called the Pudding Hurl. The idea was to take a spoonful of pudding in your mouth, stand sideways, a predetermined distance from the commissary wall, and whip your head around, letting the chocolate pudding fly out. Points were given for how far you stood from the wall and the magnificence of the splat. I still feel guilty about the Rorschach test of pudding that we left behind. Vanilla wouldn't have left such obvious residue but, *please,* it simply didn't have the right consistency.

If there was one part of *Family Ties* that the entire cast loved, it was the occasional wraparound show. That's what they called those episodes in which the characters sit around — in our case, usually on that ubiquitous living room set or at the kitchen table — and recall memories that are really just introductions for clips of favorite moments from previous shows. News of a wraparound was cause for rejoicing because they were scheduled right after taping a regular show on Friday nights, and we'd get paid for two shows taped in one night. Cool!

There was no time to memorize the scraps of dialogue they'd write for us, so we often didn't. We'd stick our scripts beneath the couch cushions for easy access or, just for fun, I'd tuck my lines in Michael Gross's shirt pocket.

We'd ask for popcorn and ice cream; I'd get a glass of white wine and stick it on the floor out of view of the camera lens. Except for wraparounds, I wouldn't usually have alcohol on the set while we were filming. But to me there was something so laissez-faire about these shows — there was only a slim story, just us tossing out lines like "Remember the time when we . . ." so I made it an exception to the rule. There were a few occasions when the silliness would get out of hand. I was just a glutton for having as much fun as possible and I admit the alcohol might have blurred the lines of acceptability for me a few times. I got carried away one night; my fooling around was dragging the taping on much later than required and, having already done one show, everyone was exhausted. It seemed that honking popcorn out of my nose *yet again* had ceased to be funny and I was reprimanded. Lightly.

Though it was customary for many of the cast and crew's friends and families to attend Friday-night tapings, David never came. Not once. Seven years, 175 shows; he never came. For the first couple of years when people asked about him, I'd just make excuses for why he didn't come . . . he's *so* busy . . . important business dinner, whatever. It was his absence I felt more than anything, his lack of interest. The truth is, eventually I stopped wanting him there; I would have felt terribly self-conscious. I'd have felt his judgment.

I came to relish the occasional after-show nights when we had refreshments. It was well past 10 p.m. so back at my house, even my older kids were probably asleep; this was solo time for me. Chalo, the prop master, would put out some wine, beer, and pizza and some of that white wine made me reluctant to head for home. The writers, actors, crew, families, and friends would mill about rehashing the show, yammering, enjoying another week wrapped. I hated to see an evening end. There were nights when I would be the last one to leave. I'd be having a great time and the next thing I knew I'd be standing out in the empty parking lot trying to find my assigned spot, just me and the security guard.

On an occasional Friday a few years into our run, after we finished the performance for the audience but before we started retakes of some of the scenes, I'd go to Chalo and very sweetly ask him if I could have a glass of wine. Since he was the prop master, and I was the star, sort of, what else could he do but pour me a glass? I don't know if he went to Gary or if Gary went to him, but after several months of this they laid down the law: "No more wine on the set."

This was okay with me. I had an office near the nursery by this time that came with a mini refrigerator where I could stow my own chardonnay. Now I could steel myself before going home Monday through Thursday, too, and I didn't have to bother anyone. On many a late night I would tuck a large tumbler of wine between my legs, hop into my white Mercedes sedan, and head home on Wilshire Boulevard. Along a particular corridor I liked to see how long I could keep the speedometer at 70. Today I'm appalled that I drove so recklessly; what a selfish menace I was on the road. Back then, I saw it as a challenge. I thought the wine made my instincts more acute. I don't know how I didn't get pulled over. I *really* don't know how I never had an accident. And thank God I never hurt anybody.

In the early part of the week, I would often be home in time to make dinner for the kids and read them stories. I'd pull into the garage, still feeling good from the day, and then I'd get to the back door. As soon as I touched the doorknob my whole body would sag with apprehension and defeat. I could hear Kate playing the piano and the little guys playing upstairs in their room; I'd want to go to them, I could feel their pull, but I was bent with depression. I didn't want to walk in that house.

I was grateful for the wine but it got in the way those nights. I could manage okay through dinner, but those stories presented such a challenge. I'd fall asleep or start talking gibberish as I was reading. That confused them. They'd cry and shake me. They knew there was something wrong. I wasn't very present for any of them. There were mornings I had no memory of driving home or reading to the kids at all.

If you asked anyone on *Family Ties* if my home life was anything less than idyllic, I think they'd have been shocked. On the set, I always doled out personal information sparingly. Years after *Bridget Loves Bernie,* the press were still giving David and me the perfect-couple treatment, which we were always happy to prop up with the right fairy-tale-romance answers. So it must have been very startling for Michael Gross when one day before Christmas of 1988, we were standing behind the set during a rehearsal waiting for our cue, and I had what could only be termed as a bit of a breakdown.

David had been away in England for about six weeks making a movie and Michael said to me, "Oh! David is coming home soon!" My eyes welled up and a few tears slid down my face. David had been gone long enough that an air of peacefulness had settled over our household. The kids and I were so happy together. I was so wound up with panic and anxiety at the idea of his coming home and upending it all, I couldn't help but start to cry. Michael misunderstood my emotions and said sympathetically, "You must miss him so much," and that's when I totally lost control. I burst into tears and cried and cried. I heard my cue to enter the scene and I stayed put and just sobbed. I was holding on to Michael or I'd have dropped to the floor. When Michael couldn't calm me, he sat me down backstage and went to tell the producers I wasn't well and I had to leave. I guess he was released as well.

All I remember then is following Michael to Emilio's, a restaurant that used to be near Paramount. I sat at our table and cried and cried as I vomited up what felt like unending pain. I told him about the slapping, the nonstop belittling, the rages; I told Michael *everything.* I told him about why I stayed in the marriage, about not wanting to break up the children's home yet *again,* about how hard I was trying to just be a different person so that maybe things would be better. My idea of becoming different seemed to entail trying not to feel so wretched all the time, which would result in being a less fearful, better mom; drinking played no small part in achieving that. It helped the unbearable became bearable. Very slowly, alcohol was revealing itself to be more and more of a solution to my problems, but I was years away of understanding that it was becoming a problem in itself.

I cried all the way through dinner; it was a surfeit of tears. Michael called his wife, Elza, and said, "I'm bringing Meredith home with me." I followed Michael, weeping in my car all the way out to La Cañada Flintridge, and when I saw Elza, I was surprised to feel the tears start afresh; it was an avalanche of misery that had been unexposed for years. They were so loving and sympathetic. Elza held me and just let me cry and urged me to stay the night. We all got on our knees in their living room and they prayed with me for clarity and courage. I felt they heard me and didn't feel less of me for having broken down. They urged me to seek out couples therapy.

I remembered Michael telling me several years before that he and Elza were seeing a therapist together. I was so alarmed — "Oh no! What's wrong already? You've just been married a few months!" He told me that nothing was wrong . . . they just wanted to learn how to communicate well so things didn't go wrong. He suggested that David and I try it. It was possible, I thought. This was a ray of hope. Elza made up their guest room for me and for the first time in a long while I went to sleep with some optimism.

I could have slept under my car that night

and not noticed, I was so blind with fatigue and emotion. The next morning, my swollen eyes and I got up very early, drove back to my house, and immediately I wrote David a letter in England telling him how I felt: that things had not been good between us for a long time and that I wanted us to get into couples therapy. Then I sat in dull anticipation of his return and his reply. When David got back from England, he told me that if I wanted to get into therapy, fine, but since I was the one with the problem, he wouldn't be coming with me.

I did start therapy for myself, but unloading all my trouble on Michael and Elza was one thing. That was a tidal wave; I couldn't have stopped it if I tried. But being that coherent and revealing to a stranger in planned 50-minute sittings was surprisingly difficult and I didn't get too much relief because I didn't yet know how to be completely honest. At home there was a quiet détente for a while. Things weren't great, but they didn't get worse until I signed up for the seventh year of *Family Ties*. Each of the actors was originally contracted for six years, but when they offered a seventh I jumped at it, mainly because I couldn't bear the prospect of having no place to go every day. I never asked David's permission, I never discussed it, I just signed up. No matter how angry it made him, I wasn't going to give it up.

I had some complaints over the years on *Ties,* but the truth is that when the show finally came to an end, I forgot about the sting of feeling underused. I was just incredibly sad to see it go. I remember when I read the script for the final episode, I was so dismayed. It was so *not* up to the task of being the ultimate script, the culmination of seven years of the Keatons. It was about Alex landing a job on Wall Street and moving to New York and how his departure affects the Keaton family. A fine premise, but there was no heart, no resonance, no majesty. And oh . . . we wanted, *we needed,* to go out on *majesty.* I expect the writers had trouble addressing The End themselves, didn't want to say good-bye to their beloved characters. Each rewrite they sent down from their offices was more disappointing than the one we'd read before. Everyone felt it, most acutely the writers, I expect. I'm imagining it was like penning their own obituaries. We rehearsed and camera-blocked this very lackluster show and I remember going home on Thursday night and thinking, We're missing it . . . what a sorry, dismal way to go out.

When we came in on Friday morning we were handed yet another script; and, oh, it was *killer*. It addressed all of the emotions, the loss, I'd experienced when Ted went off to college two years before: the pain a parent feels when a child moves away, of having to say good-bye, about the closing of one door as another door opens. In that one episode they took on loss and abandonment in the face of another's opportunity and excitement and the deep love and commitment between the family members. And the words they gave us (and I could feel their tears in the ink as they put them down on paper) became ways to channel the love, respect, and regret at seeing it end among the cast at the same time. They honored those relationships they created and forged over seven years of hard loving work. They gave us majesty.

I'd never experienced anything quite like the taping that night. Whenever we'd go to the dressing rooms for a costume change and we'd walk past one another, I remember we'd reach out and touch hands or stop for a brief tender hug. It was much quieter than usual back there. We were all in the same deeply emotional place of "We will never pass this way again." Every exchange onstage put us one step closer to that final moment.

When we finished the taping, we all collected backstage as usual. I was on a complex high from finishing a profoundly moving show and trying to grasp that this was, inconceivably, *the end.* Andrew McCullough introduced us, again as usual, calling out the cast's names one by one, as the studio audience applauded. I was the last one out; I came out applauding for the audience and to my peerless peers, my comrades in the trenches, these darling, funny, accomplished people. As we stood there beside one another, I remember Michael Fox and I fell into each other's arms and began weeping. And with that, my *Family Ties* era was over. What a tremendous experience it had been.

CHAPTER 11

One undeniable plus of being on a hit show like *Family Ties* was that it raised my profile. In television, having a recognizable name can translate into job offers. In the mid-1980s, *Family Ties* was seen both in its weekly prime-time slot and in syndicated repeats Monday through Friday during the day; my old series *Family* was being aired on cable, and I had various TV movie reruns airing. I've forgotten which entertainment publication determined that roughly 80 million viewers saw me every week, making me, for that small window in time, the most watched woman in America. They also might have been the ones to dub me Queen of the TV movies.

Back in the TV movie days, the three networks were making about one hundred telefilms a year. During my hiatus I always made a point of going to Jack and saying, "Pleaase get me something else." I loved

TV movies because they were good money and basically took less than five weeks to shoot. But I also knew that in this town you're known for what you did last. So if *Family Ties* made people think I was a comedienne, I put extra effort into finding dramatic roles during the hiatus. And thanks to the Movie of the Week format, I've played a sexy cat burglar, a concert pianist, a woman on the lam, a Civil War femme fatale, a jilted lover, a breast cancer survivor, a little woman in *Little Women,* a district attorney mom, a Donner Party mom, a lesbian mom, an alcoholic mom, a drug addict mom, an unfaithful mom, a schizophrenic mom, a psychotic mom, a murdering mom (twice), an avenging mom (three times), and Winnie, who lived in a mental institution.

I have a theory about why I often landed juicy roles: I wasn't a stunner. I was *accessible.* I didn't inspire fear or jealousy. I was average. People could identify with me. Not only that, I didn't mind parts where I behaved or looked unattractive. Looks weren't what I was trying to sell.

For example, in *Winnie,* one of my favorite TV movie roles, I wore a crooked, discolored prosthetic tooth and brown contact lenses, had mousy brown hair and a gangly walk, and talked in a garbled, high voice because the character I played was slightly deaf, as well as mentally challenged. But more than anything, I wanted the audience to be in touch with the humanity of the character, to identify with her. That was important to me, no matter what character I was portraying.

It always appeals to me when some research is required in prepping for a movie. I feel that enables me to bring more than the same old Meredith to a role. I spent time at Camarillo State Mental Hospital to learn more for *Winnie.* I went to a group home where the residents could work and go to school. I sat in the classes with them. I had lunch with them. I had endless conversations with them. It was eye-opening and heartbreaking. I got to see how very guileless and trusting they were. I never felt they projected or assumed; the group I was so blessed to work with were accepting, loving, and without judgment, qualities the mentally *un*challenged could aspire to.

Before I showed up at the group home, I'd been told, "Look, they watch a lot of television so if you want to be incognito, fool 'em; disguise yourself." I put on a curly reddish wig and a pair of oversize glasses. As I was driving away from my house, I passed the nanny as she was bringing the kids home from school. She looked at me with a puzzled squint like, "Who is *that?*" And I thought, "Yes! This is good!"

When I arrived at the home, they were still in class. I sat down at a lunch table out on their patio and fussed with my wig and busied myself with my brown-bagged snacks, waiting for them all to come out. I hoped they'd think I was a new girl! At noon the doors burst open and their voices were boisterous. "Oh, it's Meredith Baxter! Look, it's MEREDITH BAXTER!" So much for my disguise.

In *Kate's Secret,* my first big TV movie, my suburban housewife had an out-of-control eating disorder. Nowadays everyone knows what bulimia is, but back in 1986, no one was talking about it. I'd never even heard the term; it could have been the capital of Romania. When I told David what the new project was about, all he said was, "If you want to be the person known for throwing up on television, go ahead."

The truth is that bulimia was such a forbidden topic back then that when the producer of *Kate's Secret* — Andrea Baynes, who also produced *Winnie* — first started contacting male directors to determine interest and availability, some declined immediately. They found the idea of a movie that showed a woman vomiting on-screen too upsetting. Steve Weiss, the NBC executive who actually green-lit the project, didn't understand it and said it made him uncomfortable, but one of the women he worked with told him, "You've *got* to make this picture."

From the moment I started working on *Kate's Secret* I felt that it was clear that the sexes were divided on the subject. Men might have been disgusted or downright baffled by it, but most women seemed to get it instantly. Bulimia is about anger, hostility, loss, insecurity, lack of control, and seizing control when you're bingeing and purging.

Andrea and I used to talk about the fact that every woman and many men has some kind of eating disorder. For a short period in my life, I flirted with anorexia. I was trying so hard to lose weight that I just sort of stopped eating. Looking back, I feel like it had something to do with my mother and it came from my own lack of self-worth; it was a desire to take up less space. I know that within my marriage, there was no such thing as my being thin enough. David often called me an Amazon, referring to my height, five-seven, *and* my weight, about 135.

To prepare for *Kate's Secret* I read case

histories and spoke extensively with Dr. Murray Zucker, an eating-disorder specialist who served as the program's medical adviser. I went to several eating disorder clinics and spoke to lots of people who were in recovery. The stories of how they kept their binge-purge cycle hidden from the people in their world were both fascinating and terrifying. One woman told me about having six friends over for a dinner of Chinese food, after which they all planned to go to see a film. When it was time to leave for the movie, she told them she wasn't feeling well and wanted to stay home. As soon as everyone left she ate all of the leftovers. Then she called the same restaurant, ordering the same items, and when it was delivered, she ate until the precise amount was left as when her guests departed. Then vomited. Unbelievable.

When it aired in November of 1986, *Kate's Secret* was a huge success — it got the highest ratings of any TV movie that NBC had shown all year. It also had a huge ripple effect. Many people have told me that *Kate's Secret* had a deeply profound effect on them. On planes, flight attendants have come up to me, dropped down quietly at my side, and said, "Thank you so much for that movie. I didn't think anybody knew."

In Eva's boarding school back East and many other private schools, *Kate's Secret* was shown in health classes, often followed by animated discussions. Prior to this movie, I don't think bulimia or eating disorders in general had been a part of the public discourse, but it was about time.

For several months in 1987, David had been working on a project for the two of us: he was editing and adapting some of Mark Twain's shorter works and letters into a two-character play, *The Diaries of Adam and Eve,* which he would also direct. The plan was to develop it at David's alma mater, Dartmouth College, perhaps try it out at other venues, then present it at the Plaza Theater in Dallas, Texas, in the spring where, after a short run, it would then be taped from the stage and shown on PBS's prestigious *American Playhouse* series.

I had a mixed time at Dartmouth with the play; Ted was in school there and I loved coming to see him and the mutual friends we had who lived in Hanover, but mounting the play was very discouraging for me. David had done a great job marrying Twain's pieces into one solid presentation; it was moving and very funny. I liked the piece, but working under him was demoralizing. Every day felt like an exercise in futility. I performed my lines under a barrage of his sneering criticism and fault-finding, rarely productive and never supportive. I knew nothing but to endure it.

By the time we got to Dallas, though, at least the play was looking good. On the morning of our first rehearsal, I left the hotel room early to get a run in before having to spend the whole day inside on the stage. I trotted out into the parking lot, trying to get the lay of the land, see which was the best path to take, and I promptly stepped into a hole, hidden between two cars. I heard the snap. My right ankle was swollen immediately. I hobbled back into the hotel, where I could see several people standing, waiting for the elevator. The idea of being recognized *and* being injured (i.e., vulnerable) felt abhorrent to me so, to avoid detection, I walked up the stairs to my floor. David was just waking up and I showed him my ankle. At first, as we headed to the hospital, he was quite conciliatory and kind. As soon as the doctors determined I'd broken both my ankle *and* my foot, he was furious.

This was going to totally distract from his play and the quality of his production. He felt that the sight of me hobbling around on crutches would attract all the attention, that everyone's focus would be on "the little darling," as he mockingly referred to me.

My only response was to be secure in my lines and drink whenever I could. Some nights, after the show, David, some of the crew, and I would gather and "redo" that evening's performance over wine and beer. Once we were at someone's apartment and I got so drunk that all I remember is coming to in a cul-de-sac, lying on the grass along the sidewalk with my feet in the gutter. The next thing I recall is being back in our hotel room, coming to the next morning with Peter, who was about four at the time, nose to nose with me, saying in a high, frightened little voice, "*Mommy?* Are you all right?" I was unbelievably sick; I must have had alcohol poisoning, because I wasn't even standing till midday.

It was great that Peter and Mollie and a new nanny were with us in Dallas for most of the duration, which made being away from home so much easier. I remember being out by the hotel pool with them one day. I was a vision in a bathing suit and knee-to-ankle cast, watching them play in the water with a few older kids. One of them splashed over to Peter and, looking at me, asked him if I was Meredith Baxter-Birney. Peter looked at me, then back to the boy, and shrugged. "I don't know."

I was just Mommy. That made me so happy!

Who knows what causes the switch to flip in a relationship, why one minute you can tolerate the situation regardless of how punishing it is and the next minute you have passed the point of no return. Sometime before Dallas, when we were vacationing on Cape Cod and David and I were out together at night, there was another hitting episode. He slapped me about the face and head. At the end of that night I'd said, *"Don't ever hit me again."* When we were back home in Santa Monica, I heard on a radio program that if your spouse struck you, you could call the police. What? Really? Then I *wanted* him to hit me; I prayed for it. But he never hit me again. And you don't get to call the police just because someone's a miserable person. I should have told him not to hit me years ago.

During the fifteen years we were husband and wife, David was physically, verbally, and emotionally abusive, and, though I had no proof at that time, I knew in my bones he was unfaithful. But the end was Thanksgiving dinner, when I realized I could not do it anymore.

It was 1989, and in truth I only remember it as a series of dark flashes: David in the kitchen before dinner bad-mouthing me as I made mashed potatoes, until I was crying; sitting in misery at the dining room table, unsure what had brought on the rush of his angry words at one of the kids; David sitting in the kitchen after the guests had left, launching into an acidic postmortem that began with "How are we going to avoid next year being a disaster like this year?" What I do remember clearly: I was standing at the stove taking the turkey off the bones for soup, and Eva, then twenty, having sat through that dinner and many others like it, passed by on the other side of the counter, and she leaned through the hanging copper pots, looked in my eyes, and asked, *"What are you waiting for?"*

Holiday music was still playing on the radio. The steam from the soup was bubbling up in my face as I cracked the back and breast bones apart to fit in the pot. I'd already put in the clove-studded onion that lent such a great flavor to this potage that, as a vegetarian, I didn't even eat. I knew nothing would ever be the same. I said to David, "There's not going to be a next time."

I don't think he understood at first that I

was serious. Initially, he was patronizing, as if I were just pouting over poor restaurant service. I mean, *I* wasn't sure I was serious, but the words had come out somehow and damned if I was going to take them back! But once we both realized I meant what I said, he asked that we not let the public know until after April 26, five months from then, when *The Diaries of Adam and Eve* was scheduled to air on PBS. He felt that the news of our breakup would distract attention from the show. I foolishly agreed to keep it quiet. I also found a lawyer and at least got the paperwork started. For a while, a temporary détente again descended upon the house.

But it didn't take long for the name-calling to resume, and the tension in the house once more became unbearable. I held out for as long as I could, but when it became untenable, I pushed the issue by having my lawyer file. In March, our publicist released one of those typical statements — we'd decided to go separate ways, these are tough times, yada yada yada. I have no idea what the fan reaction was, but Whitney made a point of letting *People* magazine know that everyone in our inner circle saw it coming. (I didn't think we *had* an inner circle.) When asked by the reporter if she was surprised that we were getting divorced, my mother said, "Well, not exactly."

Even after the announcement had been made, David did not leave the house for another *ten months.* Of course, this had to unfold his way and on his terms. The gloves were off. Everything he said to me was so discounting, laced with menace and contempt. He'd talk to me through the kids, saying things like, "Well, if your mother knew anything about putting a dinner on the table then she wouldn't have made *this . . .*" or, when the housekeeper asked what he wanted for dinner, he'd reply loudly, "I don't know . . . ask the bimbo."

And I bit my tongue. I said nothing, as always. I recall sitting at the dinner table, looking into my son Ted's eyes after David had made yet another series of disrespectful comments to me. I remember wondering if he was learning that *this* is how you treat a woman. Are my boys learning how to be men from watching *David?* And what do my girls learn from watching me? That you just take it when your partner is ugly to you? That you cry and say nothing because that's what Mommy does? Will they pick partners by my example?

A couple of years earlier, I was watching the news and there was a terrible story that had riveted the nation about a man, Joel Steinberg, who had murdered his six-year-old daughter. His common-law wife, Hedda Nussbaum, was attracting almost as much attention for not protecting the child and was claiming also to be the victim of Steinberg's abuse. There was a media and public frenzy around this: they were asking her, "If he was so bad, so cruel, so abusive, why didn't you just *leave?*" I was sobbing, watching these news shows.

I knew why. David was by no measure the monster Joel Steinberg was; but I knew why. Hedda didn't leave because she didn't know she could. I hadn't left David because I *didn't know I could.* I was stripped of self-confidence; I was fearful and uncertain. I felt as impotent in my own house as Hedda seemed to feel. I don't mean to be claiming some victimhood greater than what I experienced, but I think the emotional dynamics between me and the Heddas of the world don't differ all that much.

David took his sweet time finding a new place to live. He was working with a couple of Realtors, one of whom had actually called me on the set, back when I was still filming *Family Ties*! She had been showing him places for months, knew about our situation, and wanted me to know that in her opinion, David was *not* looking for a place to live. He was killing time, being difficult, and frustrating all the Realtors who were working so hard for him. I suppose if it were so bad, I could have moved out of the house, but I would never have left without the children and I had no permission to take them away from him. There was nothing for me to do with this information except let it go to my stomach. Everything was agitating me; my stomach was hurting constantly from a small ulcer, I had lesions on my gums, and my hair was falling out . . . all a combination of stress and drinking. I'd added sake to my cupboard staples; I'd heat it in the microwave and it served to keep me warm and foggy on difficult nights.

David finally found a great place in Santa Monica on the beach, which he couldn't move into for about eight weeks because he wanted to remodel it. Just as I was picturing another two months of our cohabiting hell, he got a six-week job in Czechoslovakia. Sweet relief. Out of town was better than the police.

Before he left the country, we divided up the furniture, Post-it notes identifying his piece or my piece. He left all of his clothes hanging in our closet and said he would leave them there until he got back from his job. He wanted his Post-ited furniture, all his stuff, to stay where it was since his new place wouldn't be ready until he was back in the country and his remodel finished.

The day of his departure to Europe finally arrived and I watched David load up his suitcases and walk out the front door. As his car drove away, I burst into surprised tears of loss and failure. I had wanted so much more and didn't know how to get it. Once again I'd sent my children's father away. I felt like such a loser, that this was the best I could do after fifteen years of marriage. I was totally unprepared for my reaction; I'd expected to feel joy and jubilation, FREE AT LAST, FREE AT LAST, and dancing in the streets. I must have cried for at least an hour.

Then I called a storage facility and asked them to come pick up his portion of the furniture, his clothes, everything the next day. I wanted every reminder of him removed; I was not going to live in a state suspended between marriage and divorce with his furniture and all his clothes until he returned in two months. Recovery from David, I knew, was going to take me a very long time and I felt I needed every day I could wrest for myself. And finally, doing something in a way that suited *me* instead of just *him* felt mighty fine.

I went upstairs and into the closet we shared. Much of it was filled with his custom-made shirts and meticulously tailored clothes. David ran regularly and was a pretty fit, handsome man who dressed in a manner that he felt flattered his lean physique. But when I looked at his clothes, this is what I was remembering: times we'd be traveling, in a hotel, and the lining of his suit jacket might have come untacked — and he'd fling it at me to fix on the spot; times when he'd disparage me for wearing long skirts and boots because of the "message that I was sending." I was feeling the weight of his arrogance and vanity and I got really angry.

I got a ladder and lugged it up to the closet and perched on the uppermost step, even with the top tier of David's jackets and shirts. I moved aside some old corduroy number and found one of his newer, nicer jackets and opened it up, exposing the silky lining. I took my seam ripper and gently snapped every third stitch out of the base of the lining along the bottom of the jacket. Addressing the back of the jacket, I very carefully snipped about every third stitch in the center seam at the tightest section below his shoulders. I repeated this with a few other blazers, then turned my attention to his pants, loosening back seams where they took the most stress. My fantasy was for gaping holes to occur not immediately but once the clothing had been on for a while, in public, miles away from the house, perhaps. And that this would happen repeatedly and unaccountably, striking him in his narcissistic self-regard. My warped satisfaction from this sophomoric act came from years of strangled silence and impotence and it makes me sad that this was the only recourse I felt I had.

In the end, our divorce dragged on for more than eight long years. There were scrutinized in-home visits from child custody evaluators, sessions with court-appointed therapists, rafts of scathing, accusatory letters fired off between attorneys. We both used the children as pawns and whoever had possession of them for the moment won for that moment. At the time, I was desperately upset when the court determined that we would share custody. Today I feel it *was* ultimately for the best, but the whole process was awful — punitive and rife with suffering for all parties. I swore I'd never get married again.

I have some misgivings about revealing so much about my life with David here. But so many women have been in situations similar to mine, I'm hoping that by seeing how I, too, participated in the abusive dynamic, others will recognize the pattern, realize they are not victims and do have some power, and find a way out.

In no way is it my intent to hurt him any more than I think he intended to hurt me. I think he acted in the only way he knew how, to take care of himself. I don't think I was the target; I was just the one there. I do feel that if he could have done better, he might have.

CHAPTER 12

Gone does not necessarily mean forgotten. Furniture, clothes, shoes are all easily boxed and stored. Harder to capture, contain, and store were the memories, the feelings that lingered long after the Porsche pulled away. In the absence of the abuser, we often abuse ourselves. It's a dirty job but someone's got to do it.

David used to stand in his bathrobe at the bedroom window, one shoulder higher than the other, wineglass in hand, surveying the front yard and our neighborhood. What I read in his stance was power, decisiveness, certainty. I never questioned that's what he felt because that's how I experienced him. *We,* the rest of the world, were wrong; *we* were stupid, *we* weren't up to the task. And *I* wanted that certainty that he seemed to have. I took to standing at the window or wandering around the yard, always with the glass of wine, trying to tap into the power that was surely as available to me as it had been to him. Okay, if it's not in the yard, it must be in the glass, so I committed myself to the search for fearlessness through alcohol.

I was forty-three years old, mother of five, and single for the first time in more than fifteen years. The world had a new and exciting patina to it; I decided to think of it as my oyster and treat it as such: I went looking for pearls. I hadn't really navigated the dating scene, and the idea of having to meet someone, tell him *my* story, listen to *his* story was seriously fatiguing. I felt reckless and in a hurry; I wanted to cut to the chase. I wanted to feel attractive, desirable, *desired.* I wanted an affair. Not having any confidence in my seduction muscles, I picked three good guys, friends I'd known and worked with over the years. All of them were safely married. I approached each individually, one after the other, and basically proposed that we have an affair.

Each rejected me very gently, without shaming me, saying in various ways, "Thank you. I'm very flattered. But I'm in a good place with my family and my wife and I don't want to do anything to threaten that." I'd picked those rare birds who valued their relationships. The lovely part is we're all still friends today.

At least I had my work. I was excited that I had a new agent. In casting off the bondage of my marriage, I thought I might as well be thorough and let go of the other men I was tied to who felt like weights to me. I held my own Saturday Night Massacre and relieved myself of Jack Fields (my agent, my stepfather, my agent, my stepfather) and a nice but ineffective man who had been my press agent for many years. I wanted to start clean with people I could count on who didn't have any agenda with me.

Through my new agent, John Kimble at the William Morris Agency, I was offered a fun, edgy role playing a serial baby-snatcher from Atlanta in a made-for-TV thriller called *The Kissing Place*. It was the story of a young boy who discovers that the woman he calls his mother (*moi*) abducted him as a toddler from a New York playground. Not only did I get to be Southern, but my character, Florence, who becomes Crystal, was subject to violent mood swings where she'd be talking softly with her son one minute and, seconds later, seething with anger and planning his death. She was pretty creepy but I identified with the wild, unbridled fury that governed this character

308

and I wanted to walk around in her skin.

The Kissing Place was filmed on location in Toronto, Canada, and the group I was working with was great. I met and became fast friends with Suzanne Benoit, our Oscar-winning makeup artist. She *was* an artist, a French-Canadian character with great style, intellect, and vivacity, and this was the first of many movies we did together.

I liked living in my hotel suite in the middle of Toronto. I think I was living out the fantasy of being a young single girl working in the city. I'd whip up some spaghetti with a hotel room–version, garlicky marinara sauce and balance that with a couple of glasses of wine, usually white. After dinner I'd most often go over my script for the upcoming week's work. I liked to be a few days ahead in memorizing my lines and it was important for me to have a strong sense of the story's arc. Or, I might sit at my window on the twentieth-something floor with my chardonnay and look out at late-night Toronto and cry and miss Kate and Mollie and Peter.

The twins were five; Kate, fifteen. Peter and Mollie were out of the country with David and near impossible to reach. Kate was in school in Los Angeles and because we had a lot of night shooting, even connecting with her was very hard. I've never been great on the phone anyway and I think I put guilt first in all my conversations. Eva was finishing her senior year in boarding school; Ted was in college.

It's hard to explain separation with little ones, and when location took me away from them, I used a method I'd hit upon that I hoped would smooth their understanding of the elapsed time and to *know,* to *see* when they would have me back home. I drew a tree and attached small cutout leaves equal to the number of days I'd be gone. Every night at bedtime, they would remove one leaf from the tree until it was bare . . . then I'd miraculously walk in the door. I have no idea how effective it was for them but it helped me.

It was second nature to start pouring the wine as soon as I got back into my hotel room at the end of a day. I didn't have to be sad, or overtired, or in a divorce depression. I just liked it. I felt I deserved it. I liked the way the wineglass stem felt between my fingers. I felt this was *how one dealt with the adversities of adult life.* I was posturing as an adult.

As the filming progressed, I was anticipating a tough late night when shooting the final scenes of the movie where my character, Crystal, gets pretty nuts and the scene climaxes up on a high fire escape. I didn't have a lot of confidence in how to play the scene, felt the dialogue didn't really help, so I was a little *out there* as the night approached. I usually liked to have a good tall chardonnay on hand in my trailer before hitting the set, especially when there was a gritty scene. I hadn't had time to get to a package store so the morning of the dreaded scene, I was reduced to begging a teamster to pick up some wine and bring it to me later on location. The early filming went okay but I was wound really tight from anxiety about the night work. When my friendly teamster delivered the wine, I was stupefied. It was red. He brought me *red wine,* which was simply not going to do the trick. *White* took me to where I needed to go; I couldn't imagine *red* doing much of *anything.* How the hell was I going to pull this off with *red?* Okay, drink two. Problem solved. I chug-a-lugged two tumblers and changed into my stunt wardrobe.

I never nailed the scene. It is dark; I drag the little boy up the fire escape to avoid the police, who are climbing up from below, then yelling, yelling, dialogue, dialogue, throw myself over. (Okay, I *fake* throwing myself over; a stunt woman does the real thing, shot from a lower angle, falling onto a very thick stunt mattress below.) It was pretty tricky, pretty highly emotional, and it took several trips back to my trailer to make sure I was on pitch but it never came together for my satisfaction. It was a disappointment. I should have had white. Damned teamsters.

Once at a press junket, a reporter had asked Andrea Baynes if we were ever going to work with anyone else. But the truth is, she'd produced three movies with me and we were a great team. I loved her, loved her grasp of story, her humor and perception. When she came to me with a fourth project, a TV movie script for a steamy melodrama called *Burning Bridges,* I signed on immediately. This character was light-years from mentally disabled Winnie Sprockett or Crystal, the child menace. I played Lynn Hollinger, the wife of a college professor and mother of two little boys, who has a sizzling fling with a married doctor. I finally got to play a character with a sex life! This was also network TV in 1990; her affair leaves her so racked with guilt that she ends up having a nervous breakdown.

There were so many things I loved about making *Burning Bridges* — we shot it in picturesque Vancouver and the material had the potential to close the book on my whole-some Elyse Keaton image. Always looking for validation, I also started a real affair with my handsome Dutch "doctor" costar. He was blithe about the fact that he had a wife and three sons back in the Netherlands, and I got the impression that he was no stranger to location romances.

On the downside, I found the adult content far more difficult than I could have predicted. The director, Sheldon Larry, wanted me to be topless for some of the love scenes, totally nude in another — which I found puzzling because ABC's Department of Standards and Practices wasn't going to allow nudity to be shown on prime-time TV.

I balked and said I wanted to at least be wearing a bra. Then one of the executive producers — not Andrea — came to my dressing room and bullied me, taunting me about my modesty, calling me a schoolgirl. By the time she'd left my trailer, I felt humiliated, powerless, and childish and caved in, agreeing to be topless and wear nude-colored underwear.

I decided that if this was what I'd signed on for, I should just get fortified: do it and shut up. I abandoned any boundaries I'd drawn about not drinking on the set. I made sure I had a tumbler of white wine within reach or in my hand at all times. When they called for first team to come in, I'd hand it off to Stacey, my fabulous costumer, and saunter onto the set. Drinking during a scene was the next natural step and because I was playing a visibly distressed character anyway, a nice glass of wine made sense. As it turned out, being topless only applied to one long love scene with the Dutch actor, and whenever my bra was off I was safely pressed against his chest. And blind with alcohol.

I didn't really flaunt my drinking, but I never tried to hide it either. I actually thought I cut a rather rakish figure as the well-oiled, number-one-on-the-call-sheet actress. Hadn't I earned the right? Do you *know* what I'm going through? Haven't I just been so good for so long, why the fuck can't I do what I want now? I'm showing up, saying my lines, I'm not falling down, what's there to object to? I'm turning in a great performance. I am being who I've always wanted to be! These might have been the same things Lana Turner was saying to herself during *Bittersweet Love* — when I swore I'd never be like her.

The truth is that I got through it and I was inordinately proud of my performance.

So much so that a month after I got home and found out that *Burning Bridges* was going to have a screening at Paramount Studios, I invited my mother and Allan to come see it, which I had never done before. I was always afraid of her judgment, but this time, I wanted Whitney to see what I considered to be some of my finest work.

We all gathered in the theater, the lights went down, and as soon as we started watching the movie, the tears began rolling down my face. I was moved less by the painful saga of my character's personal awakening than I was by reliving how agonizing it had been for me to risk looking foolish, to play a sexy and complicated woman and really put myself out there. I didn't see on the screen the brilliance I was expecting to see, the splendor I'd *felt* while I was performing, but I didn't have a critical eye for myself that day.

When it was over, I was standing with a few friends in the sunny parking lot talking. I was anxiously awaiting my mother's reaction and she was taking a long time coming out from the theater. "Well, Meredith," she said when she and Allan finally emerged. "It's time." Then she placed two fingers on the upper part of her cheekbones and pulled the skin back — the universal semaphore for "face-lift."

That was it. No congratulations, good job, or I can tell that you're stretching yourself as an actress. I never spoke to my mother about my work again.

About a month later, Andrea Baynes invited me to meet her for lunch at The Mandarin in Beverly Hills. We were talking about *Burning Bridges* and rehashing our adventures in Vancouver when she asked me if I thought I had a problem with alcohol. I stopped breathing. I had ordered a glass of wine with lunch but, sensing some kind of scrutiny, I'd barely touched it.

"Andrea!" I said, genuinely floored. "How can you *say* that? On the basis of *what?*"

She explained that during the filming of *Burning Bridges,* as the editors were piecing together a rough assemblage, they often had to cut around me because my eyes weren't focused and they couldn't understand me. I'd not noticed *any* of this during the screening! She said they'd held production meetings at the end of the day and asked themselves, "What are we going to do about this?"

What were they going to do about *me?* The idea that they were sitting around talking about me, that I was being perceived as a problem, just shocked and *appalled* me.

Being the focus of such negative attention was agitating . . . horrifying.

Andrea suggested that I get into a program for recovering alcoholics and gave me a couple of names of women she knew who might take me to a meeting.

I was thinking, "A *program?* For *alcoholics?* Isn't that a little bit over the top?"

But even one person in the industry thinking I had a drinking problem and talking about it was untenable. It never occurred to me *I* had a problem . . . I just had to deal with their *perception* of a problem. Word travels very fast in Hollywood. This was not good for business. As I drove away from The Mandarin, I decided, Well, I've got to do something to get them off my back.

When I got home, I called Helen, one of the names on the list. She was the wife of someone I'd worked with in the past. When she answered, I unaccountably burst into tears, said I thought I had a problem, and asked if she'd take me to a meeting. I have absolutely no idea where those words came from. I certainly didn't believe them. She said she had been hoping to hear from me for some time.

The meeting we attended was for women and was in the Pacific Palisades, and outside of *Days of Wine and Roses,* I had no idea what to expect but I knew I wouldn't like it. I had contempt *prior* to investigation and *after*ward. People raised their hands and said, "My name is . . . and I am an alcoholic." I was aghast. I thought, This is the most hideous, ridiculous thing I've ever done.

I could see women recognize me and turn to whisper to their neighbor. I was dying; I felt so exposed. They were going to think I *was* an alcoholic because I'm at this stupid meeting. I saw a woman in production I'd worked with years before. I saw a woman I suspected David had had an affair with. I put my head down and met no one's eye. Inside, I was screaming, Don't look at me like I'm one of you. I wanted to shout, You don't know me. You don't know ANYTHING about me. Leave me *aloooone!*

I kept drinking. But a few mornings later I met Helen at another meeting. I just sat there silently howling, Don't give me your telephone number. Don't say hello. Don't *hug* me, for crying out loud. Don't don't don't. I wasn't on what you'd call good behavior. People would come up to me and say so kindly, "Oh, you must be new." I'd say, "How the fuck do *you* know?"

The speaker at this second meeting was a woman who had written and produced a

318

movie I'd done. At first I was frantic that she'd see me and wonder what *I* was doing there. As I listened to her story I remember thinking, She's telling *my* story. Someone called ahead and coordinated with her to talk about *me.* I thought I was going to drop through the floor in humiliation. I was so angry I was trembling. Months later, I realized none of the facts in her story paralleled mine. But I had heard and totally identified with the feelings of sadness, separateness, and devastation. And I wouldn't admit that to myself or others for many months to come.

I left that meeting before it was over and went home; God knows I wasn't going to be saying any prayer at the end with these folks. I was tense and unnerved as I repeatedly circled the long counter in my kitchen. It felt like they were all telling me what I could and could not do *as if they knew me.* I opened up the refrigerator, poured myself a very tall tumbler of cold white wine, and downed it in anger *at them.* I was shaking and crying; I just had to get out of the house. For no reason, I drove to Beverly Hills, parked my car on a tree-lined street next to a church, put my head back, and fell asleep.

When I woke up, I realized it was time to

pick up Mollie and Peter from kindergarten so, woozily, I made my way up to their school.

That was my last drink, April 4, 1990.

CHAPTER 13

I kept going to meetings but I didn't really think I had a problem. My daughter Kate might have commented once or twice in the past about how much I consumed but I just thought she was being overly observant and worrying about nothing. I simply moved the wine bottles up to my bedroom closet so as not to agitate her; it seemed the thoughtful thing to do.

I had a hard time identifying with stories I heard in meetings about people trying and trying but not being able to stop drinking. I'd never tried to stop drinking because I never felt it stopped working. I didn't identify with those who spoke of losing their homes, livelihoods, or relationships due to their drinking. Nope. Nope. I never drank like *that*. A few glasses of wine, a couple of nice margaritas, are what made my life possible. Sure, I'd had a few incidents when I'd had way too much, might have blacked out, but I was pretty sure that was the same for most people. Alcohol wasn't my problem; *David* was my problem and promised to be for many years to come. Alcohol was a refuge, I didn't have to feel all the pain. I thought it *was working for me!*

Here's the odd part: although I absolutely did not believe I was an alcoholic, I stopped drinking. I really didn't want industry people to be talking about me; I didn't think a 12-step program would work for me; I didn't see how the joy and laughter and freedom I saw in these people's faces could ever be mine, but I was so lonely, so desperately lonely, and without any other ideas, I took steps I did not believe in so I could stay among them. For the first few months, without the alcohol, I was agitated, angry, and cried a lot and I ate lots of hard candy to replace the sugar, but I stayed with it.

Slowly, I could see that my life seemed better just because I wasn't drinking: I didn't fall asleep reading to the children anymore, I had more energy, I wasn't forgetting appointments as often, I felt more present, perhaps, but there was nothing to take the edge off my anxiety. I knew I was supposed to be doing some kind of writing, to figure out causes of the anxiety, but I didn't go in for the self-examination stuff.

It seemed too heady, tedious; it made me sag with fatigue at the very thought.

After a while, I came to understand I was a *periodic,* which was why it was so hard for me to identify with much of the daily drinking stories. I didn't always drink every day. But whenever I drank, I almost *always* got drunk and frequently blacked out, which I later learned was another good indication that one is an alcoholic. It made me think of passing out on the Cherry County stage when I was a teen, blacking out after that party in Dallas, the many times I'd no idea how I got home. Having more evidence that I belonged in the 12-step program helped combat the ambivalence I still struggled with.

Even so, I'd go to meetings as often as I could, racing to get there on time, desperate to be there among the people. Against my will, I started to feel the hope and the love in the rooms. I was frantic I'd arrive late and have to walk into a full room where heads would turn and I'd be seen. When I felt so exposed with all the eyes on me, then I had a hard time listening. I felt I didn't get to enjoy the anonymity most of them took for granted and that made me angry. I felt because I was *known,* people thought they knew something about me and *that*

323

made me angry; I was so self-absorbed and focused on how I *felt* all the time, I could hardly hear what was being said. Sometimes I'd stand outside the closed door, knowing the meeting was starting, unable to turn the knob. It was like standing outside my mother's bedroom. I could feel the tears come but I didn't have permission to open the door. Usually another latecomer would open up and then I'd slide in behind, hopefully hidden from view.

I loved the laughter inside. A guy told a story of his home being foreclosed on, his car being repossessed, and his family leaving him all in the same day, while he observed it all in detachment with a highball in his hand . . . and everyone in the room was falling out of their chairs in uncontainable hysterics. I saw how they didn't take themselves so seriously and I came to understand how very self-centered I was, how very insular my world. I could see the warmth and acceptance that was available to me if I could bring myself to trust it.

I barely followed suggestions. I'd been told to get a sponsor in the program, someone I admired and could confide in, someone I'd allow to guide me. I thought this was a revolting idea. There was no way in the world I'd trust anyone enough to confide in them. I recoiled from and immediately dismissed any concept of a higher power; I was not at all interested in addressing how I might have caused harm to others, drinking or sober; I was confident I'd been done wrong almost all my life and saw no reason to question that belief.

Eventually, in an effort to appear compliant, I decided to pursue a sponsor — the woman I thought had had an affair with David. I figured we had something in common. She was an actress who had worked with him a few years earlier and had even had dinner at our house a few times, although she had to remind me of that. She quickly straightened me out and assured me there had been no affair with David. I just wanted someone who understood what my life had been, someone who might feel sorry for me in the process, and she seemed as likely as anyone. She was great and agreed to work with me and gave me some general directions, which I followed, generally. I think I saw myself as a profoundly emotionally damaged person. I didn't hold out much hope that any program, any kind of *self-analysis,* was going to resolve the deep-seated pain and trauma I'd felt over my lifetime. I'd put myself in the hands of multiple therapists over the years, with little to no results. How likely that some woo-woo program was going to fix me? I was willing to stay for the meetings and the support because I really had no place else to go, but I put in only the most cursory effort.

A Mother's Justice was my very first movie job after getting sober. It was about a young woman, played by Carrie Hamilton, who is raped, and I played her mother who acts as a decoy to catch the rapist. I deeply identified with wanting to stand up for and protect my children . . . not really what the movie was about, but so what? That was *my* subtext. This was also shot in Vancouver and I knew that many of the crew members had also worked on *Burning Bridges* and probably witnessed some of my alcoholic behavior. They had no way of knowing I had gotten sober. Since I was desperately afraid that people would be talking about me, waiting to see me sneak a drink or hide in my dressing room, I was pretty quiet, sat and read out on the set *where I could be seen* between shots as much as I could. And I was word-perfect and clear as a bell.

I only had one instance of anxiety on this movie: when the director asked me to create a more emotional, cathartic moment in a final scene where there's just me, no dialogue. My immediate response was no, wrong choice. But the truth was I was fearful of my ability to produce the desired effect without first priming myself with wine. There was no time to call my actress-sponsor for guidance, because the director just whispered, "Action." So I silently envisioned wanting a drink, feeling shaky and desperate, and making a call to a sober friend in the program. I wept emotionally and cathartically as I silently imagined her words of support and understanding. "Cut." It was okay. Actors will use *anything* to get the job done.

It was a heady period for me. I was feeling good about myself: I *was* in the program, responsible for myself and making a very good living. I've always been attracted to jobs that challenged me, grabbed me where I lived, and another movie came up, *Bump in the Night,* that fit right into that category. We shot in Pittsburgh, and I played a boozy, once-famous New York reporter named Martha "Red" Tierney. When her eight-year-old son is kidnapped by a pedophile (played by Christopher Reeve), she is forced to quit drinking because she needs to be clearheaded enough to track him down, which of course she does.

Like so many times before, the universe

sent me a movie that struck an important chord then playing in my own life. It often seemed to work that way. *Kate's Secret* demanded I look at my self-esteem and self-image arena; in *Kissing Place* I got to tap into the almost psychotic craziness I was feeling in my home at that time; and *Burning Bridges* resonated with the lies and deceptions of my dysfunctional relationships and reliance on alcohol.

Ironically, playing an out-and-out alcoholic in *Bump in the Night* worked for me, too. We were shooting in Pittsburgh. My character, Red, was struggling with trying not to drink. At one point she's ready to cave and finds herself sitting in a mirrored dive bar with a highball in front of her. I sat on my stool at the bar as they adjusted lights and took still photos when it suddenly dawned on me, Oh! I'm six months sober today! I hadn't really planned on staying in the program; I just didn't take a drink one day at a time and, hey, I'd put six months together! To celebrate, I called my sponsor and then walked across the street during my lunch hour and I bought a $1,500 Omega watch as a gift from myself to me. I've had that watch for twenty years.

It is especially important that I go to meetings when I'm out of town and away from my support system. That night, I went to a meeting at a large church some distance away. There were many doors off a main hall and I had no idea which one led to my meeting. An older church woman was bustling toward me and I could have asked her assistance but I didn't want to betray my reason for being there; I still didn't want anyone *to know.* I stood with my ear cupped to each door until I found the one I wanted, then slipped in.

Here's another irony: I remember many instances when I had no problem *regaling* people with wild stories of drinking escapades and dumb stunts I'd pulled. That was just telling things I'd *done.* But if someone knew I was sober, I thought that meant they'd know who I *was.* All my life I'd been reticent and had a terrible fear of being known, and at that time I had no willingness to change that.

Back in Los Angeles, I'd met some new people in the program, one of whom was Carla; she was terrific. She'd invited me to lunch after a meeting with her and a group of women at their usual gathering spot. The waiter greeted them warmly and they introduced him to me in passing and then, as he was taking their orders, they started discussing the meeting. Any bonehead hearing them would know without question that they were recovering alcoholics and they'd already introduced me as one of them and I thought I was going to expire on the spot because now *the waiter kneeew.* What would he think of meeeeee? It's sad and fatiguing to think back on the degree of self-centeredness I suffered. Being a recognizable person only exacerbated my anxiety and self-focus, rendering me panicky and secretive in situations that were totally benign and friendly. It took many, many years for this to change.

Before I was cast in *Bump in the Night,* I'd been deep in divorce activity and it picked up again after the movie was over. I just resumed a life of legal combat. I had selected a woman lawyer over a guy who'd been recommended to me as a *barracuda* because I didn't think I could stand dealing with another arrogant, pushy, aggressive, dismissive male. David's phalanx of lawyers took my deposition several times and each was a harrowing experience. I remember his lawyers as sneering weasels, dripping with sarcasm and innuendo. They did it so well that it must have been old hat to them, but I would occasionally have to excuse myself, go to the bathroom, and kneel on the cold tiles to cry a prayer to stay present, not crumble, not take it personally, although it was all excruciatingly personal. I recall no particulars of what was said in the depositions, but I do remember what I wore.

I'd found all the depositions so threatening that the only way to deal with them was to wear what felt like armor; I dressed in a very masculine style. I wore blazers and slacks with casual buttoned shirts and wing-tip oxfords. Honestly, I never thought, I'll dress like a man, I just did it; I was angry. I was seething with anger but felt very vulnerable, and somehow I'd decided that jackets and wing tips would protect me. And I'd cut my hair short, as many women do when they've ended a relationship, even buzzed it up the back a little. I'm sure, in retrospect, this deserves some probing as to what degree this foreshadowed my ultimate coming out, but I can promise you, I was just trying to disguise myself as cold, unflappable, indomitable as I deemed most men to be.

One day in early 1991, a terrific TV director named Dick Lowry and a writer named Joe Cacaci asked me to meet with them. They'd bought the rights to make a film based on a series of newspaper articles about Betty Broderick, a forty-two-year-old La Jolla socialite who a few years earlier had murdered her ex-husband, Dan Broderick, and his young wife, Linda, shooting them to death as they slept.

Betty's motive — that after supporting Dan through medical school and law school and assuming full responsibility for raising their four children, she'd been cast aside for a newer, younger model — turned her into an unconventional figure of empowerment for casually discarded women everywhere. The title was *A Woman Scorned: The Betty Broderick Story.* Dick and Joe wanted me to come on board. I didn't hesitate for a minute. I was in.

I had no trouble understanding the story of a woman done wrong, feeling I was one myself. I was now in my second year of sobriety and really getting in touch with my anger toward David and the life I'd been living. I identified with Betty's point of view. I too felt resentful, unappreciated, targeted, passed over.

As soon as I knew the agents had sealed the deal for the movie, I went from the production office straight to the Mercedes-Benz dealership and headed for the biggest sedan they had on the showroom floor. It could probably sleep four. The doors were so heavy it took both hands to open them. It offered lousy mileage but had an incredible sound system. It was white. It was beautiful. I loved it. I didn't know anything about bargaining. I just said, "I'll take it." It was ridiculously expensive; I'd never indulged myself like this before but I thought I'd feel powerful if I drove something that could drive over David's Porsche, should the need arise.

For me, Betty Broderick's world was a great one to walk around in. She was privileged, so there were great sets and wardrobe. She was arrogant and entitled, so there were many scenes of her self-centeredness and demands, and she was angry, so we got to see her act on her self-pity. It was *great!* I identified on *every* front. What a character! A woman with no boundaries of her own who certainly didn't respect anyone else's. I read everything I could get my hands on about Betty, tons of magazine and newspaper articles and interviews. And I found I held a certain amount of sympathy for her; I wouldn't have chosen to kill two people, but I felt I understood what brought her to that point. I think there was a fair percentage of the female public who felt the same way at that time.

If I had to pick one scene that I found

most therapeutic, it was the one when Betty, at Christmastime while her children are at their father's, drove her Suburban SUV up over her husband Dan's lawn and straight through the front door of his new house. Again, I wouldn't have done this, but I understood it from the twisted perspective of having been in a harsh custody battle with David and the sense that if you have the children in your possession, then you are the winner. And Betty's children were at their dad's and happy to be there, so she was the loser, impotent and unsupported.

It was cold and foggy the night we shot that scene. Our crew was gathered outside a beautiful corner house in Hancock Park, a very upscale section of Los Angeles. The company had built a false front entry onto the house that extended out about four feet; that was my target. It was very dewy and the grass was slick. The stunt people gave me very clear directions. Then I climbed behind the wheel of the old Suburban, my walkie-talkie at my side, got the car into position near the middle of the intersection, and waited.

Usually they don't put principal actors behind the wheel for stunts but they needed to clearly see it was Betty driving, even in the long shots. I'd been lucky and pulled off some nifty car stunts before in other movies and felt confident I could handle this. I was *eager* to do this. I was driving a big mother of a car and the engine sounded ominous under the best of circumstances, but this night the rumble sounded like an imminent stampede and I was tingling with anticipation. From a distance, I heard them yell "Rolling," I tensed and waited for the camera's pan to include my car, and at "Action, Meredith" from my walkie, I stamped down hard on the gas. The wheels spun on the wet asphalt until they found a purchase. Then the car shot over the pavement, bounced up the curb, up the grassy incline, across the lawn, and crashed into the front door, knocking a spectacular hole in the false front to reveal the foyer. And there stood the family, as if for a family portrait, except for the looks of fear and astonishment on their faces. It was perfection!

It was everything I had wanted it to be: the anticipation, the rumbling, the wrestling of the SUV over the slick ground surfaces, the crash, the shocked faces. I got to do it over and over again as they shot it from several angles.

This scene was followed by Dan coming out of the house and physically attacking Betty; we were really going at each other, swinging, punching, swearing. Not many jabs hit their mark in all our flailing but because we both totally committed to it, we were torn, bruised, and breathless by the end of the night. Stephen Collins (my husband from *All the President's Men*) played Dan and he was just marvelous. He threw himself into this with a passion that matched my own. What made working together especially intense was that in some ways we each held the same strong points of view as our characters and I think our identification with their opposing sentiments that night propelled us into the fury of their conflict. It may have been a cold, misty, foggy night but *we* were white-hot.

I'm embarrassed to say how cathartic that was for me. I think I was more in touch with my anger than I'd realized. The good thing is that I got it out of my system while driving someone else's car and play-thumping an actor. I didn't have to use my huge new two-bedroom music system as a battering ram after all. It was a physical and emotional purging. I was calmer for a while.

A Woman Scorned ended up being CBS's highest-rated TV movie of that season and landed me an Emmy nomination for my performance. CBS had ordered a sequel to the Broderick story, which we were shooting when my nomination was announced. I found out about it when I returned to my motor home, which the producers had *stuffed* with balloons and streamers. A month before the first movie was shown, Betty was convicted of second-degree murder and sentenced to thirty-two years to life. Our second movie, *Her Final Fury: Betty Broderick, the Last Chapter,* which was shown less than nine months later, focused on the stretch of time between the killings, both trials, and the outcome.

In the interim between the two movies, I was excited to have a chance to read the court transcripts, which I knew were going to be very revealing. I was stunned. Betty had duped me. When I first came on board I'd read everything available in print written about her. What I had not realized was that when she was put in prison, she had immediately hired a publicist and gave interviews to every single periodical that would talk to her. So, of course, everything I read had *Betty's* spin on *Betty's* story — a very sympathetic spin, which had seduced millions of women sympathizers across the country to her cause. Including me.

Where before, I had believed she had been victimized, manipulated, and bullied, I came to see *she* was the ruthless master manipulator. Psychiatrists showed her to be a nine-point narcissist, seemingly incapable of considering anyone's needs unless they coincided with hers. This was a woman who acted *solely* in her own interests, regardless of her voiced concerns for her four children's welfare. Our second movie, *Her Final Fury,* put me in the wonderful position of being able to correct a misconception I had myself embraced and put out there for others. Actually, maybe I got that Emmy nod for *A Woman Scorned* because I *was* so committed to Betty's self-assessment and could embody her with absolute certainty.

While I was filming, I was only getting to my 12-step meetings on weekends, but I still went regularly. I liked the meeting at Cedars in Los Angeles that my new friend Carla introduced me to. It was a very social meeting, late on Sunday morning, so I still had time to run beforehand. My comfort level there would come and go, depending on the day. Many times I'd arrive early enough to get a good seat but I'd still sit with my head buried in the *New York Times* Sunday crossword — anything to keep my face down and people at bay. My stepfather Allan always did the puzzle in ink, so I did too, hoping I looked as smart and confident as he. So, I guess I didn't want anyone to get to *know* me, but I still wanted them to have good assumptions *about* me. Once, I was sitting, trying to appear engrossed in my puzzle, as the speaker started. I heard her mention a prayer she sometimes used, that started, "Dear God, please help me for I am too little," and I sat there while tears ran down my cheeks, blurring the ink on my puzzle. That's how *I* felt, too small to bear this room of strangers, too small to deal with divorce, child custody, and my deep sense of damage and neediness. I felt so powerless. I started using that prayer.

I grew to really enjoy this meeting and Carla. I loved her conversation, wisdom, and especially her irreverent humor. We frequently talked on the phone during the week. She had been sober more than ten years, and I relished her insights into the program, especially as she talked about emotional sobriety. She listened with great compassion to my own story and we talked at length about our mother issues. I felt seen and heard in ways I never had before.

I think it was about 1992 when I was going for full custody of my youngest children and I was at the end of a second long and dreadful child custodial evaluation. A team of family analysts had come to both David's and my house to make a critical assessment of our individual parenting skills with Peter and Mollie, who were about six at the time. It seemed that months went by before the results were in and I spent many anguished hours with Carla, wailing in fear and apprehension. She had become really close with the kids, engaging their trust, and I came to rely on her wise counsel.

The day I got the results I think I kind of lost my mind. I was devastated that the official evaluation determined that we should maintain the custody division *as it was*, which I perceived as a loss; I still had the kids only four out of seven days a week. Not only did I feel it was a repudiation of my claims of David's abuse of the children, it also felt like an indictment of my relationship with them. I'd lost my fight for them as I was feeling crushed and engulfed by the endless divorce. I didn't know what to do with the huge feelings that came up. I didn't want to drink . . . I wanted to die, bury myself somewhere. I just got in my car in despair and drove up the coast, no destination in mind.

This was in the days of car phones (no cell phones yet) and mine rang so many times I turned it off and rode in silence except for my crying. I had no words for the devastation I felt. I thought I'd failed the children; once again I wasn't able to defend them. Somewhere north of Santa Barbara I turned around and headed home in defeat; there was Carla, waiting for me in front of my house, worried that I'd been unreachable for so long. Over the next few weeks, she talked to me about acceptance. She said it wasn't personal and that the kids had their own path and being in David's life meant they would grow to know and understand him as they wouldn't, *couldn't,* if I had sole custody. I really struggled with the possibility of a picture bigger than the one I could see, one that didn't focus solely on my sense of calamitous loss. Carla said I was severely limited by my inability to imagine that the arrangement might not be a calamity and (this was hard) I had to allow that the children's own higher powers had necessary lessons in store for them.

I trusted her words, and many years later, I can say there was such truth in what she said. I *personally* might have chosen different lessons for them in less painful ways but . . . who asked me? No one put me in charge.

Carla and I became fast friends and the kids were delighted that she was like part of the family. It had been a long time since I'd had a close friend like this. We did movies, museums, holidays, and a number of road trips together. The constant was laughter.

One Fourth of July, Whitney and Allan invited the kids and me to spend the night at their Malibu beach house and watch the fireworks. It was only natural that Carla was included. We'd all had a great day on the beach with Peter and Mollie, barbecuing and watching the big show. A few of the Broad Beach home owners regularly got together and hired a crew and barge to come up from San Pedro loaded with fireworks, sit offshore, and put on a huge, indulgent, excessive, and extravagant display for everyone. It was over-the-top phenomenal.

Late that night after the twins were asleep, Carla and I were lying in bed laughing softly, and talking about the day, and I kissed her. It felt very organic. I just loved her; I loved how she was such a vital, fun part of our lives; I loved what a good friend she was to me, how loving and present she was, how generously she gave of her time. It just felt like the right thing to do. I couldn't think of any better way to express my depth of feeling for her. I can't talk about the kiss in terms of sexual attraction because it wasn't about that — which is probably what the problem was from the start.

It became a sexual relationship. I was thrilled to be close to someone whom I loved and felt safe with, trusted and enjoyed so much. We just laughed and laughed. I never questioned my sexuality because making love felt like the next natural step in our singular relationship, not an expression of my desire for a woman, even this particular woman. This was no awakening. No penny dropped. I was simply happy to be with her.

I don't know how long I would have remained in this unexamined state were it not for the fact that, over time, Carla fell in love with me. I tend to back off when I feel that people have expectations of me. And in truth, I think I had already given just what I'd wanted to give. At that time, that was all I could do. But of course, *how would she know that?* I hadn't said there were limitations to my involvement. I hadn't *thought.* I hadn't *considered* . . . I had just acted, impulsively and, I guess, selfishly. I think I didn't see it as selfish at the time because it was reciprocated; but I understand today, those are separate issues.

Carla was amazingly honest. She had learned a lot in her years of sobriety, and I learned how to be fearless and thorough in relationships by her example. And I could be really honest and clear with her, which was unusual for me. I wasn't in love with her. But I loved her. I wanted to be in her life because I valued her friendship so much. That, too, was selfish, wanting what I wanted even in the face of her deep feelings and hurt, but I'm slow. We broke it off. I told Carla that I thought I really wanted to be with a man, which was true as I knew it.

Carla and I continued trying to redefine our friendship over the next few months, despite wanting different things, and at the same time a guy from the program named Michael Blodgett began pursuing me. He would often come up to me at meetings and make oily overtures, telling me how beautiful I was, asking if he could walk me to my car. It felt weird, slimy. I remember once asking Carla, "Who *is* this guy? My god, he's so creepy. And my car's *right there;* I don't need him to walk me to it." But somehow, at some point, his attention and flattery stopped feeling unctuous; I actually started considering him. He was tall, built like a boxer, and very pretty, in a B-movie, sleepy-eyed matinee idol kind of way. In what felt like a relatively innocuous gesture, I invited him to go to a play with me at the old Westwood Playhouse. That was when Michael told me he was married.

Hold on a second.

Married? What?

This man had been hitting on me for months. There was nothing that ever indicated to me that he wasn't single. He told me he didn't always live with his wife; he had an apartment in West L.A. Oh. Okaaay.

I wore a skirt with boots and stockings to the theater in a quasi-unconscious effort to appear well protected. Our first date and something tells me to protect myself? With panty hose? It was odd — I was beguiled and repelled by the same thing: his intense sexuality. He knew he was attractive and counted on that to draw me in. It obviously had worked for him for years and it was the only currency he dealt in. We basically only saw each other at meetings, where he never failed to comment on my appearance, and at dinners after evening meetings, usually with groups of people. I was trying to keep it cool between us; I wanted other people around. I was very confused, feeling seduced by his powerful charm and allure, yet really put off by his calculated, fawning remarks.

It was this same spring of '94 that Elizabeth came to work with us as a nanny. She was from England, funny and capable, which got my heart right away. The kids immediately loved her and she became my trusty substitute when I was working or traveling. Elizabeth is one of the few people who saw the entire Michael Blodgett debacle in all its glory from the beginning to its sad, inglorious end. I think Elizabeth answered the door the first time he came to my house. She saw the looks, his and the ones he gave, that were often unnervingly intimate; she felt the pursuit and told me later it was a forgone conclusion: "You didn't have a chance; he was going to get you."

My part in that, because I always have one, is that somewhere I decided not to be perturbed by the salacious intent of his looks or flattery. In an uncomfortably familiar way he reminded me of Jack, how *he* looked at me, always assessing my appearance. I decided to view it all as *sincere* and *heartfelt.* It took some contorted effort but it filled a need in me; I desperately wanted to feel desired and, taken from that vantage point, how could I not? So, somewhere along the line, I thought, I'm not going to fight this anymore, and we began having an affair. Which was immediately awkward.

Although I still resisted some of the program, one of the first things I did embrace was the tenet of rigorous honesty: I really wanted to stop lying to myself and to other people; we were as sick as our secrets. Hiding that I was involved with Michael definitely fell under the category of deception and it upset me. I hated that I'd fallen into secret-keeping, it was so antithetical to whom I'd wanted to be. I had said to Michael, "If this is what you want, you've got to *say* something to your wife. What about rigorous honesty?" But he didn't tell her and I didn't stop seeing him.

There was fun and excitement with Michael. No one had ever pursued me like he had and he lived up to all the sexual promise. I had adjusted to being a sort of afterthought in romantic moments with David; with Michael I was the most important person in the room. It was the only time in my life I'd felt such an erotic connection with a man. That was the fragile basis upon which our entire relationship was balanced. And it was all fraught with lies.

I never knew what to tell people about Michael's background except pieces he'd told me. He'd been arrested a couple of times, usually around fights in bars. He seemed to revel in his "drunkalog" stories, which included colorful and often violent episodes involving alcohol. I got the feeling he could be a very nasty drunk and was grateful he had been sober about eighteen years when we met. People in Los Angeles remembered Michael as the dreamy, barechested, blond, curly-haired host of *Groovy,* a beach-party music show that aired on a local channel in the '60s. He had acted for a while but by the time I met him, he'd switched careers and was a screenwriter. He'd cowritten the movies *Turner & Hooch* and *Run* with a writing partner; he'd also penned a few sex-and-mayhem novels — *Captain Blood, White Raven,* and *The Hero and the Terror.* Michael had three daughters, one from each of his marriages. The youngest was about seven at this time and he brought her over once or twice. She was a smart and darling little girl.

One Saturday while we were still dating (is it dating if it only happens around meeting rooms and the bedroom?), Michael dropped by my house unannounced when Whitney, Allan, and my brother Dick were visiting. I was totally flustered with his sudden appearance and unsure how to explain him away. I think I omitted his last name in the introductions in an effort to obfuscate but had to leave him with my family out by the pool while I was getting some food ready. I watched from the kitchen window and I could hear Michael reeling off his credits to impress them, mentioning *Captain Blood, Turner & Hooch* . . . how he had all these great deals going and that he was expecting a phone call from Sherry Lansing any minute, yada yada yada. I could see the cool skepticism settling over Whitney's and Allan's faces. Finally, Dick got up, loped into the kitchen, and said to me, "Well, he seems just too good to be true," a small quizzical smile on his face. I could only shrug and sheepishly acknowledge, "Yes . . . I know. He's something, huh?"

One afternoon, I took the kids to Palisades Park for a picnic along the bluffs, and though Michael had joined us for a little while, he had to leave early. When it started to get dark, I packed up our things and got ready to leave, but Peter, who had been fractious with me much of the afternoon, wouldn't stay in the car. I can't remember anymore why he was angry, but he kept leaping out of the backseat and running off. After going through that hair-raising parent evaluation I had no confidence how to proceed. Could I pick up my child and toss him in the car if I thought that was the only way to get him in? He wasn't even ten at the time and I was beside myself with agitation.

Then Michael appeared, dressed to go for a run. I'd not answered the phone at home or the car phone and he was concerned. I told him what was up with Peter and he found him where he was hiding in the bushes. Peter took off running along the bluffs, in the direction of home. As Mollie got buckled into the car, I could see Michael run slowly after him. I circled the block and when I saw them next, they were running apace, talking and laughing. I drove home and waited. Thirty minutes later, Peter panted in through the door. They had jogged the entire way home. He came up and hugged me, pressing his face into my side, saying, "Hi, Mommy. I'm sorry."

Finally, Peter was interacting with an adult man who just listened to him, wasn't making him wrong, wasn't yelling at him, who wasn't being physically abusive to him. I thought, Here's a man who treats Peter like a respectable human being. He uses persuasion, not pressure. That really got my attention.

Not long afterward, Michael showed Mollie the same respect. He and I were standing along the sidelines at one of her weekend soccer games and she was goalie. At the end of one play a girl from the opposing team slammed into Mollie as she stood protecting the goal, absolutely wiping her out. A mass of players joined the collision and when the dust cleared, Mollie was at the bottom of the stack. Now, no one is allowed to enter the field during a game except referees or coaches, but Michael ran onto the field as the girls were getting up, swept up Mollie, and ran back to the sidelines with her in his arms. I could hear her protesting all the way, "Michael, you can't *do* this, take me back, you can't go on the field!" As he deposited her next to me he said, "Relax, this is largely symbolic. I just want you to know I'll show up for you."

Okay, he broke the rules, but I read it as a profound gesture. I was thinking how David had been so harsh with little Teddy and Eva both before and after we were married and how I'd longed for a different kind of influence for my children. Michael *was* different. I was seduced. I'd been wooed through my children.

We'd been seeing each other for about six months when the call from Michael came: "She knows," he said, explaining that his wife had followed him to my house, had confronted him when he got home, and now she was kicking him out of their house. "What shall I do?"

What? No, no, no. This was so *not* what I wanted. I remember being on the phone, standing in my redwood bedroom with late

351

afternoon sunlight streaming in, already feeling the loss of the serenity I usually found there. *Ever since I found out he was married, my fantasy was that he leave that marriage, if that's what he wanted, and for us to spend time together as single people . . . find out who we were together and see if we had a future. I knew that Michael was shrewd and didn't want to leave the safe boat he was in until he had one foot securely in another boat, that he'd push off from the first only when he absolutely had to.* I knew that without question my actions had led me inexorably to this moment I was not ready for. But I had put all this in motion; once again I thought I had no options. I said, "Come."

Our lives changed very quickly. Michael was a whirlwind. He was not a rules guy and earned the kids' immediate devotion by inviting them into our bedroom to watch television with us. I'd always had them on a pretty short TV leash, having grown up with the same: no watching until homework was done, a certain amount of reading attended to, etc. Michael was a great proponent of "kicking back," which was how he referred to any nonwork, nonproductive activity, with which my house now abounded. I didn't argue much because I could see that the kids, particularly Peter, seemed to thrive on being with Michael. This was a totally different way to be a man from the model Peter had grown up with. There was something lacking, to be sure — not a shred of intellectual stimulation to be gotten here — but the concept of not being found wrong every time there was a misstep was a revelation.

Michael was also very social and we started having lots of parties. Michael would invite people from the program over and we'd eat and play charades. It was fun to open my home to people and know how much they enjoyed being there. And the kids were a vital part of the parties, too. Michael's youngest daughter was spending time with us on occasion and the three children got on famously, putting on plays for the crowd or leading the crush into the swimming pool.

We had a nice thing going; it was smoother than I'd anticipated. Michael was trying to work on selling some scripts. We went to meetings together openly now. No more hiding. I still liked going to meals with a bunch of friends after our Tuesday-night meeting. Michael would help out and pick up the kids at school once in a while or drop them at soccer practice. Just *that* was huge for me. I could never ask David to help me out during a day; he was *not* available for that.

I did another TV movie around this time, *Betrayed: A Story of Three Women. Betrayed* had a light side and was an easy shoot, working with Swoozie Kurtz, who was lovely. The only odd part was that Michael would show up on location; he'd unexpectedly appear in the yard of the house where we were filming. He'd look nice and presentable, but I wasn't sure about having someone *around* like that, just watching. I liked to be with the film company when I was on a job. I didn't have guests come; I felt they distracted, interfered. But he liked it so I didn't say anything.

Then Michael brought up marriage. I never wanted to get married ever again and had been very clear about that from the start. To me, marriage to David was when I lost my voice, I lost my autonomy, my identity. I felt I lost *everything.* The divorce continued to be hugely expensive and I made sizable monthly child support payments. I had no intention of getting married to Michael. But at a certain point, I'd hear Michael talking with the kids about marriage. His daughter was becoming more of a fixture and the three children were jazzed by the idea. He'd say, "I think we should be married *for the kids.*" What for? Because it's moral? Are we concerned with morality now? And wait a minute . . . he was still married! We were going to have to deal with *that.* I don't know what he said to the children, but he definitely planted the idea of our becoming a storybook blended family because suddenly they started begging us and begging us to get married. Finally, I gave in. I couldn't keep up the argument. It seemed to mean so much to Peter and Mollie. I knew they loved Michael and loved our new life together.

Michael had to get a divorce and it became imperative to deal with it right away. Walking on the beach one day we had a disturbing talk about what lay ahead. His daughter and ex-wife lived in a sweet little house he owned in Brentwood and Michael was talking about selling the house because he was low on money and didn't seem to have any coming in. It's noteworthy that I at no time asked Michael if or how he would share living expenses with me. He seemed to expect that I would just pull that wagon, so I think I accepted that as my obligation, but never even asked him if he had any. He didn't seem concerned where or how his family would live on only half the money from the house. She had little income; there was no way they could support themselves.

It felt so heartless and really triggered my feelings of guilt about having contributed to the breakup of their family. I couldn't bear the idea of compounding their anguish, so I volunteered to pay what was left on their mortgage so they could stay where they'd been living. I wasn't trying to be a hero; I was trying to avoid a horrendous, untenable situation. I knew Michael was going to be looking at lawyer's fees and some kind of family support and I couldn't conceive of how he was going to handle all that since he wasn't earning any money.

I just remember us walking barefoot in the surf; my head was down, watching the small waves wash over my feet. These problems seemed unassailable and we had barely begun to scratch the surface. I knew this was going to be a very expensive venture. Every little wave that pulled back across the sand to the ocean was part of my savings disappearing. But I reminded myself that I was earning good money at the time and I just thought, Okay . . . I can do this. I *have* to do this. It falls to me. I'd better get a series.

And I did, actually. Within a short time I was coexecutive producing and starring in a new ABC Productions show called *The Faculty*. I thought it was a great concept — a half-hour comedy shot in front of a live audience (my favorite) and I played the vice-principal of a middle school; I was surrounded by a very talented cast of actors who played teachers, administration, a school nurse, and principal. Our writers and producers were terrific, seasoned professionals, which was important; we needed people there who knew what they were doing. I had no idea how to *produce;* it was just important to me that I had a say in many of the major decisions on the show. I did love that *The Faculty* sort of became a family affair. Almost every Friday that we taped, Michael and Elizabeth would bring the kids to sit in the bleachers and laugh themselves silly at our stellar cast of performers. I was proud of *The Faculty;* I thought it was well written, sharply directed, and wonderfully acted. I felt strong and accomplished and very grateful. Every night before our metaphorical curtain went up, the cast would gather backstage for a quiet cheer. I would whisper a prayer to just be a worker among workers; I didn't want my ego messing with the close relationship I'd forged with my fellow actors; we were all in it together.

If I looked only at the little things, there was much that made me think Michael could be a viable partner. With David, either he was seizing all the power or dumping all the responsibility on me. It was extraordinary to me that Michael helped with the kids on occasion, or that when we began to send out wedding invitations, he sat there and addressed the envelopes with me! I think I grasped at anything that gave me a sense of partnership. That's what made me think, Oh! This is what a marriage is! Because I had so little experience actually sharing a task with an equal partner, it felt safe. I told myself that *addressing envelopes together* is what marriage is all about.

I did everything I could not to focus on the larger things, because they gave me pause. The lying was very difficult. I had found myself telling half-truths to my children or friends about Michael being married. I'd hear him rattling off his credits again to someone, *anyone,* telling of some imminent job, which I knew wasn't true. Carla had even asked me once after a meeting, "What about the fact that he lies all the time?" I responded, "Yes . . . he does dance, doesn't he?" as if he were a precocious child. I mean . . . what??? I knew he embodied the concept of "hip, slick, and cool" as a preferred profile. He needed to *appear* to be a player; fact was preferable but not an issue. It made me queasy but I let it go.

When I think about why I made some of the decisions I made, a pivotal memory stands out. We were driving to get our marriage license in Norwalk, a gray, industrial suburb of Los Angeles, and we got lost in a tangle of freeway exchanges. I had a *Thomas Guide* on my lap, but I had arrived at an age where I couldn't read the tiny map and I had no glasses. Michael kept asking, "Do we take the 105? Do we get off there?" I just couldn't read the map and my tears started coming. I was so afraid to tell him I didn't know where we were. Years earlier, David and I were driving at night in Cape Cod, and I was reading the directions from a piece of paper. I could feel David getting angry and frustrated at what I was reading, and he began hitting me with his free hand. Then he pulled over to a parking lot, got out and came around to the passenger side, reached in and began slapping my face. So when Michael started asking me similar questions — "Where do we go?" — I guess I was triggered back to that incident and I was projecting the same outcome. Michael could see how upset I was so he eased over onto the shoulder of the freeway. He held me and said very quietly, "I know what's important."

That single extraordinary gesture made me feel seen and safe; I thought, *This is love.* So much of what followed over the next few years was ameliorated by the profound feelings he engendered in me that day.

He wasn't David. Michael got untold points for just not being *that.* In retrospect, it wasn't much of a hurdle: don't hit me, don't denigrate me, I'm yours.

There were a few people in my life who weren't so sure that marriage was the right decision for me. One day I was working at Paramount and my brother Dick showed up. Apparently he was there as a result of a family meeting, which had been held without me, where everyone agreed that my marrying Michael seemed like a terrible idea, but that I seemed too happy about it for them to try to stop me. Dick, my designated savior, was sent on a mission from the whole family: his job was to make sure I got an airtight prenuptial agreement so that when things fell apart, Michael wouldn't get half of everything.

I did as my family advised and got the prenup, although I felt acutely uncomfortable about it. It really upset Michael. It was the first time I'd seen him visibly angry; he said it showed a lack of faith in him. I was secretly happy to have the agreement but felt timid and guilty that I wanted that protection; somewhere I didn't feel I had the right to claim and protect what was mine, what I had earned. I don't remember what the particulars were, but the idea was that, should we divorce, he would not share in anything I had prior to our marriage. Right.

On October 21, 1995, after Michael and I had been together for a year, and his divorce was final, we were married at Westwood Presbyterian Church. I have to say, it was an extraordinary day! From the moment I got up that morning, I floated everywhere I went. I was in another world. I was so happy. I had found someone who loved me and I felt safe and cherished and everything was going to be fine. All five of my children were at home; it was a wonderfully joyous melee of activity as we girls all had our hair and makeup done by a friend. Peter had a sleek new suit and, as Michael's best man, combed his hair straight back, creating a startling resemblance to the groom.

During the ceremony, my eldest daughter, Eva, was my radiant maid of honor and stood with my stunning girls Kate and Mollie alongside me; opposite were Michael and

Peter. Ted and Allan had walked me up the aisle and I felt so confident and grateful for the strong relationships we all had. After we said our vows, we had a sumptuous reception at the Hotel Bel-Air. We had a buffet dinner for about a hundred friends and family members, a live band and singers, and hours of dancing. The whole thing was ridiculously expensive but I felt expansive in my happiness.

I was embarrassingly ingenuous about money. I only knew I earned it. David and I never discussed it. I didn't really spend very much (except for that Mercedes). I'd abdicated responsibility for it and didn't understand investments, taxes, accounting, IRAs, insurance, pensions or profit sharing, or endless etceteras. I had a business manager handle it all. Self-esteem, guilt, irresponsibility all played a factor. I didn't actually know how much money was there, but I hoped that somehow in the miasma, it would all work out.

Once we were married, I felt even more financially responsible for Michael. Although he always talked about some script or project he was working on, he had no income, and I didn't want him to constantly be asking me for cash for fear of shaming him. Having him be responsible for himself never occurred to me. We devised a plan where he became my "manager" (in name only, thank goodness), and I would pay him a salary that I could deduct from my income. I hated the cliché of this but it seemed like a plan that gave him some freedom and dignity at the same time. I also gave him a credit card.

Right around this time the lease was up on my car and I was planning on getting the new model of my current Mercedes, having developed a taste for them. Michael drove a huge old Cadillac with torn roof fabric and a reluctant engine. It was well past time to replace it and I had gone with him to peruse the Cadillac dealership for options. He'd liked several but here was my dilemma: I wouldn't be comfortable if I had a more expensive car than he did. *I* would have felt shame, then . . . as if I were showing off, even if I had earned it, as if it weren't right for me to have one if he didn't. Michael told me when he moved in, "In my old house, *I* was the star in my family," and that contributed to my feeling that the only thing I could do would be to lease Michael the exact same $100,000 Mercedes that I was getting. I was spending so much to mitigate my low self-esteem, it made my stomach hurt.

Despite some good reviews, *The Faculty* lasted only one season. But movie scripts were coming my way — some of them good, some less good. I was tired and interested in taking some time off, but my business manager made it perfectly clear that I was not in the position to be picky. He said to me, "You cannot turn anything down. You are hemorrhaging money." What?

I could see how that might be true. There was ongoing child and spousal support to be paid, divorce lawyer's fees that were still being paid, three private school tuitions (thank goodness David paid half for Mollie's and Peter's school), Kate's college tuition, Michael's ex-wife's expenses, our regular household expenses. And Michael had planned some pretty swanky vacations: the Ritz-Carlton in Hawaii with the kids, the Waldorf-Astoria in New York with the kids and several times without, always first-class. This was more lavish than I was used to traveling but I couldn't argue that the kids enjoyed it — prudence never won out. We made three trips to Lake Powell over the years, twice with some of the kids and us on a long houseboat, and once, most extravagantly, with about twelve of us on two houseboats, all trips requiring air and ground transportation. I knew it was pricey but I did so love having all the family together and we had incredible, memorable times on these trips. They became legend and we tell tales of them to this day. There were probably more prudent ways to have traveled but I couldn't really regret any of it. I figured I'd just have to get another job.

Michael had family in Minneapolis, where my brother Brian and his wife and kids lived, so we'd often go there to see them too. Brian often referred to Michael as Mr. Big Big Big because of how he'd go to the local market and bring home HUGE porterhouse steaks for ten or fifteen people at dinner — a couple of hundred dollars just for the meat. His need to appear generous and effusive overrode any of my objections.

What was harder was what felt like a growing irrationality on Michael's part. We stopped going to after-meeting dinners with friends because I'd become so uncomfortable with his behavior. There'd be about ten of us at a table and when the sizable check came, Michael would grab it, plopping down his credit card, saying, "It's on me; I just got a residual." No he didn't. *I* was paying for that meal. He lied, even when he knew *I* knew the truth.

It didn't seem to bother him that people

knew he lied. He seemed kind of proud of it. I once went with him to our little local branch of Union Bank, where he had an account, and the manager greeted him with a warm hug. He was cashing a check. It was made out to a fictitious name for $600. He told the pretty cashier, who also seemed to know him, that the payee had done some writing research for him but wasn't able to get to a bank; could they please cash it and Michael would get the money to him. She seemed to know the routine and didn't hesitate; he signed the phony name on the back, she handed him the cash. He passed a $100 bill to her as he pocketed the rest, saying, "Thanks for your help, honey." It all felt slippery but I wasn't clear it was illegal. A couple of years later I learned that this was called *check kiting.*

In 1998 at the Revlon/UCLA Breast Center, I was diagnosed with ductal carcinoma in situ, or DCIS, in my right breast. My DCIS was at zero stage, caught early through my regular mammogram. DCIS, the most common type of noninvasive breast cancer, occurs when the cells that line the milk ducts calcify, become cancerous, and overproliferate. I was having none of it — I was very much in denial and was determined to find some alternative to the surgery they were suggesting. I mean, it's stage *zero!* I figured if I didn't give it any credibility, I could get away with just being annoyed. However, my daughter Kate, then a student at Yale, was the research queen, and she determined I had no alternative but to proceed with the needle core biopsy the doctors recommended. I capitulated.

Michael, on the other hand, started flipping out. Michael was a breast man. He really valued my breasts. He was afraid that *he* was going to lose my breast, or that I might be misshapen, which would be calamitous for him. The doctors assured him that the object was to remove the disease but leave my breast intact. Which they did, but they couldn't get clean margins, so I had a second surgery. In total, they removed the equivalent of a medium-sized cupcake from my inner right breast.

During the course of this Michael became so panic-stricken that he scheduled an appointment with the doctor and insisted that if she would remove only the tiniest amount possible he would make a big donation to the hospital. *Of course* she removed as little as possible, as she would have even without his extravagant overture. I sent ten thousand dollars to UCLA to fulfill his promise, but I was resentful and agitated by his behavior. I had been in touch with my old friend Suzanne Benoit all through this and she had to remind me, "*You* are not your breasts." I had lost sight of my value; my husband was measuring me by my bra cup.

I got another movie, *Wednesday Woman,* being shot in Vancouver, and I was enormously grateful for a break from that cancer scene. Luckily, I needed neither chemo nor radiation, so I was free to go film in Canada. Michael now came to all of my location jobs, traveling to Toronto, Vancouver, Arizona twice, and North Carolina twice, and he was having growing discomfort with scenes that called for me to be physical with another man in any way. Fortunately, most of the movies were simple stories where romance never figured. However, doing *Holy Joe,* in North Carolina about six months before, he'd started grinding me about simply hugging John Ritter, who played my pastor-husband, in a benign scene *that called for me to hug him.*

Well, *Wednesday Woman* presented more of a challenge for him, because in it I was married to John Heard and having a heated affair with Peter Coyote. Michael had ideas. He's say, "Instead of going into this big clinch with Coyote, and kissing him, have them put the camera at this angle and then just *hug* him and they won't see the difference. You're the star; you can make them do this." This was making me crazy. He had no business butting into my work. This kind of interference, coming from someone who supposedly understood show business, was ridiculous and astoundingly immature. I felt invaded, disrespected, and bullied. I made none of the adjustments he wanted, which infuriated him.

I didn't always know what to expect from him. One day I came home from work and he was nowhere to be found. Hours later he showed up, dragging himself in, acting dopey and looking terribly sunburned. He had gone out to write in the park and had fallen asleep. He'd written nothing, but he never did, no matter how much "work" he seemed to bring with him.

Michael had a walking, brooding resentment against me even when I had harmless scenes with the men; I could feel the tension even on days I wasn't working. We were in Frazier Park one afternoon and he told me he was thinking of writing a movie about lap dancing. "I think I'd better go try out some lap dances just to see what it's about. Don't you think? I have to do my research. What do you think about *that?*"

So this threat was quid pro quo? He was equating his fucking around with my doing my job? He was threatening me with this? I was terribly upset by the inference and the verbal aggression. He might be able to receive a lap dance, but I knew he wasn't capable of writing anything anymore.

Back home, a good friend in the program who'd been acting as sponsor to Michael for a while, told me that his downhill slide began during my cancer scare and picked up speed. I had to admit, I'd known it had started years before. When Michael first moved into my house, along with his clothes came a shallow cardboard box full of about twenty different yellow and clear pill bottles. I looked at them and found many of the labels torn half off. I immediately suspected he was trying to hide the drugs' names but no . . . the drug was clearly visible. They were mainly painkillers and tranquilizers, Roxiprin, which seemed to be his favorite, Ativan, Percocet, Klonopin, Xanax, and others. The pharmacy, doctor, and patient names were missing, which I much later learned was a method used when playing the pharmacies by getting prescriptions under fake names or fake doctors, both of which he was doing. I *had* asked what all the pills were for and he said, "Oh . . . I get migraines . . . from the accident," referring to a bad collision he'd had some years before.

Pretending was easier than questioning, because what would I do with the answers? I didn't want to know what was going on.

Then came the behavior that was difficult to ignore. We'd go to parties, and Michael rarely let me out of his sight. Or he'd disappear and later on I'd find him passed out in a bedroom. Once, during an event appearance in Daytona Beach, I found him all alone down by the ocean, vomiting into a towel, fighting withdrawal.

Elizabeth and I tried to monitor Michael when we were home because he couldn't tell when he'd had too much. Then Mollie and Peter were telling me stories about what happened when Michael had picked them up at school. Coming home, he would stop at an intersection, forget what he was doing, and let the car slowly roll into oncoming traffic while they screamed in terror from the backseat. That was the end of that. I never let him drive them again.

I started feeling crazy. I was trying to manage him and it made me nuts. I'd hear the rattle of pills in my sleep and be up like a shot to find him with pills stuck on his mouth or chasing them through the air, his fingers plucking at nothing. His behavior became so erratic and unmanageable that I began attending 12-step meetings meant for the friends and relatives of alcoholics. I needed counsel and direction. While I was there I bumped into a man who knew Michael very early in his sobriety and I filled him in about what was going on. He told me, "You need to get him out of your house."

I was looking for permission. I was so grateful to be told what to do because I was at a loss.

As soon as I got home, I started calling around trying to find a bed at a rehab center. The closest one I could find that also had a medical facility was the Rehabilitation Center at Scripps Memorial Hospital Encinitas. But when I told Michael he had to go there, he refused.

I told him I didn't care where he went; he just had to pack up and leave. Immediately.

Thank goodness the drugs had rendered Michael malleable as opposed to belligerent. But drugged or not, he chose the high life; for the next week, Michael lived in a $600-a-night room at Shutters on the Beach in Santa Monica.

One morning he called me and said he was in trouble; he was having difficulty standing.

"Are you ready?" I asked him. "I'll only come to take you to rehab *now*."

He said okay and I told him to be ready downstairs; I called and made arrangements at Scripps, got to Shutters and somehow wrestled him into my car, and we made the two-hour drive to Encinitas, a town near San Diego. He kept passing out on the drive. A couple of times, I thought he was dead.

When I came home from dropping Michael off, Elizabeth sat me down and said there were things she'd been afraid to tell me for some time. She said that Michael's behavior had been getting more bizarre over the years and he'd approached her frequently, quite possibly while he was drugged, and the instances had been hair-raising: Michael offering her money in exchange for oral sex; Michael quietly asking her to show him her breasts for money, often when I was right there in the room or on the phone; Michael coming downstairs, high and waving a loaded handgun; offering the cleaning lady money to find the jar of Roxoprin he'd hidden but then could not find. Elizabeth told me that she'd kept all this secret because she worried the information would be devastating to me. She was also afraid I might not believe her and she'd lose her job. She was feeling lost and abandoned as well.

The weight of this new information, combined with having denied all that I knew for so long, was crippling.

He called that night, sounding steadier, but I could hardly speak to him. He said, "You know why I started using, don't you? That fucking prenuptial agreement." What?

I asked him, "Are you going to stay in rehab?"

"If I stay, are you going to be there when I come back?"

I said, "No."

He said, "I'm outta here." He hung up, called a limo company, and got a ride back up from San Diego.

I called my lawyer.

CHAPTER 14

Now I was moving Michael out of my life. I sat on the sofa in my living room and just howled with grief. What was I doing with myself? I was fifty-three and even with all I had been through it appeared that I'd learned nothing. I was in the same place as with David, just over a decade ago, except this time the divorce was going to be twice as expensive. I had earned a lot of money during the marriage but so much had been spent. The legal fees were higher; Michael was going to get $11,000 a month in support, plus, because I was more well known, he was getting a huge chunk of cash for something called "personal good will," a misnomer if ever there was one.

In divorcing Michael I felt nothing but relief. However, it was very difficult for Peter and Mollie, who'd had none of the issues with Michael that I did and consequently, although they'd been aware of some bad behavior, in no way did it color their affection and regard for him. All they knew was that this vibrant, exciting man was gone from their lives, it was my fault, and I never asked how they felt about it but I could tell they were very angry with me. I felt like I was in a tough position. Although I knew they loved him, I felt if they were going to understand why I'd made him leave, I'd have to give them the litany of behaviors that made his staying untenable. Which would be crushing to them. So I said nothing. I had such a huge ax to grind, I selfishly could only take in feelings that matched mine; I had no room for their missing him.

Right around this time I went to my regular Thursday-morning women's meeting to mark my anniversary of being sober for ten years. I stood up and started weeping, haltingly revealing where I was on that day. With ten years I'd have hoped to have more solutions, more serenity in my life, but I had none. At the end of the meeting, a friend came up and suggested that I might benefit from counseling and gave me the names of three therapists. She said, "Make an appointment with each of these therapists. Tell your story to each one and see who you respond to. Then pick one and start going." And she said, "Michael is not the wound; he is only the sword in the wound," the meaning of which eluded me for some time but I understand it today.

For the first time in the history of my sobriety, I did *exactly* as I was directed because I had no solutions. There was something about one of the therapists — Sarah — who made me feel like she really listened to me. I had thought my pain was so huge I wouldn't find someone to help me contain it all. I felt Sarah could do that. I've been seeing her ever since.

While I was fumbling my way to stability through divorce and therapy, Whitney was in the middle of a horrible couple of years. It began with a simple bit of clumsiness and went downhill from there. In 2001, she and Allan were at their Malibu home working when my mother tripped outside of her office and couldn't get up. Allan found her lying flat on the ground, immobilized by what turned out to be a broken right ankle and torn ligaments in the left. She spent nine months in a wheelchair, sleeping in a hospital bed in their living room, with Allan doing his best to nurse her. Whitney had always been a tough woman, but I think this was when she started to soften a bit and really learned to appreciate Allan and the loving way he tended to her.

When 2002 rolled around, we wanted to help my mother put that painful year behind her, so Dick, Allan, my mother, and I all met at The Lobster in Santa Monica on February 20, 2002, to celebrate her seventy-sixth birthday. Over coffee, she mentioned that she'd been diagnosed with esophageal cancer. She talked about it so lightly as in, "I don't think it will be a big thing. I'll have to do *this* and have treatment for *that* . . ." But it got my attention enough that I went home and, after I called all the kids, I did a Google search. There are two kinds of esophageal cancer and hers, squamous cell carcinoma, was the more serious variety. A bit later, Kate called me; she'd found some more technical online medical sites and they all indicated that few people with squamous cell esophageal cancer survive beyond two years.

For the next several months, Whitney and Allan crisscrossed the country — to the Mayo Clinic, Memorial Sloan-Kettering, anywhere they could think of — looking for clinical trials my mother might participate in. When they were in Los Angeles I would drive her to the doctor's appointments, which afforded us some time together.

These were usually quiet, nonchatty drives, punctuated with her moans of discomfort. Whitney's health began to deteriorate, but she was not without her humor. Once when they were at Brigham and Williams hospital in Boston, a nurse said to a thin, white-haired Whitney, "And this is your son?" and pointed at my lean, bearded, broad-shouldered stepfather, who had a couple of years on her. Allan froze, terrified that Whitney would be insulted. But instead my mother just burst out laughing. There was always relief when Whitney laughed.

There weren't a lot of bright spots, though. Mostly she was in pain, with difficulty swallowing due to the tumor in her esophagus. She had to spend several nights at Cedar-Sinai Hospital and Allan, Brian, and I took turns sleeping on a cot by her bedside. For the first time in years my mother and I had some quiet time together. I was still tentative around her, unsure of my moves, so I decided to just get her talking; ask her anything. We talked about her childhood and when she started acting; she was quite animated and warmed to the topic, but she tired quickly and would just get quiet.

She said that at times it felt like she was getting ready to let go, even though this was only three months after she'd been diagnosed. She talked about acceptance. She said that stimuli seemed to come from a very narrow source and she was trying not to look outside that source. And that is how I experienced her: a very slow shutting down, seemingly lost to interaction for long stretches at a time. Then she'd give a start, awakening to having been awake but gone — she was so often disoriented.

Allan told me his worst moment was telling Whitney he was planning on hiring hospice care for her because that was when she finally grasped that she wasn't going to get better. Allan did his best to persuade her that the care workers would only be there so they could help him out, but she didn't believe him.

Kate, Ted, and his wife, Cheryl, were at the Vineyard with Allan many times over my mother's last weeks. Kate had told me of one afternoon trying to change the bed linens with Allan while Whitney was still in the bed. She was floating in and out of sleep and was connected to humming medical equipment, so she was no help, obviously. Kate peeled back blankets, and Allan gave a tug on a sheet and fell backward, stepping on the cord of Whitney's oxygen apparatus. The room sank to immediate silence and

Kate and Allan looked at each other in shock, wide-eyed, aghast. Kate gasped, *"You pulled the plug!"* And they fell about laughing so hard, desperate to dispel the weight of the moment as they hastened to plug the machine in again. I love my family so much for their black, macabre humor. No*thing* and no *one* is too precious to preclude being a target, particularly when the need to laugh is great, even if it's at my dying mother.

It's absurd for me to sit here, as a healthy adult woman, and tell you how I'd have *preferred* my mother had handled her impending death. However, I wish she'd have allowed us all to talk about the looming loss of her. But because she couldn't acknowledge it to us, we couldn't bring it up, couldn't talk about our feelings, try to clean any slate. I didn't feel like she was putting up a front for us; to me it felt like denial, and in the face of that, I didn't feel I had permission to say anything. I could only sit with her; be with her, acting like I was waiting for her health to improve. Even as she was dying, I was still wanting from her, thinking, *Look, even now at the end, you have nothing for me* . . . as if she were withholding from me. I think of that now and I wince with shame that I was still so self-absorbed.

Whitney was at their home on Martha's Vineyard when she died — just seven months after her diagnosis — on September 28, 2002. She was seventy-six. As per her wishes, she was cremated. We had two memorial services — one on the Vineyard and one in their home in Malibu. The first one, in Malibu, was very informal: we invited friends and family and anyone who wanted to could stand up and share memories of her. Back in 1987, once the acting jobs were not forthcoming, Whitney had reinvented herself one more time. She produced and directed a documentary called *Reno's Kids: 87 Days + 11,* about Reno Taini, a California high school teacher who helped troubled students turn their lives around. Reno and his wife had stayed close with my parents over the years, and he spoke quite movingly at the memorial about the importance of Whitney's documentary and what a deep and natural connection she made with all these troubled teenagers.

My mother? Gifted at working with *young* people?

Were we talking about the same person?

I just lost it. All I could think as he eulogized my mother was, Then what was wrong with *me?* Why could my mother be so loving to these kids, these strangers, while ignoring and emotionally abandoning her own children?

Here was a lovely gathering meant to honor and celebrate this woman whom so many loved, and all I could contribute were tears, frustration, and longing. I was devastated by Whitney's death. I was a walking protoplasm of pain, plagued by a profound sense of loss and rejection my whole life. I must have been hoping until the very last that *something* would give, but with her death I realized that ship had sailed. There would be no healing with her, no being made whole. I'd been so slow to learn that *nobody* could fix me. If it were going to happen, I would have to do it myself. It was an inside job.

My divorce from Michael was finalized right after my mother was diagnosed. I was relieved. I prefer one battle at a time. I'd reconnected with Carla at an art opening that same month and we started spending time working to repair and restore our friendship. She had been a great support and source of wisdom for me while my mother was dying and had come to the memorial service. Carla noted that because I'd avoided much of the self-examination process suggested in the program, I'd not laid to rest many of the issues that brought me into the program in the first place ten years before, the primary issue being my mother! Drinking had been but a symptom of my alcoholism; I used drinking to solve my problems, but my problems were caused by my *thinking,* my selfish, self-centered, self-seeking, self-pitying thinking, and the destructive feelings and resentments that resulted. This way, I developed and preserved a belief system that filtered all information through a warped prism of being unwanted, unloved and unlovable.

So Carla started working with me, putting me through program steps to dispel that belief system and create a new one. She helped me find clarity around the deep resentments I had clung to since I was a kid. I resented that my brothers and I had to stop calling our mother Mom or Mommy in favor of her stage name. I resented that she didn't acknowledge us as her children for a long time. I resented that she basically gave us to our stepfather, Jack, to raise while she pursued her career.

My job was to try to understand her, figure out who *she* was, learn what kind of mothering/role modeling *she* received, what did *she* want that she didn't get, what were *her* disappointments in life and how did she deal with them? And why did she make the choices with her children that she made? After I'd written about all of that, I heard something at a meeting that clarified a lot of it for me. A woman was talking about our parents as wells and that we were wired to go to our parent-wells for nurturing and sustenance. Many of us found our parent-wells were empty, but they weren't empty *at us.* They were just *empty.* Although my entire life I had experienced myself as being *the target* of her empty well, there was no fact to support it; they were just my feelings.

The next part of my job was to learn to have compassion for my mother's empty well, to accept my mother's limitations and forgive her. Well, as soon as I started thinking of ways I had disappointed my own children, I quickly had a much better perspective. I thought about being too fearful to protect them from David, times when I traveled and worked when they probably needed me, times I left them with nannies, times I, like Whitney, had chosen work over my kids, times when I'd had too much to drink to be useful to them in any way — the list is endless. I could honestly say, however, that I did the best I could given the tools and information I had at the time, and therefore I had to allow the same for Whitney.

What I came away with was a sense of understanding Whitney and appreciating her in ways I wouldn't allow myself to before. In truth, she gave me the very best she had. What *I* thought of it at the time is not important because *I wasn't in a position to know.*

Many of what I think are my best traits as a mother were developed *as a protest* to what I had experienced with her. Working or not, she never came to any school function or play that I was in. So, I was very attentive with all my children. When not working, I was with them all the time, making breakfasts, packing lunches, doing carpool, play dates, homework, projects, school breakfasts, soccer games and practice, gymnastics, baseball games and practice, swim meets, piano, violin, track meets, open houses, teacher meetings, performances. Every single one was an effort to *not* recreate what had happened with me. I understood that my *absence* had more power than my presence. They may not have cared so much if I saw a particular play or recital. But my *not* being there could be devastating to them . . . and besides being very interested in what they were into, I wanted to come anyway. Thank goodness, I learned to love doing it all. I am grateful for a gift my mother never knew she gave.

With an eye toward broadening my world, my therapist Sarah had encouraged me to branch out, take chances, do something different to draw people into my life, assuage my loneliness. Being less a warrior than a copycat, I threw myself into dance classes. Sarah was a ballroom dancer and she'd spoken so passionately about her challenges there, I thought I'd give it a try, too. When I first started at L.A. Dance Experience, I probably wrestled with my teacher, Russell Adcock, more than danced with him. I recall early on, after a particularly strenuous tour around the dance floor, he walked me to the side, patted my hand, and said, "Okay, next time, I'll lead." So for many years, I worked to be still and feel his subtle lead. That in itself was a form of surrender. I loved it and continued dancing for several years.

About a year after my mother died my twins got ready to go off to college. Peter went to Dickinson College in Pennsylvania and Mollie was going to Skidmore College in upstate New York, with her first six months in London. All five of my children chose to attend colleges on the East Coast; besides the attraction of their respective colleges, I think it was a prudent and effective move to escape parental oversight.

Never having gone to college myself, I was dying of jealousy. Years they had spent or would be spending traveling, learning, experiencing, broadening their minds, were the years I spent taking drugs, getting married, and having children. In no way do I regret having my children — they've brought me more happiness than I would have thought possible. But I do regret that I didn't have the discipline or drive to pursue a higher education; in my fantasy, it would have given me greater self-esteem, made me smarter, given me answers. Kate told me once that all college taught her was where to look for the answers.

So my last kids were going; the oft-mentioned empty nest was looming. Many times I'd told friends of when my firstborn, Ted, went off to Dartmouth. I had been in a depression for weeks in anticipation of his departure; we were very close; he was just a little younger than I'd been when he was born. He had been a great energy and life force to be around and I was missing him desperately long before he left. I realized that he was the last buffer between me and

David. I drove him to the airport and in those days, nontravelers could walk up to the departure gate, too. First, I was hanging on his neck sobbing; then as he tried to get on the plane I might have been clutching his ankle trying to retard his progress, getting dragged with each step down the chute. I didn't care about all the stares; I was bereft at losing my boy.

Eva had gone from boarding school to Wheaton in Massachusetts and the transition felt seamless and good. Kate, also, had gone back East to boarding school at Exeter, then to Yale. So by the time Peter and Mollie were ready to take off, I was pretty much an old hand at launching my offspring. Now it was just " 'Bye! I love you! 'Bye!" Although I was going to miss them acutely, I felt healthier, more grounded than when the others had moved on and less like I was being abandoned. I don't have to do that drama anymore. In another way, this was a profoundly exciting time for me: I was fifty-five years old and I'd never lived alone in my life.

I have a one-bedroom guesthouse in the back over my garage that I've rented off and on over the years. As my youngest were wafting off to college, a young sports coach contacted me through mutual friends. Paula was thirty and gay and wanted to know if the guesthouse was available. My eldest daughter, Eva, had recently separated from her husband and she and my granddaughter, Sophia, were living in the house with me for a while. (Okay . . . I still wasn't living *alone,* but the truth is, I wasn't directly responsible *to* or *for* anyone for the first time since 1967!) I told the young woman, "Fine, come check it out," which she did and voilà, Paula became my new tenant.

As tenants go, she was ideal — very quiet, polite, and respectful of my privacy. It was a perfect setup for any renter: private street, gated property, separate from the main house, separate entrance, lots of trees and privacy all the way around. *I* could have lived back there happily. Paula had an independent schedule and I never knew when she was there. But she was also available when I didn't feel like going somewhere by myself. Occasionally, we'd wind up going to a movie or taking a walk, finding we had a common love of reading.

I was half heartedly seeing a guy for a while and on occasional Thursday nights we would go to the Santa Monica Pier and listen to music. Paula joined us once or twice, dancing with another friend, Keith. I never danced to rock music, so my date and

I sat on the side and I just watched Paula dance. I think it started then. I couldn't take my eyes off her. After that, whenever I was at home, I always watched for her; I wanted to know where she was. If she was out by the swimming pool, I'd go out there, or just check on her from inside the house. She was blond, tan, and very fit, so attractive. I loved that she was a reader; we'd swap books and talk about our favorite authors. I felt giddy and silly and was thrilled to have someone so responsive living so close.

In August, about six weeks after Paula moved in, I left for a short business trip to Daytona, Florida. While I was gone, we started sending texts to each other, texts that were fun, flirty, cryptic. And, I thought, inescapably provocative.

I remember one night there, standing on the balcony of my beachfront hotel overlooking the long, flat, deep beach of Daytona; the sunset was brilliant and I was afroth with confusion. What was going on? For one thing, I couldn't believe the way I was reacting to this young woman who was *twenty-five years my junior.* We seemed to have a great time together. I remember sitting next to her at a comedy performance and I would swear that sparks were leaping between us. But it wasn't until I was in

Florida and the texting began that I could no longer deny that *something* was going on. But was it only going on *with me?* Was I making this up?

The first morning I was back I asked her to go on a walk and we headed down to the beach. And I put that very question to her, as if she were responsible . . . what was going on? And she kissed me. And the highway was behind me and the lapping waves were in front of me; the whizzing cars blended with the gulls overhead as she kissed me; I held my breath to prolong the suspended moment.

"I can't do this," I said as I pulled away. "This isn't going to happen." I was in *shock* — that she kissed me and that I had liked it. I wished that I'd had the guts to do it first. I don't even remember walking back up from the beach, going home, anything. I felt as if I were wearing a beekeeper's bonnet with the bees *inside,* crazily buzzing all about my head. I couldn't think; I couldn't focus; yet I was not confused. Despite my denial, I wanted to be with her.

I made love with Paula for the first time late on a Saturday afternoon in her apartment over my garage. I remember this because afterward I went to a dance upstairs at the Hollywood Club, where my dance group occasionally gathered. Sarah was there. The dances were usually held at the Westwood studio of L.A. Dance Experience, where the setup was vaguely reminiscent of high school dances. Men and women gathered around the perimeter of the dance floor waiting for either a dance they recognized or an invitation to the floor. Neither was actually required, judging from the range of dancers gliding around the room. Many experienced couples could skim over the floor with style and finesse, their progress occasionally hampered by the likes of me, struggling to master a sequence of steps.

At the Hollywood Club the whole setup was different. There were several café tables arranged where you could linger upon arrival, change into your dance shoes, get yourself a beverage, survey the room. Here, for some reason, I felt the therapist rules were different. In Westwood, at most I'd nod or smile hello to Sarah but would rarely engage in conversation and never hang out. But once in a while in Hollywood I might sit at her table with her friend, also named Meredith. This night, *this earth-shaking Saturday night,* I ran up the stairs to the studio, breathless, flushed, heart pounding, on *fire.* I felt delirious and out of my mind with excitement and a secret I was dying to tell but knew I couldn't. I could barely croak out hellos as I threw myself, wild-eyed and red-cheeked, into a chair at their table. I was sure anyone looking at me could tell, "Why, she's just slept with a woman and has been turned inside out!" I think Sarah just took me in, eyebrows raised. I might have muttered something about having "just met someone."

Oddly, I danced better that night than most. A nice man I knew named Tom asked me to waltz with him and I felt a strength, confidence, and abandon I rarely did on the dance floor. I was dancing with a secret. I was giddy with discovery. He spun me out and I twirled as a jubilantly just-born woman. He dipped me low and I leaned back gracefully as the lover of a woman. I felt more fully, comprehensively alive than ever before in my life.

I want to be clear. This was not a revelatory experience because I'd had great sex. The sex was fine. And I'd had great sex before without this feeling. Something shifted in me; there was a quickening and I understood that it was with a woman that I would find myself.

It's like when I was a kid. I had always struggled to see. Close up was a snap but anything further than the length of my arm dissolved into softness and blur. I had no concept of my sight in relation to how others saw. I thought this is how everyone sees things. One day when I was about twelve, I was sitting outside in my backyard with my friend Maxine and, on a whim, I tried on her glasses. I sat up straight and my mouth fell open in wonder. The trees, which had before always resembled lollipops, now had *leaves.* Individual *leaves!* I could have cried. Oh, so *this* is how the rest of the world sees? Being with Paula was like putting on glasses and being delivered to the real world. Suddenly there was clarity and I felt singular and exotic and untouchable. I saw leaves. I *fit.*

Of course, at the same time I had this prickly problem of being a quasipublic figure. I liked my life private. And the truth is, I couldn't have planned for this to have unfolded in a setting more conducive to secrecy, totally private and insular. It probably happened the only way it could have. No one had to know. I was very concerned about our relationship becoming known in the business, although I was hardly someone the paparazzi tracked. I did think the general public would have a very difficult time embracing me as a lesbian when I'd been a sort of "favorite mom" figure for so many years. It would just be so confusing. *I* was confused; why wouldn't the public be? I wasn't unhappy with my self-discovery but I wasn't sure what it meant. Was I gay? Or was I just Paula-gay? I couldn't tell and the truth was it did not matter. I was right where I wanted to be.

However, Elizabeth had to know; there was no way she wasn't going to be suspicious because she was in the house five days a week, now working as my personal assistant. I do *not* hide my feelings well, and I didn't want to have to lie if my car was home but I was not to be found. I was nervous, braced myself, and told her, expecting God knows what kind of Catholic blather from her. She just dismissed me with a wave, saying she thought as much, she'd seen the signs. "As long as you're happy," she said, "and she's so much better than Michael. She's so cute it makes me wish *I* were gay!" What? Boy, gotta hand it to the English, poker-faced *and* unflappable!

I told Eva because she had a right to know, living in the house, and she would have to be blind not to know anyway. Eva did not surprise me with her acceptance; she's always been a most open and laissez-faire girl, but I didn't know that included her mom in a lesbian relationship. I got to see her in a new way, too. Eva's only comment was wondering about Paula's age, which I was trying to downplay. Both Eva and Ted were older than Paula, which made me blanch, as if I were a lesbian cougar.

I would have loved that age question to disappear, but not one of my friends who knew about Paula let it pass. I am one of the older ones in my group and the fact that she was *so* much younger than all of them gave them pause. And made me feel defensive. I just found someone who has turned my head around; why would I care about her age? I was seeing life in a new way.

I actually saw *everything* in a new way, even the book I was reading: When I went to go visit Peter at Dickinson that fall for the first Parents' Weekend, I was reading Jeffrey Eugenides' extraordinary novel *Middlesex.* When I got to the part where the intersexed heroine Callie has a lesbian relationship with her best friend, I was just exclaiming, "Oh, my God. Oh, my God." I had started reading the book as an adult but was thrilling to it like an adolescent. Reading that and knowing that Paula was just outside my door at home made all the passages feel very real to me.

In absolutely every way, being in an intimate relationship with a woman felt totally different than when I was with a man. I felt seen and accepted as a whole person, not just for surface, shallow reasons. I felt a connection and a safety; I had more of a sense of who I was. I felt equal. Now, in truth, it could have been the men I chose, because, face it, I wasn't a very good picker. I had felt a quiet panic that dictated I had to be with any man to have value. I remember a woman telling me once about a lawyer she'd been referred to about a personal matter and I *immediately* thought, "I wonder if he's married?" I was both arbitrary and desperate. It seemed to have nothing to do with who they were or what they were like. I remember Sarah asking me, when I'd just begun therapy with her, what I looked for in a man. Well. That stumped me. I sat there for a minute and started to answer, then stopped. Tried again to offer an answer, and stopped again. After a few moments of silent, tense deliberation, I had it. "Hair," I blurted. "He has to have hair." Character, honesty, integrity, fidelity, or kindness never occurred to me. I'd never asked for them and never got them.

A good friend of mine who is gay invited me and Paula over for a dinner party. After all of the tightly controlled secrecy I maintained, this felt like a tiny bit of freedom and validation. We were in the company of other gay women and it felt safe and exciting to be so relaxed and uninhibited. It was not lost on me that the other women there were, for the most part, with peers, partners around their own age. I was glad no one made any comments; it's a very accepting lot, but I felt an imbalance. The age thing was starting to get to me. The sexual tension with Paula had been a powerful glue but as that initial heat subsided somewhat, I was beginning to notice a callowness, appropriate to her age, perhaps, but not particularly palatable to me. On a few occasions, I'd gone out with Paula and *her* friends and the age disparity was an inescapably looming issue. I felt even *her* friends looking at me oddly.

What was I looking for in my life? What was important? I wanted love and connection and I felt like I was experiencing that in a totally new way that was open and liberating. That all felt right and good until I took the next step and considered what I wanted *down the road*. How likely was it that I could build a life with Paula? Why in the world was she even with me considering the age difference? I didn't want to be a mother figure; it didn't seem like a promising basis for a sexual relationship. I was interested in something healthy and mutual but Paula was just moving into her powerful years. I wanted to be with someone solid, with maturity and self-knowledge that only come with age. This was not tilting in my favor. I was in anguish. For a few blessed months I got to live with what felt like *the answer,* and now I had to acknowledge the absurdity of that idea. I had to consider letting it go. I had discovered the wheel and was seeing it didn't fit on my little bike. But I knew. I *knew* no other wheel would ever come my way. Part of me fervently wanted to put it on anyway. *Let* the bike be lopsided, just don't let her go. *This will never happen for me again.*

But in April, after months of indecision and despair, I asked Paula to move out and then lived with the horror of what I'd done.

CHAPTER 15

As it turns out, looking for a woman works the same as looking for a man: you ask friends, you go to places where you might meet people with mutual interests; you go on dates and see if you click.

My world has always been very small and lately most of it centered around recovery, so I was reduced to telling women I knew from the program that I was looking and open to meeting someone. When I first started seeing Paula, my sponsor, who is lesbian, had suggested I check out gay meetings, saying it was good to be around like people. I'd been going to one particular women's meeting for a while and a friend there knew I was looking to get out into the women's scene a bit. After this meeting, as she was giving me a squeeze good-bye on the front lawn, she got a good hold on me, lifted and rotated me around, saying, "The blonde in the white shirt and shorts said she was interested in meeting you. Are you interested in meeting her?" and she plopped me down in position to view said woman in shorts. I replied in the affirmative; my buddy passed on my number to the blonde. She and I subsequently spent two or three afternoons together just walking and talking, getting to know each other enough to realize we had already peaked. So we went our separate ways. I found that's generally the way it goes.

I met a couple of very nice women and even dated one really terrific woman, Debbie, for several months. She had a huge, eclectic circle of friends. They were lively and intelligent and had all sorts of different jobs — musicians, fine artists, a chef, a radio personality. They had dinner parties; a lot of drinking was going on but that was okay, I could navigate through that.

Debbie introduced me to gay-centric events like the Halloween parade in West Hollywood, which was wild and fun and we had a ball. I really wasn't going to great lengths to hide I was there.

I didn't know people who had gangs of friends like Debbie had. I saw people having a social life, a community of friends, and it was totally different from my frame of reference. Being in a group of smart gay women made me almost light-headed. I knew that no one was taking an oath of silence at these parties — anyone who saw me could tell a friend or leak it to the press if they could find someone interested. But in truth, I was willing to live with that risk in exchange for drinking the experience in.

Here were these fun, smart, talented people and I didn't have to tell them I was gay. I was *at the party.* They *knew.* Which reminds me of a silly joke I'd heard years ago: Which would you rather be, black or gay? The answer was, *Black, because then you didn't have to tell your parents.*

There was no turning back. I felt fully committed to being gay. And it was time to tell my parents. I told the ones I had left.

One afternoon at tea at the Peninsula Hotel, I broached it with my stepfather Allan. "I want you to know that I'm dating women." He studied his Earl Grey for a moment, looked at me, and admitted, "So am I!"

I often call my stepmother Ginger in Virginia Beach on Sunday mornings and this time I had some clarifying to do. "I really need you to know something I haven't talked to you about. I told you I've been in a relationship for a bit."

"I think I know where this is going," she

403

said. "I think you're going to say you're with a woman."

"Whoa! How did you divine that?" I sputtered, absolutely floored.

"I asked you if there was someone special in your life and you said, 'Yeah, there is . . .' but you were always gender neutral and vague about who it was. You never referred to *him*." This was not the response I expected from my dear stepmom in Virginia, with Baptist roots and a conservative look at the world. But she was totally supportive of me, gay or not. Wow.

So, Eva already knew; Kate and Mollie didn't seem invested either way, but being honest and up front about it was primary for them; Peter was so sweet, said, "Mom, I just want you to be happy!" And Ted, whom I refer to as the family smart-ass, said, "Oh, I already knew." What?

Meanwhile, I was expanding my gay universe by microscopic increments. I went from being gay only in my house to being gay in my house, yard, and sometimes in the cul-de-sac and at meetings and parties.

I wasn't sure that being gay out in the world was a safe thing for me. Debbie was out and comfortable with her sexuality. But she was very respectful about the fact that I wasn't. I remember one night we were at the theater and I had my hand on the small of her back and she took it away and said, sotto voce, "Careful."

Debbie and I had a nice, easy connection but it didn't seem like we were developing into anything. The good thing was that I felt we were totally honest with each other when we decided to go our separate ways. There was no anger. It just wasn't happening. This was novel for me . . . breaking up without tears of accusations and resentments. Unheard of! Then about six months later, she called me for some reason, I can't remember what, and we started seeing each other again.

One night we were on a theater date at the Music Center. We'd arrived early and were people-watching when my cell phone rang. It was a woman named Nancy Locke. Several months earlier a mutual friend had given her my name and phone number: Nancy was toying with the idea of getting sober and our friend suggested that she contact me if she wanted to talk to someone about sobriety. Subsequently, Nancy and I had talked on the phone numerous times. After a certain period, she decided she had other priorities and her calls had stopped. But there she was on the other end of the line saying in that distinctively happy voice of hers, "Hi! It's Nancy, remember me?" She said she wanted to give sobriety a second try. I'd always enjoyed our conversations — she had a ready laugh and an engaging way of listening; I always felt she was very present, that she was genuinely curious about other people. We were comparing schedules, trying to figure out a good time to get together, and she said, "I can't tomorrow. I'm getting ready to drive up to Santa Barbara tonight to make dinner for a friend."

And I had the strangest feeling. A wave of longing and maybe even jealousy swept over me. I'd never even met this woman. But I thought to myself, I wish you were making dinner for *me.*

We agreed to talk later in the week. I hung up. I went back to Debbie and had a perfectly lovely evening.

When I talk to someone about getting sober, I share a lot of my own personal stories. I'd say, "This is what happened with me . . ." and hope that something resonates with them. It's never the actual specifics as in "I drank a bottle of this . . ." or "I passed out there . . ." I talk about the feelings that are involved, about the *thinking* and the choices I made, and how the program affected me.

Those are the kinds of conversations I'd already had with Nancy on the phone. So when I received her Music Center call I already knew her a little and liked her. We agreed to meet at 4 p.m. the following Thursday. Talking to her about sobriety was almost secondary; I was eager to make friends with other women; *I* wanted to build *my* community.

All I knew about Nancy was that she was gay and a general contractor. But aside from my first name and that I was many years sober, she knew absolutely nothing about me. Ten minutes before we met for the first time — at a Starbucks near my house — Nancy realized that she didn't even know what I looked like. She called me on my cell and said, "How will I recognize you?" I wasn't going to say something boneheaded like, "Have you ever seen *Family Ties*?" and I liked the mystery of neither of us knowing so I said, "Let's just see if we can find each other."

I was there before four, and Nancy was running about five minutes late. Finally, I got up to grab a book from my car. The part of the story that Nancy likes to tell is how she was hurrying in the front door of Starbucks and passed me heading out, and she thought to herself, "Oh, there's that actress from TV. What's her name again? Meredith Baxt . . ." and — *ding!* — *"Meredith?"* she blurted out. And I said, "Nancy?"

What I remember the most about our conversation that day is that it felt instantly easy. She playfully gave me grief about being so mysterious. She said, "Don't you think you could have told me who you were?" And I said, "What was I supposed to say? 'Oh, by the way, I'm Meredith Baxter, you've probably seen me on TV.' " Blech!

She had great, twinkly aqua blue eyes and I loved her ability to ask questions because sometimes there's a big silence in me that I have a hard time getting around. I remember that Nancy told me a really beautiful story about growing up blue-collar and her close relationship with her mom. So I thought I should describe my mirror-opposite childhood: lacking for nothing in the Hollywood Hills except that I was virtually alone with little connection to my parents. And I guess that's when I started crying. Nancy didn't seem put off. She didn't see anything wrong about the fact that I barely knew her and I was sitting in a coffee shop weeping that I didn't have *her* mother. She was moved that I felt comfortable enough to let my guard down. She didn't know I would always cry about not having her mother.

We hung out for about an hour and a half, talking and laughing. When we got up to leave, I said, "This was really fun. I had a great time with you. Let's do this again." But I wasn't ready to leave yet; I hadn't told her that I was gay. I don't know why I felt this was so important to tell her *right this minute* but I really liked her and wanted to see her again. So I tried to discreetly wedge it into the conversation by saying, as if as an afterthought . . . "And the woman I'm seeing . . ." To which Nancy replied, "Whoa. Whoa. *Whoa.* Back the fuck up!"

She looked so startled, I just started laughing. We both sat back down and she said, "Are you *gay?* Don't you think that's maybe something you should have told me?" I said, innocently, "Why?" And she said, "Because that's a big part of who you are."

Later Nancy would tell me that when I told her about Debbie her spirits sagged. Ten minutes earlier, it hadn't crossed her mind, because she didn't know I was gay. Now she was saddened because I wasn't available.

So my friendship with Nancy began as a series of meetings involving cups of coffee at Starbucks, long intense conversations about life and the program, and submerged feelings of attraction, with me feeling skittish. When we'd part, Nancy would always have to say, "When do we get to do this again?"

In late December, Debbie and I broke it off for the second time. The truth is that we had run our course; it just didn't feel right to continue. So I was single and looking at New Year's Eve. Michael Gross and I were scheduled to appear in a special production of a live 1940s-era radio play version of Frank Capra's *It's a Wonderful Life.* It was running at the Pasadena Playhouse over several nights including New Year's. I sent Nancy an e-mail and offered her a couple of free tickets. She wrote back accepting my offer. She was bringing her elder sister, Kate. I helped arrange for them to get seats close to the stage and after the show, I walked them out to their car. Nancy looked *good* outside Starbucks.

Soon after that night we went to a lecture at the Hammer Museum. Then to another play. In between there were lots of awkward moments, sparks of something not yet easy to define and hesitations at the end of the night where it felt one of us was supposed to lean in and kiss the other, but neither of us did. I vacillated between feeling desperate to see her and being aloof and a little unavailable. This went on for weeks. In retrospect, I think I could sense the buildup of feelings for Nancy and they sent off warning signals to my reptilian unsure-how-to-have-a-relationship brain. My knee-jerk reaction was to wear my imaginary six-shooters (which I was very fond of) and not let her get too close.

I didn't want to let anyone new in. I had never even invited Nancy over to my house. I wasn't sure I was ready for romance in my life. Casual fooling around was one thing. But I could sense some real feelings growing here and I thought that would make me vulnerable to someone taking over my life. I wasn't sure I'd recognize if that were happening or how to handle myself, *so you just watch yerself, little lady!*

Some part of me must have thought I was ready because I called Nancy and told her I'd bought a tapestry that needed hanging, I didn't know how to do it . . . could she help me? Of course, now, I realize I sounded like a damsel in distress, but I really just wanted to see her in her carpentry bags.

That night Nancy put about a million holes in my wall trying to locate the studs. I was distressed with how she was aerating my dining room, but then I was easily

411

distracted by how fetching she looked in cords and a Black and Decker. This was a no-sweat task for her, studs aside, and once she finally got the damn tapestry up, we went out to dinner, had fun, and ended the night with our time-honored dance of who-is-going-to-make-the-first-move.

A week later, when we got together at our usual watering hole, Nancy, being bolder and more adventurous than I, decided to come clean to me about her feelings. She said, "I think I'm not being honest with you. Over these last weeks I realize that I've become extremely attracted to you. I don't want to ruin our friendship. So if this makes you uncomfortable, I think we should talk about it because then I can put my feelings in the proper place." And I said, "I feel the same way." It was so exciting to proclaim our interest in each other that we were both instantly seized by shyness. "I have a suggestion," I said as I boldly ventured when none had trod before. "Maybe instead of saying 'Let's meet for coffee,' we can say, 'Let's have a date, because I'm sick of coffee.'" Yep, I was pretty audacious.

One of Nancy's true gifts is storytelling. Even though I have heard all of her best yarns countless times, I don't tire of listening to her. I love watching people watch

Nancy relive outrageous tales from her past. When she gets to the punch line and everyone throws their heads back and laughs, it just thrills me.

By the time I got together with Nancy, she was fifty-one years old and had a lot of stories to draw upon. She was born in Portland, Oregon, and raised by an engineer father and homemaker mother in suburban Glendale, California. When she was growing up, she always excelled at sports. There was never a time that she didn't assume she'd become a physical education teacher.

Nancy had her first experience with a woman when she was twenty-one. At the time, she was living with a man, planning to get married, and working as a bartender at a place in Pasadena called the Sawmill. Somehow a girl she knew from junior high school tracked her down and made a pass at her. Their one drunken night together scared Nancy so much that she left town. The next day she packed up her things and enrolled at the University of California at Santa Barbara, abandoned her marriage and physical education plans, and refocused as an art major.

Once at UCSB, she did one of the things she does best: she made friends. On the Fourth of July, she went to the local softball field, sat in the stands, and tried to pick out the team that had the cutest girls on it. Then she asked if they needed another player.

Through the softball team, she met a group of girls who called themselves the Cowgirls after Tim Robbins's novel *Even Cowgirls Get the Blues*. They surfed together. They went on vacations together. They drank together. They went to women's music festivals together. They were her posse.

In 1977, I was on *Family,* the mother of three, and struggling to make my second marriage work. In 1977, Nancy was young, experimenting, and running through lots of girlfriends. You tell me which of us was having the better time.

It was after an art professor suggested she take a woodshop class that Nancy discovered she loved knowing how to run a table saw, how to use tools, how to make things. That led to her dropping out of school, driving to Santa Rosa in Babs — as she called her red Volkswagen van — and working as a no-pay gofer on an all-women construction crew. She showed up in khaki pants, a Hawaiian shirt, and flip-flops and was greeted by a group of hardworking, muscular gals in flannel shirts and crew cuts.

At first they just had her drag lumber from

414

one side of the construction site to the other. Six months later, when she returned to Santa Barbara, she had acquired all the necessary house-building skills, but no one would hire her because she was a woman. So she started as a laborer, often the only woman on a construction crew, and kept at it until she was supervisor. By the time I met Nancy, she'd had her general contractor's license for more than twenty-one years and had built Nancy Locke Construction into a successful company that specialized in residential home remodels.

Once we finally got together, we took it slow. Very slow. High school coed slow. We were each seeing my therapist, Sarah, independently and she told us to get to know each other first. There was a lot of kissing, but we waited five weeks before we actually slept together, a personal record for us both. Even after that, things moved at a glacial pace. I never let her sleep over — and her commute from my house to her home in Los Feliz involved three freeways and, at best, a forty-minute drive, often in the dead of night or pouring rain.

As you can tell, I wasn't exactly prime girlfriend material. See, because my feelings were engaged, I felt at risk . . . to *myself* . . . to *my own thinking.* With David and with

Michael, I'd witnessed evidence of their undesirable behaviors, *which I ignored,* to my detriment. I had pretended not to notice how I was spoken to, pretended that I wasn't aware of how they perceived me or treated me. This time I was with a woman, but it was still me in the equation. And I was afraid I'd start pretending again. Whenever Nancy and I spent time together, I was *vigilant.* What am I seeing? What is she saying? Is she consistent? Is she getting too close? Am I making up stories about her? What am I pretending *not* to see? I didn't want to reveal too much about my feelings. *Aloof* felt just right. I was not going to give her *anything.* I did not want to be taken advantage of. I didn't want any presumptions. I couldn't ask her to stay over because I wasn't anywhere near ready to wake up next to another person.

Poor Nancy paid the price. When I finally did ask her to sleep over, I wouldn't allow her to keep so much as a T-shirt at my house. She was constantly in a state of unpacking and packing her things. She'd venture, ever so shyly, "You know, it would be a lot easier if I could leave a few things here. Maybe sweatpants. Do you have maybe a *shelf* where I could leave a pair of sweatpants?" Now, I live in a five-bedroom house, but the question felt too invasive and panicked me; I blurted, "I don't have any room." And the subject of Nancy bringing her dog, Scout, along with her so she didn't have to race home to Los Feliz in the morning to feed or walk her? Forget about it!

As a contractor, Nancy drives a big Ford F150 4×4. She has to haul lumber. I was worried about my neighbors seeing a truck parked out in front of my house overnight and then a woman climbing into it in the morning. I asked Nancy to park her truck around the corner so no one would get any ideas. What? I was so loony. Was I afraid they'd think I had a friend with a truck? This was the one time I remember her balking. Her eyes narrowed. "My truck is part of who I am. Deal with it." Right.

One minute I'd be drawing Nancy toward me and we would have the absolute best time, laughing, loving, and the next minute I'd get cool, step back. I'd get triggered and think I was going to lose my voice, so everything had to be on my terms. It was totally, patently, desperately unfair. It must have been horribly confusing to Nancy; I don't know how she tolerated it. But it was the only way I knew to do it.

About a year and a couple of months into our relationship, Nancy reached her breaking point. We'd been to a meeting together where Nancy had rested her hand on my thigh. This was more PDA than I was comfortable with at the time. We hadn't even told many people we were together. On the drive back to my house, Nancy made a comment about a sober women's retreat we were planning on attending. She said, "I'm looking forward to being somewhere where we don't have to hide who we are." I told her the truth. I said, "I'm not ready to tell people who we are."

Being out was where Nancy's world and mine collided. There was never a time Nancy proclaimed, "Hey, world! I'm gay!" She just stopped hiding it. She felt that if someone were uncomfortable with who she was, that was his or her problem. On the other hand, she didn't have to worry about photographers or tabloid reporters or working in an industry that isn't necessarily terribly accepting of gay women. Either way, Nancy hated our being in the closet and she hated my vacillating behavior toward her. Everything she'd been keeping inside tumbled out. That night we argued, got into bed, didn't touch, didn't talk. The rigid stillness was oppressive. At one point in the night I reached out to her to cross the divide and she didn't respond. She ignored me.

The next morning, Nancy got up and left without so much as a good-bye. I felt utterly abandoned. Once again, I felt old family rejections and the emotional abandonment in my marriages. My wound. I had long ago decided no one would ever make me feel that way again, and that no one included Nancy.

Nancy called after two days of silence. I asked her to come get her things and give me back my key. I was completely shut down. I was *gone.* I'd decided — and apparently so had she — that we were not together anymore. That was *it.*

Over that next week, I took walks with friends and coldly reported Nancy's crimes. Then I started writing, trying to see what I was feeling besides *wronged.* I talked to my therapist, Sarah, who helped me see that I was reacting to old feelings from situations in the past, not necessarily to Nancy's actions. She thought that Nancy and I had felt deserted by each other and we each spun off into our own orbits of pain. I cautiously took contrary action. I wrote Nancy an e-mail and said, "I have come to realize that you are not the wound. You are the sword in the wound."

I had to go out of town for some business and talked to Nancy while on the road. She mentioned that she'd been to see Sarah, who had asked her what kind of relationship she wanted to have with me: was Nancy just looking for a gal friend to go to dinners or movies with and have casual intimacy? Or did she want a spiritual relationship, in which we both could grow together, have a real intimacy by being thoroughly open and honest and have trust in each other?

Nancy wanted to know what my answer would be. Apparently I sat in silence on the phone and eventually said I wasn't really interested in any spiritual relationship. I was going with the movie kind. I neither understood nor saw the attraction in the other; it seemed like a tough road with little promise. I could hear the dispiritedness in her voice, but I was afraid I wasn't equipped to offer or accept more than that. Once home, in my next session with Sarah, complaining about feeling like I was disappointing Nancy by not being emotionally available to her, Sarah put the same question to me about what kind of relationship I wanted to have. "Oh, the movie kind. Really," I said again, without a moment's hesitation.

Then I had to think about most of the previous relationships I'd settled for, where I'd been so lonely, lying to myself, pretending I wasn't hurt, trying not to feel, not being able to share, not showing up. Now I was with someone who *did* want more, who was ready to share that path with me. Would I never let go and be willing to be known, even though I was frantic with longing in the isolation I'd created? Was it possible . . . might there be a power greater than me who could guide me, give me the courage I needed? I was willing to consider there was. It was at that point we began to slowly repair our relationship. We started going to couples therapy together. We worked on communicating. I told Nancy, "This is very difficult for me. I know you're not getting what you want. I'm asking if you can be patient with me." And she said, "I can."

Nancy always says that I changed so quickly, it was almost alarming. I wanted to change. I had started praying to be open to Nancy, to be able to love her fearlessly, and my altered perception triggered an immediate transformation. Hearing that she would stay and be patient while I worked to change gave me such hope and relief and freed me to race to meet her halfway. She created a safe place for us to grow together, which I had never had before. We were on equal footing. Slowly I started to understand about intimacy; I could see its appeal and came to desire it for myself. In the past, when I had revealed myself, my thoughts and feelings, which I had thought was intimacy, I was really opening myself up to attack and manipulation, because of who I had chosen to be with. Small wonder I found it threatening. But someone who hears you without judgment and makes space for the way you feel without taking it personally, reflects back what has been shared, and then shares herself, understands intimacy; that is what I've come to experience with Nancy. I wasn't scared of Nancy. I totally trusted — and still trust — where she was coming from. We're close in a way that doesn't happen ordinarily; it is spiritual, singular, and precious.

There were still complications. While I never hid our relationship from anyone I felt close to, I wasn't out to the public at large. In February of 2008, when Gary David Goldberg and the cast of *Family Ties* celebrated the show's twentieth anniversary on the *Today Show*, Nancy came with me. Gary and Diana flew us out to New York on a private jet (which was just so fucking cool I couldn't believe it) with Michael Gross and Marion Ross, who had worked on Gary's *Brooklyn Bridge,* and her husband. I took this opportunity to be intrepid in the face of my old friends and introduced

Nancy as my girlfriend. Michael Gross and Diana had known Nancy for some time; everyone else yawned and said welcome. Well, that was lovely and uneventful, but my intrepidity stopped there.

This story was the biggest standout for me from that trip: It was Nancy's and my first time in New York together and we were delighted to be put up at the Four Seasons. Justine Bateman and Tina Yothers, the Keaton youngsters, and their husbands were at the hotel; Michael Gross, too. The *Family Ties* cast was to be picked up by limos early the next morning and taken to the NBC building for the *Today* taping. Michael Fox was going to meet us there. We were all so excited. To avoid unexpected questions, Nancy decided to stay and watch the show from the hotel room.

Very early the next morning I'd gotten dressed with care, black slacks, lovely white blouse, and was making a protein drink in the bathroom. Nancy was in the bedroom, watching the news in what I call her breakfast pajamas. They have toast, eggs, pancakes, and a toaster on them. I was using one of those clever Cuisinart hand mixers that comes in two pieces for easy travel. I was in a rush, as I perpetually am, had made my yummy drink, and was cleaning up after myself. At home, since I mix it at the kitchen counter, I'd have to unplug and take the mixer to the sink for washing. Here, in the hotel bathroom, the counter is conveniently right next to the sink, so I started washing up immediately after use, neglecting to either unplug or remove my thumb from the on switch. Whatever possessed me to do this is long forgotten in the spray of blood, my shriek for help, and the certainty I had cut off my fingertips. "Oh my God! Oh my God, oh my God!"

Nancy appeared in the doorway in a panic that almost matched my own. She told me later *she* thought I'd cut my fingertips off; there was blood everywhere, spattered across the mirror, the counter, on my blouse. She ran to the phone to get a doctor and I screeched for her to find our contact for the *Today Show* and tell them not to wait because I wasn't going to make it, picturing myself in emergency surgery. Nancy barked some orders into the phone, then, unable to reach our contact, raced out the door, still in her pancake pajamas, to catch the limo waiting downstairs and out front. Apparently during the off-hours, hotel security officers are sent to handle emergency situations. Two fellows appeared at my door with a very small medical case and endeavored to address the index and middle fingers on my left hand, which I could not even look at. They were trying to wrap them up but seemed comically inexperienced. If the bed were on fire, I'm sure they would have known what to do. One guy wrestled my left arm into a headlock while the other spun gauze loosely over the ends of the fingers, which now revealed themselves as intact but with multiple deep slashes through the nails. When they were through, a large silly, turban like cap that kept falling off sat atop my bound fingers and required the assistance of my thumb to stay in place.

Nancy had returned during the gauzing, having sent off the *Today* limo. Now, of course, I was calmer and not in surgical need, all ready to go to the *Today Show,* so again the poor girl was drafted, still panting and in her breakfast flannels, to go back down and grab me a cab while I changed clothes. I made it to the *Today Show* in plenty of time, asweat and fingers throbbing, but otherwise just fine. We had a great time on the show; no one noticed my fingers, but if you ever take a look at a clip of the *Family Ties* NBC reunion, you might see that bandage wad in my hand.

When it comes to the lesbian community,

Nancy is my trusty guide. Nancy has seen it all and done it all. Meanwhile, because I am a total neophyte, she has to indulge me. In 2009, she decided it was time for me to experience the annual alcohol-soaked gay girls gone wild extravaganza that takes place in Palm Springs during spring break, known as The Dinah (officially Dinah Shore Weekend). She said to me, "This is something that is really fun. It's geared toward drinking but if we could stay away from that element, would you go?" The truth is that I really wanted to go! I just wanted to *see;* I couldn't imagine what it would be like. I had never done the spring break crazy that so many kids did in high school, so again, I had no frame of reference. I was a know-nothing dweeb.

The problem was that I didn't want anyone to know I was there. I would be really exposed. Any person with an iPhone or a digital camera had the ability to take pictures at any time with no one the wiser. If I could have worn a paper bag over my head, I would have been so happy.

Nancy was more pragmatic. She sent an e-mail to a close friend, Mariah Hanson, the woman behind Club Skirts and one of the founders of parties at The Dinah. Mariah very thoughtfully decided on a red velvet rope strategy — we enjoyed the Indigo Girls from the privacy of a special VIP section. I thought, Okay, *this* is what celebrity is for. I'd often wondered.

And Nancy was right. It was wild, with good music that we took in from afar; I slipped in and out fairly incognito. We avoided the boozy pool scene that I felt thirty years too old for anyway and spent most of the time by ourselves, reading in the sun. Like we'd do at home.

As concerned as I was about incriminating photos surfacing, I had absolutely no trepidation about playing a lesbian therapist in a couple of episodes of the lesbian comedy web series *We Have to Stop Now.* No one thought I was a murderer just because I played Betty Broderick, I reasoned; I'm an *ac-tor!* The writing was really good and everyone in the cast — Jill Bennett, Cathy Debuono, Suzanne Westenhoefer — was amazing and wonderfully funny.

I met the whole cast when we gathered for the reading. Each webisode is only ten minutes long so we could easily go through the entire season in one sitting. Afterward, amidst laughter and character discussion, Cathy said to me, "You know, we'll be shooting some of this on a lesbian cruise; going to Mexico, Belize, Honduras. . . .

Would you like to come?"

As you know, I called her later and said, "We're in!"

EPILOGUE

So. The deed was done. The good thing, I realize, about coming out on national television, is I never have to come out again. Ever. It was horrible, magnificent, life-changing, and *done.* So, in many ways, that's all behind me and my job is to get on with my life, which is not just about being gay. The love of my life, Nancy, and I get up pretty early every morning and we usually have some quiet nongay coffee and newspaper time before she's off to the gym; I usually head to a heterosexual meeting and hit the equally hetero gym afterward. Our lives are exactly the same as before the *Today Show* and *People* magazine, just freer. I do experience some relief in the capacity to live without interference or censure, real or perceived. I hadn't known I was looking for this kind of emotional balance and could not have anticipated the sense of relief I've enjoyed.

Three of my first public post—*Today Show* events were speaking at Human Rights Campaign gala dinners in Raleigh, N.C., Houston, and Los Angeles. I loved being there with Joe Solmonese, who represents total commitment to sustaining equal rights for gays and lesbians and transgenders. I felt grateful for the opportunity to participate in the gay community and felt welcomed with open arms. I had an opportunity to talk about Don't Ask, Don't Tell, the government military program that practices prejudice in the guise of protecting heterosexuals . . . because they must need it. I got a lot of juice for the *Today Show* appearance (as if I'd elected to do it as a supreme act of in-your-face brio) and that's when it really sank in just how much bigger than me this whole experience has been. Whenever anyone comes out, prominent or not, it lays the groundwork for social change and acceptance. That's why it was a political act. I may be the only lesbian you know (although this is quite doubtful) and I am here to dispel, if only to a small degree, whatever fears, misunderstandings, and apprehensions you might have about the threat of a homosexual agenda. (That idea is amusing. The only agenda I know of is . . . leave us alone; don't make choices for us that we wouldn't make for you.)

To my knowledge, I've not had one negative reaction from anyone I know. However, as happens with the anonymity offered by the Internet, there were many ugly comments made about my coming out. I was warned ahead of time, *Don't read the comments about yourself in Internet news articles.* But of course, I read some and immediately understood how the Ku Klux Klan became so successful. If no one knows who you are, it's safe to do, say *anything,* no matter how mindlessly vapid, ugly, or divisive; it's a format for the powerless and disenfranchised, where they can feel some power, feel heard. So, now that those folks have their forums, maybe they don't have to kick their dogs anymore.

And those few uglies were balanced by so many wonderful, loving, championing comments. Two that stood out as being most illustrative of the way some women have identified with me I found on my own fan club's website, one from a woman in North Carolina:

Thank you so much for telling your story. I, too discovered at the ripe old age of 52 that I was head over heels in love with a woman. After 2 divorces and numerous love affairs, for the first time in my life, I felt comfortable in my own skin. I think of Harvey Milk every time someone comes out — that his death was not in vain but a liberation for all who are closeted. Thank you, thank you, thank you!

Here's another:

Meredith, I just turned 40 and have been feeling "too old" and feeling that it's "too late" for me to come out. I'm married w/ kids and I can only hope that one day I gain the strength to be true to myself and to others. With each year that passes, it is emotionally draining trying to keep this secret inside, but thank you for giving me a new spark of hope. I have a big decision to make and it's really hard. Good luck to you and congrats!

So . . . hope! If I can give hope to some, that could be enough; it's a place to start.

Suzanne Westenhoefer jokes about how surprised she was by what I did. She says, "At the end of my act, I always give a little speech encouraging people to come out. But I never expected anyone to actually go and *do* it!"

So I will end this book by echoing the

same persuasive words Suzanne used in quoting gay activist Harvey Milk.

Come out. If you're not out, come out.

Surprise me.

ACKNOWLEDGMENTS

I'm glad I didn't wait until my eighties to write a memoir; it would have involved that many more years of memories to excite and excavate, more friends and family to account for and stories and relationships to sort out, satisfy, and encapsulate. I'm thinking that rather than being an early offering, I consider this memoir timely. I am glad to have found all those spotty journal entries I've made over the years, sometimes in notebooks, often scrawled in between drawings in my sketchbooks. Unearthing my life frequently took side roads down Amateur Art Alley.

And where does my gratitude list start? With my lovely partner, Nancy Locke, who always seemed to have faith in my ability to write this despite my fears, wails, and declarations to the contrary. And next, I have to thank Margy Rochlin, who painstakingly questioned and recorded, searched and researched, prodded and pushed me and others for more stories, more details, and more connective tissue. I have great respect, awe, and gratitude for her ability to shape my stories into a cohesive framework upon which I could build.

To my friends and family, mainly my children, Ted Bush, Eva Whitney Abarta, Kate Birney, Ph.D., Peter Birney, and Mollie Birney, I offer my apologies for not being very available these past nine months due to this nonfiction pregnancy. This has been a deeply personal undertaking. Taking responsibility for my life took more thought, introspection, and willingness than anticipated; giving it the self-reflection required seemed to dictate *me on me* time over social time, and I regret any perceived slights. Please know I hunger for you *all.*

I have to thank Annie O'Toole and Nancy, who have been seemingly tireless sounding boards for me, reading and rereading, never admitting to tedium. And also to Annie for offering harrowing and hilarious recalls from our sixteen years of working together.

To dear Allan Manings, my stepfather, who let me talk and talk and talk about my thoughts and trepidations about this book. Even while he was gravely ill, he gently urged me onward, and to him I weep my thanks. He gave me many stories about my mother and their lives together and what he knew of her early years. I loved him dearly and I'm deeply saddened he didn't live to see that I took his words to heart and made it through, as he said I would.

I give thanks to my brothers, Richard Baxter and Brian Baxter, who willingly plumbed their memories to offer their experiences of our shared stories . . . but so often not the same perspectives. Of course.

And I appreciate Robert Bush for so generously giving of his time, observations, and recollections of the few years we shared, ranging from the tender and hallucinogenic to the rough and combative. Thank you.

I am grateful to Michael Gross for his great recall of our shared history; it helps to have a good friend who's such a colorful raconteur. Thank you to Victoria Thompson, who amazingly, all these years later, had physical evidence of our respective ships having passed in the night. Thank you so much for your contributions. I am indebted to Andrea Baynes, who shared not just the made-for-TV foxhole with me many, many times, but contributed background information, giving context and perspective where I had none.

My thanks must include Alan Iezman who

advised me, Dan Strone, CEO, Trident Media Group, who accepted and supported me, Diane Salvatore who said "yes," and Julia Pastore who has guided me ever since. Thanks, Julia, for championing me while keeping the ducks on the path.

Others who made this book possible are: Sarah la Saulle, Ph.D., Martha Sanchez, Leonard Goldberg, the Paley Center for Media (Los Angeles), and The Academy of Motion Picture Arts & Sciences. I feel deep gratitude for the hundreds of people, many of whom I know by first name only, who for over twenty years have shown me unconditional acceptance and honesty; they gave me the lessons for living and urged me to keep coming back.

ABOUT THE AUTHOR

Meredith Baxter has been an actress for forty years and has five children. She achieved early success in the comedy *Bridget Loves Bernie,* followed by the acclaimed ABC drama *Family* and the popular NBC sitcom *Family Ties.*

She received Emmy nominations for *A Woman Scorned: The Betty Broderick Story,* her part in the series *Family,* and her role as a lesbian mother in *Other Mothers.* She has starred in more than fifty movies for television and coexecutive-produced several, including *My Breast, Betrayed: The Story of Three Women, Darkness Before Dawn,* and *The Long Journey Home,* as well as her TV series, *The Faculty.*

She has served on the board of the CLARE Foundation for six years; CLARE is a nonprofit organization that provides recovery services for alcohol and drug addiction.

Baxter makes appearances speaking on breast cancer, domestic violence, alcoholism, and general life experiences. Meredith established the Meredith Baxter Fund for Breast Cancer Research to help support nonprofits in providing free mammograms and follow-up care to women who can't afford them.

She lives in Santa Monica, California, with her partner, Nancy Locke.

The employees of Thorndike Press hope you have enjoyed this Large Print book. All our Thorndike, Wheeler, and Kennebec Large Print titles are designed for easy reading, and all our books are made to last. Other Thorndike Press Large Print books are available at your library, through selected bookstores, or directly from us.

For information about titles, please call:
  (800) 223-1244

or visit our Web site at:
  http://gale.cengage.com/thorndike

To share your comments, please write:
  Publisher
  Thorndike Press
  10 Water St., Suite 310
  Waterville, ME 04901